J

Education and the law

This edited collection addresses a subject which is topical not only in Britain, where there has been a spate of laws and regulations affecting the structure and content of education, but also in developed and developing countries, where the overriding motivation in many cases has been to raise economic performance.

The first part of the book deals with the way legislation affects education and training both directly and tangentially, and how the law through its influence on such things as participation rates, certification, employer involvement and restructuring can affect the level and degree of economic activity. Contributors examine the education systems of the USA, Kenya, Japan, Germany, Nigeria, Britain and France to illustrate the interdependence of the elements involved. The second part focuses on the concept of curriculum control and school government. Chapters take a comparative approach to what is taught in the classroom and how the implementation of legislation affects all aspects of a country's education system.

Witold Tulasiewicz lectures in education at the Universities of Cambridge and Calgary. **Gerald Strowbridge** lectures in the Department of Staff and Curriculum Development at South Kent College. They have been, respectively, Secretary and Chairman of the British Comparative and International Education Society.

Education and the law

International perspectives

Edited by Witold Tulasiewicz
and Gerald Strowbridge

London and New York

First published 1994
by Routledge
11 New Fetter Lane, London EC4P 4EE

Simultaneously published in the USA and Canada
by Routledge
29 West 35th Street, New York, NY 10001

Typeset in Times by LaserScript, Mitcham, Surrey
Printed and bound in Great Britain by
Biddles Ltd, Guildford and King's Lynn

British Library Cataloguing in Publication Data
A catalogue record for this book is available from the British Library.

Library of Congress Cataloging in Publication Data
Education and the law: international perspectives/edited by Witold
   Tulasiewicz and Gerald Strowbridge.
   p. cm.
   Includes bibliographical references and index.
   1. Educational law and legislation. 2. Educational law and legislation –
Great Britain. I. Tulasiewicz, Witold.
   II. Strowbridge, Gerald.
   K3740.Z9E38   1993
   344'.07 – dc20
   [342.47]   93-2509
                                                                  CIP

   ISBN 0–415–08943–3

Contents

Illustrations

Contributors

Colin Brock is a Research Associate at the University of Oxford Department of Educational Studies and Chief Education Adviser to UNECIA (Universities of England Consortium for International Affairs).

Nadine Cammish is a Lecturer in Education and Director of the PGCE programme at the University of Hull.

Andrew Convey is Chair of the Teacher Education Committee of the UK Centre for European Education, and Research Fellow in the Department of Education in the University of Leeds.

Peter Downes is the Head Teacher of Hinchingbrooke School, Huntingdon.

Peter Ezeh is a journalist specializing in education and other current issues in Nigeria reporting for 'Punch', Lagos.

Teruhisa Horio is Professor in the Faculty of Education of the University of Tokyo.

Mihalis Kassotakis is Professor of Pedagogy in the Department of Education in the School of Philosophy of the University of Athens, Greece.

Alexandra Lambrakis-Paganos is a Senior Lecturer in the Department of Education in the School of Philosophy of the University of Athens, Greece.

Beverly Lindsay is Associate Dean (Academic) and Professor of Education in the University of Georgia, Athens, Georgia, and currently Executive Director of Strategic Planning at Hampton University, Virginia.

Paul Meredith is a Lecturer specializing in the Law and Education in the Faculty of Law of the University of Southampton.

Eberhard Meumann was formerly Director of the Institute for Theory and the History of Pedagogy, East Berlin.

Jack Sislian is an Educational Consultant and Visiting Professor in the Faculty of Education and Community Studies in the University of Reading.

Hilary Steedman is the Senior Research Fellow of the National Institute of Economic and Social Research, London, and currently acting as Examiner for the OECD in their Review of Educational Policy in France.

Gerald Strowbridge is Principal Lecturer in the Department of Staff and Curriculum Development at the South Kent College, Folkestone, and has represented BCIES on the Executive Committee of the World Council of Comparative Education Societies.

Dan Taverner is a Lecturer in the Department of Education of the University of Cambridge, and a former Chief Inspector of Schools.

Witold Tulasiewicz is University Lecturer in Education, and Fellow of Wolfson College, University of Cambridge and is currently Professor at the University of Calgary .

Tessa West is the Inmate Services Manager at the Wolds Remand Prison, Brough, Humberside.

Sir David Williams was formerly Rouse Ball Professor of English Law and is now Vice-Chancellor of the University of Cambridge.

Foreword

Sir David Williams

Recently we have seen a rash of publications on the subject of the law and its relationship to schools and higher education. This is significant because hitherto such books have often been collections of statutes, whereas they are now concerned with the substance of the law. We are at the beginning of a new era.

The law, of course, operates at different levels. First, there is statute law, which is critically important in laying down a framework for a system of education. It is significant that until 1988, however, there had been no major legislation in the United Kingdom in the field of higher education, and even then most of the Education Reform Act of 1988 was concerned with the schools. Even where the schools are concerned, one has to go back to the Education Act 1944 for a previous major piece of Parliamentary legislation. There has been further important legislation in 1992, but it is nonetheless remarkable that statute law was for a long time relied upon only in a fragmentary way.

There is also subordinate or delegated legislation. Schools have long been familiar with regulations, and universities are becoming more and more aware of their importance. Governmental control in the field of education is often exercised, however, not so much through primary or subordinate legislation as through circulars and codes of practice. The adoption of such methods of control is important, because in practice it makes the law much more difficult to track and consequently difficult to identify for purposes of challenge in the courts. An outstanding example of government by circular is the manner in which schools were reorganized in England and Wales in the 1960s and 1970s. The change-over to comprehensive schooling in these countries was achieved, initially at least, not by primary or subordinate legislation but through a circular issued in 1965 and subsequent circulars.

What part has been played by the courts in the field of education? Administrative law has developed rapidly in recent years, where – no doubt in part because of the fuzziness of the law and practice concerning education – the courts have on the whole been fearful to tread. There have been one or two outstanding exceptions, notably in the mid-1970s when the House of Lords struck down a decision of the Secretary of State for Education and Science in a dispute between her Department and the Metropolitan Borough of Tameside over the reorganization of schools. More recently, in a case concerning an application for a discretionary grant to attend university, the Court of Appeal held against the applicant, but nevertheless indicated that local authorities should be more open in disclosing the basis of their decisions. Public authorities should operate 'with all the cards face upwards on the table' and avoid giving merely blanket responses when questioned about the exercise of discretion.

One would not wish to argue for excessive involvement of lawyers in the field of education, but it is nevertheless important to explore the areas where duties arise and where discretion should be properly exercised. There are rapid changes taking place in the field of education (at all levels), and it is difficult enough to keep pace.

The situation in other countries is similar, as the application of statutory and delegated legislation to affect change in education becomes more frequent and the involvement of central government greater. Accession to Europe will affect educational legislation in member states of the European Community in the form of resolutions or Council of Europe conventions to be adopted. With the increasing political and economic uncertainties facing all societies in the 'new world order' one is likely to see governments at different levels having more frequent recourse to law to effect change. It would seem that educators cannot call the tune – that is being called by ministers. However, though the regulatory side has taken precedence in recent years this might not always be so.

The contributions to this volume provide ample evidence of some of the difficulties and challenges which lie ahead in a number of countries and the educational measures adopted to meet them. The application and interpretation of laws pose significant problems for those working in education.

Editors' preface

The chapters assembled in this volume are a selection from presentations prepared for a British Comparative and International Education Society annual conference held at Wolfson College, Cambridge, which addressed the theme of 'Education and the Law' and which was presided over by Sir David Williams, the Vice-Chancellor of Cambridge University.

Education and the law may be viewed as superstructures on the societal base which are shaped by that society's values and priorities. In earlier times the church or the ruler would determine the purpose and place of education and would be able to do so largely by virtue of their authority confirmed by certain undertakings given by the providers and recipients, such as entitlement to and obligations after schooling. Basic educational aims intertwined with religious and national loyalties were manifestly transparent; in any case education affected only the few. With the rise of more complex modern societies, governments began to use education more consciously and have tied it more firmly to their political, ideological, economic and social systems, using appropriate ends to achieve their objectives. Most societies, whatever their precise forms of government, reveal this shift towards increasing reliance on specific legislation, constitutions or statutory law and a vast array of regulations and ordinances and especially their exact interpretation, to obtain control over the contents of education, its providers and its recipients. In the modern world the temptation is for politicians to use the law as well as the public purse to place limits around the professionals while giving more of a say to the consumers of the service, the parents and governors of schools, as opposed to the teachers. But it can just as easily be the other way round, if the teachers are used by the government to disseminate a particular ideology. This can lead to confrontation if education is regarded as an intervention.

Legislation for greater accountability by the providers of education and training may be seen as attempts to shift responsibility for difficulties away from government and their control over the allocation of resources, and unload it on to the educators or users. When further legislation is introduced it may have precisely the desired effect, but more likely it will have side-effects some of which will be anticipated and considered on balance worth the risk, but others which may not. Indeed legislation in matters of curriculum control, for example, can cause harmful change, whether intended as under Facism or not. Social security and employment laws can have repercussions in education; in an example taken from British practice, there was the recently rescinded rule which limited the amount of time taken off for study by those registered as unemployed and entitled to state benefits to 21 hours in one week. The rule was justified by the need that they must be 'available for work' which may be offered.

The chapters in this volume provide ample evidence of problems, whether originating from nation-state education policies, or from supranational legislation such as the ratification of United Nations' conventions, interacting with sociopolitical and economic factors, such as the type of democracy practised, or the adoption of free market or centralized state interventionist economic principles or commitment to 'standards' by the governments concerned.

Legislation affects (a) the provision of education (who are the agents), (b) the structures (how is the system built up), (c) the curriculum offered (what is the subject matter taught) and (d) the teaching style (who delivers the curriculum within the existing structures) in a complex power struggle. The powers of the state affect and in turn are affected to varying degrees by the status of professionals, their associations, and professional unions, and the strength of public opinion reflecting the views of the customers of education who, unlike in the Middle Ages, are more aware of the fact of usually being the paymasters, too. The pupils are less often heard in this context, whether by design or by omission.

For decades educational provision as a topic of debate was limited to politicians and professionals, who controlled the resources, financial or experiential, with little other involvement except from special interest groups. With the arrival of major sociopolitical and economic change not only as a result of upheavals such as war but also in peacetime (recession, formation of larger economic and political units, immigration as well as ideological clashes), other agencies have increasingly become involved with their influence impinging on the educational legislation. Litigation is on the increase as the polarization grows between the forces with power and those without it, and while industry clearly becomes a powerful force, they can no longer simply be equated with government and consumer respectively.

The importance of comparison in an increasingly interactive world justifies the study of the mutual influence of education and the law in a variety of societies and situations. The contents, details and the particular individual style and emphasis of the papers, delivered or commissioned, reflect the current educational concerns and priorities in the countries they deal with within the context of the sociopolitical constraints in which they operate as seen by the writers, who examine the extent and effect of change and assess the power of legislation. The comparative element is implicit throughout the volume, although several chapters have a more explicit comparative character.

A variety of concerns are discussed. The chapters are arranged to show, in Part A the interaction between national educational legislation and ideological and economic change, and in Part B the working-through of legislation which affects the institutions, their curriculum, their government, the teachers and the pupils.

It is possible to see further groupings of chapters emerging according to their detailed contents. This has led to their arrangement in several clusters not only in the two parts of the book, but also within each part.

The editors wish to thank all the authors for their contributions, the continuing interest of the Vice-Chancellor in the publication, Andrew Convey for his advice in all editorial matters, Carol Moore, the domestic bursar at Wolfson College, and the editors at Routledge for their courtesy and patience. We hope the present publication, the latest in a long list of BCIES Proceedings published by Routledge, will be a worthy companion to the other volumes. The editors were stimulated by the variety, complexity and insights provided by the themes ably tackled by their fellow contributors to this volume which made their work so much easier and pleasurable.

Witold Tulasiewicz
Gerald Strowbridge

Part A

The law and education: economic development

1 Legislation and minority rights in higher education: American and Kenyan case studies

Beverly Lindsay

Shortly after he became Assistant Secretary for Postsecondary Education in the United States Department of Education, Leonard Haynes declared:

> We are at a historic moment. For the first time we will have the dialogue and the debate on postsecondary education . . . where the American public can discuss where we are going in the twenty-first century. We have before us . . . a decade of opportunity and a decade of action. We can make meaningful changes.
>
> (Haynes, 1990, cited in Matthews, 1990, p. 17)

Kenyan President Daniel arap Moi recently stated that education was one of the greatest gifts to a generation because it provides the necessary skills and knowledge to enhance development ('The Thailand Trip', 1990, p. 32). Undoubtedly, such lofty statements are eagerly awaited by students and parents. The fundamental challenge is to translate such declarations into authentic public and educational policies.

Public policies may be envisaged as the plans of action to accomplish goals of national and state governments. Policies encompass comprehensive methods and procedures designed for programme implementation. Executive, legislative, and judicial actions often serve as the bases for public policies which are frequently influenced by economic and fiscal considerations. Educational policies are influenced by similar considerations (Bishop, 1977, pp. 285–91; Klein, 1987; Mazzoni, 1989, pp. 79–80, 85–6; Lindsay, 1990b, p. 209).

In the United States, the role of the judiciary has been more pronounced than in other nations. Distinctions between *de jure* policies and *de facto* policies and programmes emanated from judicial decisions regarding public school segregation. The original characteristics of *de jure* policies encompassed those which existed as a result of laws or other official documents or practices. Sanctions could be applied for non-compliance (LaMorte, 1987, pp. 294, 331, 334, 444). Within the public arena and education institutions, the characteristics of *de jure* policies also encompass official written documents, oral directives from the chief executive or other cognizant administrators, and official charges that emerge from practices and procedures. Providing documentation to senior administrators or responsible agencies is undertaken to demonstrate policy compliance. In short, *de jure* policies are formal and official.

De facto policies are informal and exist by fact. In the original conditions, there are limited, if any, sanctions to be applied. When *de facto* policies continue to exist and discriminate against particular groups, the American courts have decided that *de facto* conditions have, in effect, become *de jure* policies (LaMorte, 1987, pp. 331, 334). That is, *de facto* conditions which existed as part of the institutional, local, regional, or national culture have evolved into formal policies.

Building upon this foundation, an examination of historical and contemporary conditions portrays the centrality of public and educational policies affecting American minorities *and* Kenyan women and disadvantaged groups. African, Asian, Hispanic, and Native Americans are the minority groups in the United States. Hence, throughout this presentation the salience of *de jure* and/or *de facto* policies is explicated especially as they affect the socioeconomic and educational opportunities of disadvantaged groups. Ultimately, the fundamental question is 'What higher education and related public policies can be created or altered so individual lives are enhanced and national development is improved?' Several sub-questions are explored. What are the fundamental rationales for the policies of various periods? At what level are the policies being articulated; that is, by officials in federal, national, state, corporate, or higher education agencies and institutions? And what, if any, sanctions are applied for non-compliance?

The parameters of this presentation include: (1) explicating economic issues – global competitiveness, human resources, and higher education and the economy; (2) presenting the statistical portraits of higher education in the respective nations; (3) examining *de jure* and *de facto* policies and programmes in the specific areas of access and retention, curriculum diversification and alterations, and student financial assistance; and (4) synthesizing some generic and cultural specific policies to help us extract cross-national lessons.

ECONOMIC AND SOCIAL REALITIES

In the United States, there is considerable concern with economic development in relation to the global economy and international competitiveness. To underscore the significance of the American economy in relation to global conditions, Groennings (1989, p. 3) stated that the approaching global economy 'is already beginning to rival the *civil rights movement* [emphasis added] as the most profoundly consequential long-term development since World War Two. . . . All people will be affected.' However, *de jure* civil rights policies,[1] characteristic of the 1960s and 1970s, might be eroded in the process. During the late 1980s, *One-Third of A Nation* (Commission on Minority Participation in Education and American Life, 1988, p. 15) stated that Americans were at a critical point since the questions are: 'Will we rekindle our commitment to eliminating disparities . . . . Or, are we resigned to a long-term retreat, in which the gaps between minorities and the majority will widen and continuing inequality will be tolerated?'

In a critical examination of the conditions of minority Americans, Wilson (1986, p. 2) contends that the economic, educational, and social status of minorities is the major crisis facing the United States. He further asserts that solutions to the crisis are directly related to the role of the United States in the global economy. What Wilson's contentions suggest are that ethical or philosophical bases for *de jure* public policies are still present; but, they must be closely aligned with economic realities. Altering public policy rationales and paradigms is crucial in light of changing economic and social conditions.

Throughout most of the twentieth century, the United States was at the forefront of the international economic community. Notable changes occurred in the 1980s. A trade surplus existed in 1981; by 1986, trade deficits were nearly $160 billion. The Federal budget deficits are over $200 billion per year, with over $3 trillion cumulatively. Loss of market share in eight out of ten technology-intensive manufacturing industries is occurring. Particular regions of the country, for example the South, are attempting to reverse these conditions through attempts to attract international firms and investments to promote the state's or region's economy. Over 30 per cent of foreign firms in the United States are headquartered in Georgia (Groennings, 1986, p. 7; Groennings, 1989, p. 4). Thus, federal and state policy-makers are constantly preoccupied with remaining internationally competitive and lessening and eventually eliminating the national debt.

Coupled with these economic realities are dramatic demographic changes in the population and work-force. *One-Third of A Nation* (Commission on Minority Participation in Education and American Life, 1988, p. 3) reports that in the mid-1980s over 20 per cent of the American school-age population were from ethnic or racial minorities. By the year 2000, that proportion will rise to one-third, producing the students who will comprise major additions to the American labour force. Nearly 65 per cent of the current American population are women, minorities, and economically disadvantaged people. These groups will collectively comprise 82 per cent of the 20 million new workers by 2000. Such groups are severely under-represented in the current work-force, particularly in fields like science and engineering, where they represent less than 15 per cent of current professionals (Wiley, 1989, p. 13; Fead, 1989, p. 4; O'Brien, 1989a, p. 1).

Paradigms for public policies must, therefore, include such disadvant-aged groups if *all* individuals and the nation are to be beneficiaries of economic and social viability. A wholesale abandonment of civil rights need not be evident. Instead, creative policies for inclusion, not exclusion, must be manifested.

Referring to Kenya, the stamp of *de jure* colonial policies was reflected throughout economic and related educational initiatives of the British.[2] Only two of every 100 African children entered secondary school during colonialism; consequently, few Africans moved into semiprofessional and professional positions so few could contribute to national development (Cheru, 1987, p. 41). Herculean problems confronted Kenya at its in-dependence in December 1963 as witnessed by the acute shortage of Africans practising domestically in professions: 36 doctors, 20 electrical engineers, and 17 university professors. Replacing foreign personnel was an immediate concern (Kenya, Republic of, 1972; Sifuna, 1983, p. 481). For Kenya, providing education for all was a central challenge, but it was especially so for secondary and higher education so that professionals could be prepared to address national development.

A continuous manifestation of the need for national development is the current per capita income of approximately $450, only $50 more than that in the late 1970s and early 1980s. Demographic conditions and future projections indicate that the ranks of Kenya's 23 million citizens will continue to swell given the population growth rate of 4 per cent per annum. Statistics indicate that over 50 per cent of Kenya's population is under 16 (Office of African Affairs, 1989, p. 1; Bowser, 1988, p. 11; Achola, 1988, p. 34). Thus, economic resources are needed to provide schooling, health care, and quality living conditions for the populace.

The contributions of all Kenyans will be necessary to develop and maintain a viable economy. As in the United States, many are adversely affected and are thus unable to contribute fully to the national economy. For example, in the late 1980s, Kenyan women comprised only 22 per cent of the wage labour force. And citizens from rural areas within certain provinces, for instance Northeastern, are barely represented in the formal economic sector (Hughes and Mwiria, 1989, p. 179; Kenya, Republic of, 1984, pp. 1, 35–7).

Government officials are, however, constantly preoccupied with the debt crisis so that fiscal allocations cannot address various social conditions.

President Moi asserted, 'It is as urgent as much as it is unavoidable for international development agencies and world powers to resolve the debt crisis facing Africa' ('The Thailand Trip', 1990, p. 32). African economies are ailing under the debt crisis because, for example, for each unit of assistance Africa obtains from the developed world, it pays three units in return. Hence, the gap widens between developed and developing countries. In short, altering international economic policies must be undertaken to enhance Kenyan development.

In summary, the preceding discussions underscore the necessity for integrating *de jure* public policies for economic development and competitiveness and those for human resource development. Whether in the United States or Kenya, the full participation of all disadvantaged people is needed for the nation's economic well-being. People become the policy-makers, professionals, and technicians who construct social, educational, and economic institutions for a nation's development (Commission on Minority Participation in Education and American Life, 1988, p. 30; Harbison, 1973, p. 3, cited in Hughes and Mwiria, 1989, p. 192). In Africa, this means that more than 6 per cent of the women should be engaged in administrative and managerial positions. American minorities and women should be represented by more than 15 per cent of those gainfully employed in science and engineering. In both nations, future demands necessitate further participation. For example, the predicted 37 per cent increase in faculty positions for American universities by the year 2003 commands the participation of under-represented groups. Citizens from remote Kenyan locales should be represented in the 6 million new jobs that are needed by the year 2000 (Hughes and Mwiria, 1989, p. 179; Conciatore, 1989, p. 3; Bowser, 1988, p. 13).

The roles of higher education, especially in relation to a nation's economy, are now considered.

While all of America's 3,000 plus baccalaureate and graduate institutions are concerned with instruction, scholarship and research, there are different missions and purposes among them. Over a century ago when the United States was a rural agrarian society, the creation and dissemination of knowledge and technology were deemed crucial to the international economy. Witness Senator Justin Morrill's rationale for establishing land-grant universities, 'Our artisans are to contend with the skill and wealth of many nations, and our farmers are sorely pressed by competition in . . . all markets both at home and abroad. . . . Our countrymen need fundamental instruction founded on the widest and best experiences of mankind' (Groennings, 1989, pp. 7–8). Hence, *de jure* policies established land-grant universities in every state to address agricultural, technical, and industrial concerns in relation to state and national needs.

Comprehensive doctoral and research universities continue to conduct basic research to advance the state-of-the-art in various disciplines and professions. Their research is heavily funded by the federal government and private corporations which are concerned with maintaining and enhancing national and international economic competitiveness. Such institutions conduct two-thirds of the basic research leading to the spin-off of high technology corporations. Universities are also global resources with expertise about other nations (Groennings, 1989, pp. 7–9). If the United States is to remain economically and educationally competitive, the characteristics of its various universities should be maintained and enhanced. That is, they must creatively seek to follow their missions and solve problems emanating from the larger society, including the academic and economic status of minorities and women.

Kenyan universities also engage in instruction, scholarship or research and service to the nation. As discussed earlier, an immediate mission of Kenyan universities in relation to the economy is the preparation of skilled and professional personnel for business, government, and various professions. During the First Development Decade of the 1960s, the Ministries of Economic Planning and Development and of Education provided rationales for tertiary or higher education (Sifuna, 1983, p. 481). Variables which influenced the importance of higher education included the need to create and increase a high-level national 'elite' to direct administrative and commercial tasks and the need to increase skilled personnel in agricultural and technical fields. During the 1970s and 1980s, special attention was devoted to science, agriculture, and engineering since these are the technical foundations of development. Simultaneously, considerable attention was devoted to all realms of formal education, given the tremendous need for teachers and schools. The University of Nairobi, the original university, encompasses all disciplines. By the mid-1980s, three additional universities were created: Kenyatta, Moi, and Egerton. Kenyatta University produces baccalaureate teachers and focuses on educational research. Egerton University specifically focuses on agriculture and related fields, and is concerned with applied agricultural research. Moi University has a technological focus and is to break the 'technological transfer barrier from developed . . . countries and develop practical solutions through research and teaching' (Kenya, Republic of, 1984, p. 22; Kintzer, 1987, p. 26). Hence, the collective missions of the several universities are to provide means to enhance economic and social development.

As we shall see in the next section, the avowed missions of American and Kenyan universities are incomplete since American minorities, disadvantaged Kenyans from rural areas, and women in both nations are not full participants in higher education.

STATISTICAL PORTRAITS IN HIGHER EDUCATION

The United States

During the mid-1980s, 76 per cent of African American and 65 per cent of Hispanic youth graduated from secondary school, compared to about 90 per cent of European Americans. This compares to 65, 56, and about 85 per cent for the respective groups a decade earlier. Of those who graduate, 32.4 per cent of African American males and 29.3 per cent of females (16 to 24 years of age) attended college in 1978. For European American males and females, the percentages were 34.3 and 29.2 per cent, respectively. By 1988, only 26.2 per cent of the African American male age cohort attended college. For the other groups, the figures were: 32.3 per cent of the African American women, 41.1 per cent of the European American males, and 38.6 per cent of European American women (Commission on Minority Participation in Education and American Life, *One Third of a Nation*, 1988, p. 8; Wiley, 1990, p. 8).

Once matriculation begins, the completion rates differ significantly. For instance, while over 52 per cent of the European Americans who began college in 1980 had completed the baccalaureate degree by 1986, only a quarter of African and Hispanic Americans had earned the degree. Within the general American population, about 25 per cent of whites (between 25 and 34 years of age) had completed four years of college in 1980; this figure remained constant through 1988. For African Americans, only 12.4 per cent and 13 per cent had completed this level of education in 1980 and 1988, respectively. For Hispanic and Native Americans, the picture was most bleak. Eight point nine per cent and 11.9 per cent were the figures in 1980 and 1988 for Hispanics. Only 8 per cent of Native Americans during this period finished four years of college (Magner, 1989, p. A-36; National Center for Education Statistics, 1989, p. 53; O'Brien, 1990, p. 28).

In short, retention rates for undergraduate minority Americans are not favourable. Less than 30 per cent of Hispanics and 25 per cent of Native American students who enter college as freshmen ever graduate. The overall quality of the academic environments, as evinced in the absence of academic support programmes and racial harassment are not conducive to retention. High attrition becomes the norm. Well-meaning white college administrators, according to Marable (1989, p. 24), have perceived the issue as a minority problem. However, underlying factors are not addressed.

Another key indicator of minority American participation is the earning of doctoral and advanced professional degrees between 1978–9 and 1988–9. In 1978–9, African American men earned 733 doctoral degrees, but in 1988–9, they earned only 479 degrees. For women, the numbers rose slightly from 534 in 1978–9 to 574 in 1988–9. Hispanic men earned 294 and 352 doctoral degrees in 1978–9 and 1988–9, respectively. Women of Hispanic descent earned 145 degrees in 1978–9 and 273 in 1988–9. For Native Americans of both sexes, very few degrees were earned: 104 in 1978–9 but only 84 in 1988–9. Of these, 69 were awarded to men in 1978–9 and a mere 49 in 1988–9. In contrast, 18,423 doctoral degrees were awarded to European American men in 1978–9 and 14,568 were awarded in 1988–9. For white women, the figures were 7,705 in 1978–9 and 10,327 in 1988–9 (National Center for Education Statistics, 1991, pp. 13–16). Statistics evinced for the professional areas such as law, medicine, dentistry, and veterinary medicine are also dismal for minority Americans during the same period of time. In 1978–9, only 8.1 per cent of the medical school graduates were minority Americans. By 1988–9, the percentage of minority American professional school graduates rose a little over 4 per cent to 12.2 (National Center for Educational Statistics, 1991, p. 4).

What appears quite evident is the rapid decline in degrees awarded to African American and Native American men. (While doctorates earned by white men also decreased, their career options are not as limited.) Although the number of doctorates and professional degrees earned by minority women has increased, the overall numbers are still small. The immediate beneficiaries of educational equity are European American women. Such women are increasingly attending undergraduate, graduate, and professional schools and remaining until graduation. Hence, statistical projections indicate that by the year 2000, the majority of doctoral degrees will be earned by women – primarily white (Nelson, 1990, p. 9).

Kenya

The Kenyan university system represents the apex of the educational pyramid. In 1978, there were 3 million students in primary schools, 120,000 in government secondary schools, and 5,900 students at the University of Nairobi and Kenyatta University College. By 1988, there were about 4.5 million primary school students, 500,000 secondary students, and 26,000 in the four public (government supported) universities (Olembo, 1986, p. 370; Office of African Affairs, 1989, p. 2). At each transition stage, there is a high drop-out rate. For instance, although there were about 160,000 students who entered government secondary education in 1987, there were 335,000 eligible youth (Bowser, 1988, p. 12). A wastage rate of 175,000 existed because there were not enough places in government secondary schools. The likelihood of further education is quite slim[3] for these students, primarily from rural areas.

The comprehensive examination system, which exists at each educational level, is exceedingly crucial in determining entrance to one of four public universities. In 1989, the Kenyan Advanced Certificate of Education examination was administered for the last time to nearly 41,895 students. That same year, 131,805 students took the Kenya Certificate of Secondary Education examination (KCSE), the new method of assessment that would determine who would enter the universities. In February 1990, the Universities' Joint Admissions Board agreed upon a combined total of 16,000 matriculants selected from both examinations (Lindsay, 1990a, pp. 869–70; 'The Numbers Crunch', 1990, p. 6). Hence, 157,000 who completed secondary education were not eligible to pursue university degrees. As we shall see in the following subsection, admission policies had to be altered; however, the vast number of students were still denied university matriculation.

Throughout the 1980s, women represented about 30 per cent of the university student body. This is consistent with the fact that 27 per cent and 28 per cent of the women in 1984 and 1987, respectively, were candidates for the Kenya Advanced Certificate of Education Examination. The choice of major shows distinct differences by gender. From 1976 to 1987, women constituted about 15 per cent of the baccalaureate science enrolments and only 4 per cent of those in engineering. Women represented almost 65 per cent of the education degree recipients and 68 per cent of the baccalaureates in the faculty of arts. Within education, 25 per cent of the women were studying for science education degrees in 1988 while 52 per cent were pursuing the arts baccalaureate in education. Somewhat surprising, 21 per cent of those studying medicine were women in 1987 compared to 15 per cent in 1976 (*Kenya, The Role of Women in Economic Development*, 1989, p. 46; Hughes and Mwiria, 1989, pp. 180–2). Once Kenyan students matriculate, persistence rates tend to remain high for all students – often over 70 per cent for an entering class. Though under-represented in various disciplines, earning the degree should enable women to pursue viable careers and contribute to national development.

POLICIES FOR ACCESS AND RETENTION, CURRICULUM DIVERSIFICATION, AND FINANCIAL ASSISTANCE

The United States

One-Third of A Nation maintains that leadership is the most critical factor for ensuring the participation of under-represented groups in American higher education (Commission on Minority Participation in Education and American Life, 1988, pp. 24–8; Clewell and Ficklen, 1986, pp. 52–6). Of special consideration is the role of the university president. Interfacing with external and internal groups on public and educational policies is central to the presidency. He or she establishes and maintains contacts with groups and is ultimately accountable for policy implementation. Access and retention, curriculum diversification, and finance are fundamental areas that necessitate institutional-wide policies that are clearly articulated or supported by the president (University of Georgia, 1990, pp. 11–13).

Access to comprehensive universities is largely determined by admission policies. Scores on standardized tests (for example, the Scholastic Aptitude Test [SAT] and the American College Test [ACT]) and high school grades are the most salient admissions criteria. Hodgkinson (1985, pp. 15–17) asserts that high school grades predict about one-half of the matriculants who will remain until graduation four to five years later. Numerous studies have presented evidence regarding problems associated with the SAT and ACT (Thomas, 1981, pp. 49–59; Morris, 1981, p. 73; Astin, 1981, 1982; Astin, 1988). Minorities and women consistently score lower than white males on standardized tests, often due to cultural and gender biases. The margins of error for the SAT is 65 points; hence, tests could vary by 130 points and serve as the basis for denying admission (Conciatore, 1989, p. 20).

In 1990 the Commission on Testing and Public Policy called for a critical re-examination of standardized tests. Acknowledging the limits of tests is an initial area for re-examining admissions policies. Scores should be reported with some indication of the probable error associated with that classification. Eliminating cultural and gender biases is a second area where considerable revisions are necessary. Over-reliance on testing is a third area where university admissions policies can be altered (National Commission on Testing and Public Policy, 1990, cited in Dervarics, 1990, pp. 1, 28). High school grades, school curriculum, written essays, interviews, and test scores could comprise the admissions portfolio.

The critical need for re-examining admissions policy is demonstrated by the following illustrations. Blackwell (1981, pp. 255–6) analysed selection criteria for graduate and professional schools and the arguments that minorities are not 'qualified' for post-baccalaureate programmes because their scores are lower than those of their white male peers. Yet, data indicate that the mean grade point averages and Law School Aptitude Test (LSAT) scores for minorities enrolling in the early 1980s were comparable to those for white males in the middle and late 1960s. Stiff competition forced higher LSAT scores and undergraduate grade point averages. Yet, it would now be absurd to contend that white males who graduated in the 1960s and who are currently practising law were not qualified for law school.

Wilson (1986, pp. 12–13) asserts that minorities and women should not expend so much effort contesting standardized test scores. Instead, considerable efforts should be expended in preparing for various standardized examinations. Some of his recommendations include: (1) more direct teaching of skills for test taking; (2) enrichment and tutoring programmes in the various subjects covered by the tests; (3) curriculum revisions to emphasize testing; and (4) the establishment of minimal acceptable scores and accepting candidates who meet the scores. On the surface, there is considerable merit to these recommendations. However, we shall observe in the section following on Kenya that teaching and testing for tests were major rationales for moving from English toward American methods of assessment. It would be quite ironic for Americans to place an over-reliance on methods being abandoned by others as they formulate new admissions policies.

Once matriculation begins, retention policies are to be initiated and maintained. Hence, the need to integrate policies and programmes that take into account cultural diversity and cultural specificity. For example, majority faculty and students often interact with various racial minorities as if they are a monolithic entity. The modes of social and educational interaction and learning styles differ among African, Cuban, Mexican, Native, and Puerto Rican Americans. Treatments or programmes should be individualized and tailored to meet individual and group needs (Lyons, 1990, pp. 1, 12; Institute for Program Evaluation, 1983).

Institutional policies for academic enhancement or support may be initiated. Such programmes, however, must be structured carefully to avoid negative connotations, as has often been the case. Two illustrations of successful cases are provided. A professor at the University of California, Berkeley, observed that 60 per cent of the African American students failed freshman calculus compared to 15 per cent of whites. From 1965 to 1975, no more than *two* African Americans or Hispanic Americans received a 'B' or better each year. Thus, he initiated an honours programme, although it certainly was not honours in the traditional sense. All course work and extra requirements had to be completed. This *de facto* initiative was incorporated into the University's 'professional development programme', an endeavour designed to increase the number of women and minority majors in mathematics and related fields. In 1988, there were 89 students in the honours programme. Only *two* African American and Hispanic students did not pass calculus. This contrasts with the 66 (of 123) minorities who were not in the programme that failed calculus. Similar programmes have been initiated at 15 other institutions (O'Brien, 1989b, pp. 1, 8).

Another illustration is the AHANA (Afro-American, Hispanic, Asian, and Native American) programme at Boston College where 12.5 per cent of the students are minorities. College officials are convinced that the programme's name, AHANA, helps attract students in contrast to some term that would have negative connotations. AHANA offers a range of services from academic tutoring to personal counselling. Prior to the programme's inception in the late 1980s, the graduation rate for minorities was 17 per cent; in 1989, it reached 75 per cent (Dodge, 1989, p. A-38). Students continually attest to the benefits of AHANA, although it cannot be argued definitively that it is the sole factor.

During the first two years of baccalaureate study, a core curriculum is studied which encompasses courses in the humanities, physical and biological sciences, mathematics, and the social sciences. Both *de facto* and *de jure* policies in most universities, until recently, dictated that the theoretical underpinnings of the various courses would be based upon those derived from the Western world. In the 1980s, Stanford and American Universities, the University of Michigan, and other comprehensive universities revised their core undergraduate curriculum requirements to include courses on African, Asian, and Latin American people, cultural diversity and pluralism, and international studies. That is, curriculum diversification occurred to mirror the realities of domestic and international life.

Such changes in curricular policies should present an avenue for the scholarship and creative works of minority scholars in the social and physical sciences and the humanities. For example, Africans are strategically deleted from discussions of scientific and political developments that characterized the Age of Discovery or the Middle Ages (Sudarkasa, 1987, pp. 4–13). Ignoring the contributions of minorities is equivalent to relegating them to an inferior or non-existent status since it is believed people are inferior or invisible if they have made no contributions.

Further alterations in curriculum policies and paradigms, according to Groennings (1989, pp. 10–14) and Boyer and Kaplan (1977), would enable students and faculty to move beyond the confines of particular disciplines. Comprehensive perspectives of phenomena would expand students' and professors' thinking about the interrelations between global and domestic economic conditions. The global economy could be discussed in the liberal arts; business and area studies could be linked; and foreign languages could become a requirement for all majors. In short, a kind of international education would be evinced throughout the curriculum. The independent and interdependent features of nations would be clearer to professionals whether in business, education, the social and physical sciences, or the arts.

Institutional policies to attract and retain students and diversify the curriculum are contingent upon the presence of faculty to serve as mentors and role models and to teach culturally diverse curriculum. Hence, the need exists for universities to attract and retain minority faculty. Until 1989, the oldest land-grant university in the United States, the University of Georgia, did not have a single African American woman full professor. Only three African American men were professors. In 1974, there were seven African American faculty level appointees and twenty-five in 1986 (Reid, 1987, p. 1; UGA Affirmative Action Office, 1987). A presidential initiative was undertaken in 1987 to ameliorate these conditions. Approximately $500,000 was earmarked for special initiatives to recruit minority Americans. Special endeavours were to be made to recruit and hire minority faculty in light of current and future programme needs. By April 1988, faculty level appointments would be made to 44 faculty of African descent (The University of Georgia, 1988, pp. 1–3). It remains to be seen how many will actually be tenured and promoted *and* whether efforts will be made about special funding.

It also remains to be seen whether African Americans will be recommended for key administrative positions. For example, in 1992, there was one African American department chair and one African American woman vice president (in a specially created position where a search was not conducted). In early 1992, the Dean of the College of Education took a leave of absence. The Associate Dean of Academic Affairs for the College, an African American woman, was not recommended as the interim dean, despite her comprehensive academic portfolio. According to the Dean, faculty and administrators within the College did not support her candidacy for the interim deanship. Being an Associate Dean is acceptable, but not the Dean; that is, race was apparently a factor since she had been deemed effective for five years without concerns being raised about her abilities or faculty support.

Although the foregoing may be initiated successfully, policies which provide financial assistance to students are often the factor which determines whether youth even attend or remain in universities. Several changes in federal policies for financial assistance have contributed to the decline in minority student participation. During the mid-1970s, a larger portion of federal financial assistance was available through grants rather than loans. The criteria were altered so that the 'most needy' would ostensibly still be eligible for grants. About 30 per cent of African American youth from working-class backgrounds attended colleges in 1988, compared to almost 40 per cent in 1976. Youth from middle-class backgrounds comprised about 36 per cent of the matriculants in 1988 in contrast to about 53 per cent in 1976 (O'Brien, 1988, p. 6; Winger, 1990, p. 75).

Loans tend to deter college matriculation, especially as tuition and fees continually increase. The Federal Higher Education Act (HEA), which provides a substantial portion of funding for federal student assistance, was examined closely in 1990 and 1991. The grants portion of the HEA may be altered in light of students' matriculation at institutions where there was a likely expectation of completion *and* for entering professions where there were critical shortages related to national priorities such as science and engineering (Astin, 1982, pp. 124–8, 183; Dervarics, 1990, p. 12).

Yet, at the Federal level, there are conflicting views regarding the balance between grants and scholarships *and* loans for student financial aid. These perspectives, and the shift of federal level initiatives to state undertakings, indicate that the state will assume increasing responsibility for economic and social policies and programmes. In the report, *Halfway Home and a Long Way to Go*, business and corporate leaders and higher education executives are stressing the need for scholarships and grants for needy students via state legislative or private sector initiatives (Betts, 1986, pp. 18–22). Of particular note is recent legislation enacted in Louisiana. A former corporate chief executive officer spearheaded a lobbying effort to pass legislation that would provide tuition grant assistance to Louisiana's needy students. Acceptance of the state's responsibility for college costs for those who cannot afford to attend was a central rationale. In essence, it is a matter of state public policy to educate its youth for productive economic and social lives. The potential social and economic benefits for the larger society are tremendous, both in cost benefits and savings to the state and increased individual earnings (Jacobi *et al.*, 1987, p. 5). Effective July 1989, every low- and middle-income student who qualifies for a Federal Pell Grant receives state payments of tuition and fees at public universities and colleges. In the state of Louisiana about two-thirds of college education costs are then covered (Taylor, 1990a, pp. 16–18; 'Texas Governor Signs "Taylor Plan" Bill', Taylor 1990b, pp. 10–11).

Similar legislation is being considered or has been passed in twelve additional states. Such state policies prevent or remove fiscal obstacles for disadvantaged youth and do not carry negative stigma as have other social programmes for disadvantaged people. Simultaneously, corporate leaders are maintaining or establishing scholarship trusts for needy and middle-income students, often for targeted areas in business, science, and engineering. Linking individual success with long-range corporate goals are the rationales since such students will become the future corporate professionals. University executives encourage such state and corporate policy initiatives because they supplement and complement other higher education financial assistance packages.

Judicial decisions created higher education policies affecting student finance. As part of a major judicial decision in the 1970s, the *Adams* case states that maintained dual systems of higher education were to dismantle these vestiges of segregation. Increasing the minority presence at pre-dominantly white institutions was to be undertaken by admitting a larger number of African American students and providing services for retention. Financial assistance via scholarships and fellowships for minorities was created by universities and Boards of Regents or Trustees. Hence, the University of Georgia began administering Board of Regents Opportunity Scholarships to economically disadvantaged minority students in graduate and professional programmes. About 100 state resident students at the University of Georgia received $5,000 per year scholarships during the late 1980s (University of Georgia, 1988–9, p. 1; Clifton, 1990, August 31, personal interview).

Keith (1987, p. 11) and Clewell and Ficklen (1986, pp. 52–5) discuss how leadership by top university administrators is a key ingredient in effective policy implementation to increase minority participation throughout the institution. Drawing upon our established conceptual framework, the president articulates official policies via written documents, state of the university addresses, strategic plans, and oral directives on access and retention, curriculum diversification, and student finance. Official or *de jure* policies carry sanctions if they are not implemented and/or adhered to. For example, the performance evaluation of senior line administrators (vice presidents, deans, and directors) should be linked directly to the units' success in recruitment and retention, curriculum diversification, and student finance. When non-compliance is evident, programmes under the cognizant administrator can be transferred; minute raises can be allocated; or, the administrator can be transferred or terminated. Such measures largely account for the preceding successes.

Presidents and other senior administrators are concerned with accreditation policies of national and regional organizations. If universities and programmes are not accredited, basically student degrees and other college or university activities are not recognized. Some professional bodies, such as the National Council for the Accreditation of Teacher Education (NCATE), established criteria that require cultural diversity in the student and faculty bodies, curriculum, practica or internships, and governance. NCATE has delayed accreditation to some schools or departments of education when cultural diversity has not been clearly demonstrated in the several realms (Jerrolds, 1990, May and June, personal interview).

Various regional organizations, via the auspices of the Council on Postsecondary Accreditation, provide the overall accreditation for colleges and universities which offer degrees. Two of these organizations, the Middle States Association of Colleges and Schools and the Western Association of Schools and Colleges, have broadened their accrediting policies to evaluate institutions on cultural diversity. The accreditation of Bernard M. Baruch College of the City University of New York was delayed because it failed to demonstrate cultural diversity (Leatherman, 1990, pp. A-1, A-12).

In short, sanctions by accrediting bodies coupled with those of presidents and senior administrators – in response to *de jure* or official policies – will help ensure that minority Americans are represented throughout colleges and universities. A challenge is to create and maintain official policies on diversity amid the myriad of other competing university policies.

Kenya

The Kenyan Minister for Education appointed a prominent committee to examine educational policies; and the group produced the 1976 Report of the National Committee on Educational Objectives and Policy. This report, commonly referred to as the 'Gacathi Report', and that of a University Task Force (of 1981) led to a national policy that would affect the entire Kenyan educational system. Effective January 1985, Kenya shifted from the English model of 7-6-3 years of education to the present one of 8-4-4, a variation of the American educational structure. Eight years of primary, four years of secondary, followed by four years of university education are the characteristics of the new design. Some rationales for creating this *de jure* policy included: (1) the provision of comprehensive and relevant curriculum; (2) an equitable distribution of educational resources; (3) an increased emphasis on technical and vocational training; (4) the use of appropriate assessment and evaluation; (5) the opportunity for further education and training; and (6) a greater sense of national unity (Kenya, Republic of, 1984, pp. 1–2). In this connection, these rationales highlight access, the curriculum, and associated issues such as evaluation and assessment.

Candidates of the new 8-4-4 system took the Kenya Certificate of Secondary Education Examination (KCSE) for the first time in 1989. The KCSE covers a range of subjects as prescribed in the national secondary curriculum – communication (including Kiswahili, English, and foreign languages), mathematics, science, humanities, and applied education (including industrial and agricultural education). The Universities' Joint Admissions Board policy originally established a 'B' in at least 10 subjects, on a scale from 'A' (excellent) to 'E' (extremely poor), as the basis for entrance. The Board proposed 8,500 slots for KCSE candidates and 7,500 for Kenya Advanced Certificate of Education 'A' level candidates ('The Numbers Crunch', 1990, pp. 5–6; 'KCSE: Something Terribly Wrong', 1990, pp. 28–9).

Immediate problems surfaced requiring official policy changes. Only 5,000 KCSE candidates would meet these minimum admissions criteria. In contrast, over 11,000 candidates who took the 'A' level examinations were eligible for admissions since they obtained at least three principal passes.

These 'A' level candidates believed they should be admitted to a university since they had met the admissions criteria (10 or more points on principal passes for arts students and seven or higher for science students). After deliberating these results, the Universities' Joint Admission Board revised admission policies. KCSE candidates who scored 'Cs' and 'A' level arts candidates with 12 points would be eligible for admission. Science 'A' level scores would remain at 7 points, in light of the crucial needs in these areas ('The Numbers Crunch', 1990, pp. 4–6; 'New Hope for "A" Levellers', 1990, pp. 17–18). Under this policy, additional KCSE candidates would be accommodated; the Ministry's commitment to the new 8-4-4 system and its examination methods would be demonstrated. However, over 2,000 'A' level candidates would *not* be admitted. A public outcry ensued immediately.

President Moi issued a directive to the Vice President and Minister for Finance, the Minister for Education, and the Vice Chancellors of the universities (that is, the Universities' Joint Admission Board). He directed this group to create or alter admissions policies to accommodate all students who met the original and revised policies. Thus, about 18,000 students were likely matriculants in 1990 ('New Hope for "A" Levellers', 1990, pp. 17–18). (Although 18,000 students were expected, the number reported in a 1991 article titled 'Crisis Time' in *The Weekly Review* (p. 4) actually reached 21,000.) The Minister of Education announced in May 1990 that four institutions would be upgraded to university status through affiliations with Egerton, Jomo Kenyatta, and Moi Universities. These new university colleges will help accommodate all qualified KCSE and 'A' level candidates and help prepare baccalaureate teachers ('Four More Universities', 1990, pp. 27–8). In essence, changes (in) or the creation of new *de jure* policies resulted from immediate social and educational conditions.

The examination results underscore the necessity for additional policy analyses which affect university admissions. The KCSE is designed to assess students' abilities in a comprehensive range of subjects rather than the former method of examinations in three or four disciplines. Teaching the curriculum and studying courses primarily for the secondary completion tests were often the *modi operandi* for 'A' level preparation. Hence, some subjects were virtually ignored which meant that individual development and employment options were limited if the students did not matriculate in higher education. Recurrent questions remain regarding minimum criteria for admission based upon assessments in several sub-jects. After all, if the admissions policies could be changed from 'B' to 'C' level passes, does that mean (as some Kenyans contend) that 'C' students are not really capable of successfully pursuing university degrees? Are the last groups of 'A' level matriculants more qualified than their KCSE peers ('The "Quality" Factor', 1990, p. 7; Mulusa, 1990, pp. 12–14). Is it reasonable to expect students to score 'Bs' on 7 to 10 subjects? To what extent may candidates with similar abilities be admitted or denied admission to a university, given that evaluation standards of external examiners are not the same? That is, what is a valid score? Might it be quite appropriate to consider an admission portfolio which includes assessments from individual teachers?

A host of issues affected students' performance on the first KCSE administrations. The 1989 examinees began the revised educational system in 1985. Changing the system certainly did not guarantee that all parts of the educational infrastructure were altered simultaneously. While various secondary school curricular changes were implemented, there was a shortage of books, curriculum aids, and other teaching materials. Quite crucial were the pedagogical methods of secondary teachers. Many had staff development training to teach and help prepare students for comprehensive examinations in a range of subjects. But, old methods are not easily discarded (Korir-Koech, 1986, p. 16; Mulusa, 1990, pp. 12–15). So, *de facto* curriculum and pedagogical methods continued to exist and affect students' performance.

The four-year programme for the KCSE university matriculants contains major alterations, especially during the first year of study. Similar to the American semester system, common or core courses are required for first-year students. The Director of the Board of Common Undergraduate Courses at the University of Nairobi asserts that 'the social and political realities of present-day Kenya,' are the foundations for the core courses. The core courses include: Principles of Development and Application; Institutions and Value in Kenya's Development; Science and Technology in Development; and Communication Skills. All underscore what the Minister of Education terms 'socio-economic situations of modern Kenya' ('The "Quality" Factor', 1990, p. 8).

Optional or elective courses will also be offered to broaden the students' perspectives of Kenyan development and the nation's place in the world. Two basic categories of optional courses are offered, one for science subjects and another for arts subjects. Art-oriented subjects are to be taken by science majors, while science-oriented courses are designed for arts students. Hence, undergraduates will be exposed to a range of disciplines: ethics, law, economics, ecology, biochemistry, music, anthropology, and atmospheric science. Environmental studies will be available to both groups of students ('The "Quality" Factor', 1990, p. 8). These optional courses should also help women, students from rural locales, and the small number of *harambee* school graduates,[4] in particular, expand their perspectives since a range of subjects were often not available in their secondary schools.

Because a substantial percentage of the 1990 matriculants pursued baccalaureate teaching degrees to teach in four-year secondary schools, the curriculum at the universities offering the Bachelor of Education (BEd) was altered. The intending teachers will specialize in their majors, but they must become attuned to the range of secondary school subjects. The development of secondary school curriculum courses in pedagogy, methods, and educational structure should later be translated into actual classroom practices. Hence, problems which appeared on the first KCSE results, such as students' 'inability to follow instructions and consequently giving irrele- vant answers [and] . . . they were not able to make inferences from the text' ('KCSE: Something Terribly Wrong', 1990, p. 30), may be addressed.

Introducing core courses and other curriculum alterations means that university lecturers would need to teach new courses. To prepare for these curricular changes, seventy new posts were created. Moreover, staff, ranging from teaching faculty to lecturers, were being retrained overseas. For example, lecturers who would teach the Communication Skills course were sent to England for additional training in English composition, litera- ture, test construction, and pedagogical methods. These retrained lecturers should use new teaching and curriculum material designed specifically for the Communication Skills course ('The "Quality" Factor', 1990, p. 9).

Perhaps the largest policy change for matriculants involves methods of assessment. Individual lecturers administer class examinations in the common core courses and those of the major concentration. Current indi- cations suggest that the final comprehensive examinations, administered at the conclusion of four years, will determine what type of, or if candidates will earn the, baccalaureate ('The Numbers Crunch', 1990, p. 9). *De facto* American methods of individual class assessment will be used; yet, the *de jure* comprehensive English method of examination will determine the final outcome. Undoubtedly, policy analyses will need to be undertaken to ascertain the optimum modes of providing quality curriculum and examinations.

As in any nation, student finances will be a salient factor in determining whether matriculants remain until graduation. University students have access to bursaries which are to meet tuition costs and loans are available to meet the costs of books, food, and living expenses (Achola, 1988, p. 35). Thus, it would appear that once candidates matriculate, the costs of university education should be covered. The scenario is not always rosy. In 1989, the Ministry of Education, Science, and Technology altered its policy of administering student loans, largely due to high default rates. The loan programme was transferred to the state-owned commercial banks via an agreement wherein the Ministry would allocate the funds to the banks for direct loans to students. The Ministry argues that commercial banks should have more success in administering and recovering student loans than a government agency. Receiving loans in a timely fashion has not always occurred as shown by student protests at Egerton University and the University of Nairobi ('The University Students' Loan Scheme: A Question of Management', 1990, p. 24). For students whose parents and relatives are from farming or other backgrounds with limited cash resources, delayed receipt of loans is a harsh burden. The Ministry and the commercial banks continue to explore policies for effectively administering student loans.

As in other developing countries, university fiscal resources can also hamper students' opportunities to obtain quality education. This was accentuated in 1990 with the double intake of 'A' level and KCSE matriculants where facilities were expanded, additional books and teaching materials purchased, and new lecturers hired or retrained ('The Expansion of Facilities', 1990, pp. 10–11). Some strategies may be explored to increase university fiscal resources by levying taxes on select items such as licenses; instituting an education tax on university graduates; encouraging private corporations to provide for students of employees; and requiring some universities to provide some food and related items since, after all, agriculture and technology are part of their central missions. Individuals, as expected, do not view favourably the prospects of additional taxes (Achola, 1988, pp. 42–5). Creative fiscal policy explorations must continue in light of current and projected resource needs.

CROSS-NATIONAL POLICIES FOR HIGHER EDUCATION

In elucidating the range of public and educational policies affecting universities in the United States and Kenya, three distinct, yet interrelated, issues emerge. They include: a shift in the rationales and paradigms of public and educational policies, specific areas within higher education that need alterations and evaluations, and the articulation among various sectors regarding the creation and alteration of policies.

A central concern of this chapter has focused on the relationship between higher education *and* economic and social conditions. For the United States, global economic competitiveness is an increasingly important rationale for public policies. Promoting national economic and social development is the rationale for Kenya. Policies impacting education, however, have not always been linked with economic and social conditions. Hence, the central thesis: a shift in the paradigms and rationales for *de jure* public and educational policies must occur so that disadvantaged groups are clearly incorporated into all segments of universities as minorities and disadvantaged groups. It is essential to balance the economic rationales posited by policy-makers with the ethical or humanistic rationales voiced by disadvantaged groups. The immediate consequences of failing to shift paradigms are the continued paucity of disadvantaged groups in higher education and their subsequent inability to contribute to the economic and social well-being of the respective nations.

To insure the participation of under-represented groups in universities, *de jure* policies pertaining to access and retention, curriculum diversification and alterations, and financial assistance must be changed and evaluated. In both the United States and Kenya, access is restricted by standardized or national tests. Arguments are voiced in both nations that establishing and maintaining educational quality via merit selection, as demonstrated in tests, is necessary for matriculation in comprehensive universities. Research in the United Stated belies these arguments. While there is space in American universities to accommodate most students, fiscal and space limitations in Kenyan institutions are often underlying rationales for restrictive admissions policies ('The Expansion of Facilities', 1990, pp. 10–11).

Particular lessons can be learned *vis-à-vis* cross-national contexts. There is considerable national concern in the United States with standardized tests and the measures which help students prepare for such tests. As discussed previously, one of the fundamental rationales for the Kenyan national policy shift to an American system was the likely provision of more access to comprehensive education. Under the old system, Kenyan teachers, students, and parents were preoccupied with probable examination items. Kenyans should not subsequently emulate American admissions policies, in lieu of English ones, that place undue weight on national examinations. Nor should American teachers and students begin 'teaching and studying for tests' as these *modi operandi* are ostensibly being discarded in Kenya. Both formative and summative evaluations of admissions criteria should be undertaken continually to employ a range of measures to determine viable policy alternatives for university admissions.

In both nations, evaluations of the curriculum diversification, alterations *and* finance will also be important. The evaluations will help ascertain answers to policy-relevant questions such as: to what extent are culturally diverse or international materials included in the core American curriculum? To what extent are the skills acquired in core communications courses at the Kenyan universities efficiently used in the major courses? Are the American and Kenyan teaching faculties sufficiently prepared in content and pedagogy to incorporate the curricular changes? And given economic realities in both nations, what measures can help ensure the efficient administration of financial assistance packages to students?

Enhancing social and economic development via universities hinges, to a great extent, upon the lucid articulation of public and educational policies. Given the different levels of development and governmental structures in the respective nations, policy articulation assumes some nation-specific characteristics. In the United States, there is a noticeable policy shift from the federal to the state level. Decentralization is heard throughout the country. Boards of Regents or Trustees, university presidents, and other university executives are, therefore, quite responsible for clear policy articulation within the universities and with external bodies. Sanctions for non-compliance with policies often rest at the institutional, state, or regional levels. National involvement in universities is the Kenyan reality since all universities are national ones. For example, the Kenyan president directed the Ministry of Education and the Universities' Joint Admissions Board to admit all qualified candidates in 1990. When public and educational policies are not articulated and implemented, the sanctions for non-compliance are national in scope and can emerge directly from the populace. The negative political fall-out for not admitting qualified 'A'-level candidates was a tremendous sanction.

In both nations the articulation of official or *de jure* policies provides major nexuses between the roles of universities *and* national economic and social development. Without lucid policy articulation, policy-makers and educators will continue to muddle through without meeting individual or national goals.

NOTES

1 Some of the major legislative, executive orders, and judicial decisions included the 1964 Civil Rights Act, Executive Orders 11246 and 11375, and Title IX of the 1972 Education Act. Such major legislative, executive, and judicial decisions of the 1960s and 1970s are discussed in Derrick Bell's *And We Are Not Saved* (1979); Bell's *Race, Racism, and American Law* (1980); and Lindsay's 'Public and Higher Education Policies Influencing African-American Women' (1988, pp. 563–80).

2 For additional references regarding the effect of British education policies on national development and education see Cheru (1987); Rodney (1972) and Amin (1972, pp. 503–24); Sheffield (1973); Court and Ghai (eds) (1974).

3 Approximately 60 per cent of secondary students attend *harambee* schools; that is, secondary 'second-chance' institutions for youth who could not enter government schools. *Harambee* schools are primarily financed by parents and local citizens. The facilities are usually inadequate, unqualified teachers teach, and textbooks and other teaching materials are largely absent. Only 7 per cent of the University of Nairobi students attended such schools (Shiman and Mwiria (1987, p. 369–72); Shiman (1990, August 30) letter to author to clarify statistics on *harambee* school attendance).

4 Same as Note 3.

REFERENCES

Achola, P.W. (1988). Mobilising Additional Funds for Secondary and Higher Education in Kenya. *Kenya Journal of Education*, 4(1).

Amin, S. (1972). Underdevelopment and Dependency in Black Africa: Their Historical Origin and Contemporary Form. *Journal of Modern African Studies*, 10.

Astin, A. (1981). *Four Critical Years*. San Francisco: Jossey-Bass.

Astin, A. (1982). *The American Freshman, 1966–81: Some Implications for Educational Policy and Practice*. Washington, DC: National Commission on Excellence in Education, Department of Education.

Astin, A. (1988). *Minorities in American Higher Education*. San Francisco: Jossey-Bass.

Astin, H. (1981). In G.E. Thomas (ed.), *Black Students in Higher Education: Conditions and Experiences in the 1970s*. Westpoint, CT: Greenwood Press.

Bell, D. (1979). *And We Are Not Saved: The Elusive Quest for Racial Justice*. New York: Basic Books.

Bell, D. (1980). *Race, Racism, and American Law*. Boston, MA: Little, Brown and Company.

Betts, D. (1986). *Halfway Home and a Long Way to Go* (Report of the 1986 Commission on the future of the South). Chapel Hill, NC: Southern Growth Policies Board.

Bishop, J. (1977). The Effects of Public Policies on the Demand for Higher Education. *Journal of Human Resources*, 12.

Blackwell, J.E. (1981). *Mainstreaming Outsiders: The Production of the Black Professionals*. Bayside, NY: General Hall.

Bowser, G.W. (1988). The New 8-4-4 Educational System: Meeting the Needs of the Vocationally Disadvantaged in Kenya. *Journal for Vocational Special Needs Education*, 10(3).

Boyer, E. and Kaplan, M. (1977). *Educating for Survival*. New Rochelle, NY: Change Magazine Press.

Cheru, F. (1987). *Independence, Underdevelopment and Unemployment in Kenya*. Lanham, MD: University Press of America.

Clewell, B.C. and Ficklen, M.S. (1986). *Improving Minority Retention in Higher Education: A Search for Effective Institutional Practices*. Princeton, NJ: Educational Testing Services.

Clifton, I. (1990). *Personal interview*. Athens, GA: University of Georgia, Office of Vice President for Academic Affairs.

Commission on Minority Participation in Education and American Life (1988). *One-Third of a Nation*. Washington, DC: American Council of Education.

Conciatore, J. (1989). Differences in Approach to Tests might Account for Scary Discrepancies. *Black Issues in Higher Education*, 6(17).

Court, D. and Ghai, D.P. (eds) (1974). *Education, Society, and Development: New Perspectives from Kenya*. Nairobi, Kenya: Oxford University Press.

'Crisis Time' (1991, February 22). *The Weekly Review*, Nairobi.

Dervarics, C. (1990). Congress to Seek Greater Emphasis on Grants, Instead of Loans. *Black Issues in Higher Education*, 6(23).

Dodge, S. (1989). A Center Helps Minority Students Solve Academic, Social Problems. *The Chronicle Of Higher Education*, 36(13).

'The Expansion of Facilities' (1990, April 27). *The Weekly Review*, Nairobi.

Fead, K. (1989, May 22). Hodgkinson Renews Plea for Educators to Prepare for Diversity. *Community College Week*, 1(13).

'Four More Universities' (1990, May 25). *The Weekly Review*, Nairobi.

Groennings, S. (1986, May 26). *The New South and Innovation in International Education*. Athens, GA: The University of Georgia, Institute of Higher Education.

Groennings, S. (1989). Public Policy and National Imperatives. In C. Fincher (ed.), *Planning Imperatives for the 1990s*. Athens, GA: The University of Georgia, Institute of Higher Education.

Harbison, F.H. (1973). *Human Resources as the Wealth of Nations*. New York: Oxford University Press.

Hodgkinson, H.L. (1985). *All One System: Demographics of Education-Kindergarten through Graduate School*. Washington, DC: Institute for Educational Leadership.

Hughes, R. and Mwiria, K. (1989). Kenyan Women in Higher Education and the Labour Market. *Comparative Education*, 25(2).

Institute for Programme Evaluation (1983). *The Evaluation Synthesis*. Washington, DC: General Accounting Office.

Jacobi, M., Astin, A., and Ayala, F. (1987). *College Student Outcomes Assessment: A Talent Development Perspective*. College Station, TX: ASHE.

Jerrolds, B. (1990). Personal Interview. Athens, GA: University of Georgia.

'KCSE: Something Terribly Wrong' (1990, March 9). *The Weekly Review*, Nairobi.

Keith, L. (1987). *Blacks in Higher Education in the 1980s: An Assessment*. Paper presented at the University of Georgia Conference on Minorities, Athens.

Kenya, Republic of (1972). *Ministry of Commerce and Industry*. Nairobi, Kenya: Government Printer.

Kenya, Republic of (1984). *8-4-4 System of Education*. Ministry of Education, Science and Technology. Nairobi, Kenya: Government Printer.

Kenya, The Role of Women in Economic Development (1989). Washington, DC: The World Bank.

Kintzer, F.C. (1987). *The Harambee Institutes of Science and Technology in the Republic of Kenya* (Report of a Study, 1986–1987), Fulbright Senior Research Paper, Washington, DC. (ERIC Document No.ED 280 540).

Klein, S.S. (1987, April). *The Role of Public Policy in the Education of Girls and Women*. Paper presented at the annual conference of the American Educational Research Association, Washington, DC.

Korir-Koech, K. (1986). *Restructuring Kenya's Educational System: Implications of Following the United States Model*. Paper presented at the annual conference of the Comparative and International Education Society, Toronto, Canada.

LaMorte, M. (1987). *School Law: Cases and Concepts*. Englewood Cliffs, NJ: Prentice Hall.

Leatherman, C. (1990). Two of Six Regional Accrediting Agencies Take Steps to Put Colleges on Racial, Ethnic Diversity. *The Chronicle of Higher Education*, 36(48).

Lindsay, B. (1988). Public and Higher Education Policies Influencing African American Women. *Higher Education: The International Journal of Higher Education and Educational Planning*, 17(3).

Lindsay, B. (1990a). Comparative Teacher Education: Illustrations from English-Speaking Countries. In W.R. Houston (ed.), *Handbook of Research in Teacher Education*. New York and London: Macmillan.

Lindsay, B. (1990b). Educational Equity in Cross-national Settings. In R.M.Thomas (ed.), *Comparative International Education: Issues and Prospects* Oxford: Pergamon Press.

Lyons, N.L. (1990). First Lesson in Recruiting Hispanics: Recognize that they are not a Monolith. *Black Issues in Higher Education,* 6(22).

Magner, D. (1989). Colleges Try News to Insure Minority Students Make it to Graduation. *The Chronicle of Higher Education,* 36(13).

Marable, M. (1989). Beyond Academic Apartheid. *Black Issues in Higher Education,* 6(19).

Matthews, F. (1990). Leonard Haynes: Key Person at a Critical Time. *Black Issues in Higher Education,* 6(21).

Mazzoni, T.L. (1989). Governors as Policy Leaders for Education: A Minnesota Comparison. *Educational Policy,* 3(1).

Morris, L. (1981). The Role of Testing in Institutional Selectivity and Black Access to Higher Education. In G. E. Thomas (ed.), *Black Students in Higher Education: Conditions and Experiences in the 1970s.* Westpoint, CT: Greenwood Press.

Mulusa, T. (1990, April 27). Conceptualising Administering and Evaluating the 8-4-4 System. *The Weekly Review,* Nairobi.

National Center for Education Statistics (1989). *The Condition of Education: Volume 2. Postsecondary Education.* Washington, DC: US Department of Education.

National Center for Education Statistics (1991). *Race/Ethnicity Trends in Degrees Conferred by Institutions of Higher Education: 1978–79 through 1988–89'.* Washington, DC: US Department of Education.

National Commission on Testing and Public Policy (1990). Cited in C. Dewarics (1990). National Commission Proposes Sweeping Changes in Testing. *Black Issues in Higher Education,* 7(7).

National Committee on Educational Objectives and Policy (1976). *Report of the National Committee on Educational Objectives and Policy (Gacathi Report).* Nairobi, Kenya: Government Printer.

Nelson, W.D. (1990). Women Seen Dominating Doctorates by 2000. *Black Issues in Higher Education,* 6(21).

'New Hope for "A" Levellers' (1990, May 11). *The Weekly Review,* Nairobi.

'The Numbers Crunch' (1990, April 27). *The Weekly Review,* Nairobi.

O'Brien, E. (1989a). Two New Handbooks Help Higher Education Institutions Set and Meet Diversity Goals. *Black Issues in Higher Education,* 5(24).

O'Brien, E. (1989b). Berkeley Model Proves Successful for Blacks, Hispanics' Calculus Performance. *Black Issues in Higher Education,* 5(24).

O'Brien, E. (1989c). Without more Minorities, Women, Disabled, U.S. Scientific Failure Certain, Federal Study Says. *Black Issues in Higher Education,* 6(20).

O'Brien, E.M. (1988). Need Multi-faceted Approach to Address Black Education Crisis, CBC Told. *Black Issues in Higher Education,* 5(15).

O'Brien, E.M. (1990). AAU Exhorts Federal Government to Support Minority PhD Students. *Black Issues in Higher Education,* 6(23).

Office of African Affairs (1989). *Country Data: Kenya,* Washington, DC: United States Information Agency.

Olembo, J.A. (1986). Financing Education in Kenya. *Prospects,* 16(3).

'The Quality Factor' (1990, April 27). *The Weekly Review,* Nairobi.

Reid, J. (1987, May 17). UGA Lacking in Black Faculty, Students. *Athens Banner Herald.*

Rodney, W. (1972). *How Europe Underdeveloped Africa*. Dar es Salaam and Tanzania: Tanzania: Tanzania Publishing Company.

Sheffield, J. (1973). *Education in Kenya: An Historic Study*. New York: Teachers College Press.

Shiman, D. (1990, August 30). *Letter to Author to Clarify Statistics on Harambee School Attendance*.

Shiman, D. and Mwiria, K. (1987). Struggling Against the Odds: Harambee Secondary Schools in Kenya. *Phi Delta Kappan*, 68(5).

Sifuna, D.N. (1983). Kenya: Twenty Years of Multilateral Aid. *Prospects*, 13(4).

Sudarkasa, N. (1987). Racial and Cultural Diversity is a Key Part of the Pursuit of Excellence in the University. *The Chronicle of Higher Education*, 33(24).

Taylor, P. (1990a). Pat Taylor's Challenge. *Black Issues in Higher Education*, 7(2).

Taylor, P. (1990b). Texas Governor Signs 'Taylor Plan' Bill. *Black Issues in Higher Education*, 7(9).

'The Thailand Trip' (1990, March 9). *The Weekly Review*, Nairobi.

Thomas, G.E. (1981). *Black Students in Higher Education: Conditions and Experiences in the 1970s*. Westpoint, CT: Greenwood Press.

University of Georgia Affirmative Action Office (1987). Minute from the Affirmative Action Office, University of Georgia.

University of Georgia (1988, April 27). Press release from the Office of Public Information, Athens, GA.

University of Georgia, 1988–89 (1989). Information sheet, Regents' Opportunity Scholarship, Office of the Vice President for Academic Affairs, Athens, GA.

University of Georgia (1990). *Strategic Plan*. Athens, GA: Office of the President.

'The University Students' Loan Scheme: A Question of Management' (1990). *The Weekly Review*, Nairobi.

Wiley, E., III. (1989). Stereotyping, Prejudice Hindering Hispanic Women in Academia. *Black Issues in Higher Education*, 6(2).

Wiley, E., III. (1990). International Concern about Implications of Black Male Crisis Questioned by Scholars. *Black Issues in Higher Education*, 7(9).

Wilson, R. (1986). *Black Education in the World Workplace: A Demographic Analysis*. Paper presented at the National Alliance of Black School Educators' annual meeting, Washington, DC.

Winger, P. (1990). Fewer Blacks on Campus. *Newsweek*.

2 Education, legislation and economic performance: the case of Japan

Teruhisa Horio

Japanese education, public and private, is set within a framework of laws. These are primarily those which form the Japanese Constitution of 1946, the Fundamental Laws of Education (1947), the School Law (1947), the Board of Education Law and Local Educational Administration Law (1948–56) and many administrative ordinances. Japanese education is under the rigid control of judicial legislation.

These educational laws have a hierarchical structure according to judicial order. Yet in reality the Constitution and the Fundamental Law of Education have been often ignored or distorted by regulations or administrative ordinances or governmental interpretation of these laws. From this have arisen many conflicts between administrative authority and teachers unions and there have been many cases in the courts concerning education. Thus Japanese education is anything but stable in the juridical sense. Why did the situation come about?

After the Second World War, Japanese liberal educationalists who had been oppressed during war time, supported and guided by the General Head Quarters (GHQ), instigated a drastic transformation of educational ideals and of the entire school system. In pre-war Japan, indoctrination in 'national morality', that is, of national fidelity and obedience as set out in the Imperial Prescript of Education (*Kyouiku-chokugo* 1890), was carried out under the name of education. In the post-war reforms, the new Constitution and the Fundamental Law of Education were formulated in 1946 and 1947 and educational ideas and principles were totally changed. Democracy and pacifism became the leading ideals in place of ultra-nationalism and militarism. The contrast in goals was marked: education as a duty versus that as a right, control versus freedom, conformism versus respect for individuality, elitism versus egalitarianism, and nationalism versus internationalism. The school system was changed from a multi-track one to a simple comprehensive system of '6-3-3-4'. ('6-3-3-4' refers to the division of the school system into six years of primary, three years of junior high school, three years of senior high school, and four years of undergraduate university education.) We can describe the changes that took place as the democratization and demilitarization of education.

In the 1950s, however, when the occupation by the Allied Powers ended and changes in United States' foreign policy were taking place, a move towards restoration began with declarations made of the need to correct the 'hyper-democratization' of social reform. Education was not exempted but rather was made the main target of attack. By the end of the decade the following apparatus had been devised:

1 Two Laws were enacted, first, the political Neutrality of Education Act (1954) for providing Governmental legitimacy over education, and the second, the Local Educational Administration Law (1956) which changed the composition of the Boards of Education from elected to nominated members.
2 A new 'Course of Study' and a new textbook screening system (1958) to strengthen the control over textbooks.
3 A system of teacher appraisal (1959).
4 Nationwide achievement tests in accordance with the new Course of Study (1961).

In this way, the new educational ideals which had been established following the Second World War were placed seriously at risk. This series of policies was to return power back to the State and thus contradictory legal structures arose.

In 1954 the Government set out to limit the freedom of teachers and bring their work under firm bureaucratic control. The Conservative Party-managed *Diet* passed two laws concerning the 'political neutrality of education' which made it illegal for teachers to engage in activities that could be construed as either providing support for or opposition to any political party. The aim and effect of these laws was to nullify the constitutionally guaranteed right to freely and openly engage in political activities, and to make the State the one and only guarantor of political neutrality.

Thus the meaning of 'political neutrality of education' changed drastically. Constitutionally it meant that the Government and political powers should not intervene in the 'internal affairs' of education, that is its contents and methods. Political neutrality is synonymous with the autonomy of education, but it also means that the State is the only guarantor of this neutrality. A revision of the Board of Education Law in 1956 replaced popular election of the members of the Board with appointment by the local governor.

Since then the Ministry of Education has used local Boards of Education to create an administrative network that now allows it to control virtually every aspect of school and even adult education. Thus the democratic values that gave shape to post-war Japan's educational system have been eroded by a powerful bureaucratic apparatus which promotes conformity and groupism. The Government's interpretation of the 'right to receive an education', guaranteed by the Constitution, now means a right to receive the kind of education the Ministry of Education deems appropriate for Japanese youth.

THE CONTROL OF EDUCATIONAL CONTENT

In the first Course of Study, issued in 1947, it was clearly stated that the Ministry of Education's guidelines were only intended to provide non-binding recommendations and informal assistance to teachers planning their own classroom curricula. This was thought to be consistent with the new values informing other efforts being made to create a free society and to promote a democratization of Japanese political life. However in 1958 the Ministry, with the tacit support of the Liberal Democratic Party, revised the content of the Course of Study in a more nationalistic direction by reintroducing moral education. Moreover, Ministry officials claimed that these guidelines now possessed legally binding power and that they required all textbook authors to closely follow their directives, even ordering the learning of Chinese characters. At the same time, the Ministry intensified its 'screening' of textbooks.

THE NATIONWIDE ACHIEVEMENT TEST

In the early 1960s the Ministry decided to administer a nationwide achievement test designed to examine whether teachers were actually following the Course of Study, and in order to discover the distribution of manpower for economic enterprise planning. But when teachers throughout the country refused to administer this exam, the Ministry, acting through the Boards of Education it now firmly controlled, imposed strong disciplinary measures to make sure that that would never happen again. In response to this a number of lawsuits were brought challenging the Ministry's authority to make teachers follow the Course of Study. These cases dragged through the Japanese court system for 15 years, with different judges handing down widely divergent opinions. The issue was finally decided in 1976 by the Supreme Court in the Ministry's favour, although the justices warned the Ministry not to abuse its authority by interfering with the inner workings of local educational administration or by specifying the contents of the Course of Study in an overly intrusive manner.

THE TEACHER EVALUATION SYSTEM

In 1957, the 'Teacher Evaluation System' was implemented. In the reporting document a column was included as to whether or not teachers exhibited appropriate 'Love of Education', and the results were actually used to provide the Government with information on teachers' participation in union activities and non-official educational research organizations. Promotions were denied or delayed. In more general terms, the very existence of such a system functioned to stifle free educational research and professional activities.

Thus, in the 1960s and 1970s the Ministry of Education strengthened its administrative control over the activities which teachers engaged in within schools. Consequently teachers' meetings, which in earlier years functioned as forums for democratic decision-making, have lost the spontaneity they previously enjoyed and now serve as little more than official assemblies in which the principal or head teacher tells other teachers what they are expected to do in their classrooms. More recently, government controlled in-service-training programmes have been instituted, which provide the Ministry of Education with an opportunity to indoctrinate and discipline new teachers.

THE CONTROL OF STUDENTS

Extremely detailed rules regarding students' behaviour both inside and outside of school have been set out, and regulations regarding such things as school uniforms, the colour of socks, the width of school bags, hair styles, and so on are strictly enforced. And even though physical punishment of students by teachers is illegal, it is neither officially discouraged nor recognized as such by school authorities even when it occurs. The roads children take to walk to school are prescribed, and in many cases they must go to school in groups. Furthermore, elementary school and junior high school students must wear name badges both inside and outside of the school. Other regulations even require them to eat their lunches in a specified manner.

It should also be noted that a system of secret reporting on students' behaviour – not unlike the one used to report on teachers – has been implemented to make students afraid to act in any manner other than that officially recognized as appropriate.

In short, the system by means of which education is presently controlled in Japan functions in both an overt and hidden fashion. At the level of explicit forms of control, we can find some of the laws and ordinances which enabled Ministry of Education bureaucrats to regain many of the powers they enjoyed during the pre-war period. At the same time attention must be called to the ways in which the existence of the textbook screening system, the teacher evaluation system, secret reporting system on students, and the school rules puts pressure on teachers and students to conform unconsciously to the dominant value of the dominating powers. The entrance examination system also functions as a hidden control on conformism.

These different levels of control are certainly not unrelated. The difference between them is that whereas the former constitute a naked exercise of power, the latter compel conformity without caution and sometimes students and teachers alike recognize that it is in their own interests to do so. In this sense, the more subtle uses of authority have more indefinite compelling force and therefore a more menacing threat to the democratic values implanted in post-war Japanese education.

ECONOMIC GROWTH AND EDUCATION

Since 1960, Japanese education has been influenced by the policy of economic growth and reorganized according to the demands of financial and industrial circles. Their influence is reflected in educational policy, in the guidance orientation in schools in preparation for the 'personality market', and penetrated into the people's consciousness in both overt and hidden ways. Under the pressure of entrance examinations '*juku*', the cram schools, have flourished outside of the formal school system and the so-called 'double school' phenomenon has appeared. The *juku* is a facility that prepares students for entrance examinations at every level from primary school on. They are private enterprises, costing a great deal, but have become almost mandatory if a student is to enter university. On the other hand, corporal punishment by teachers, violence and bullying among pupils and school refusal caused by psychological oppression have increased. Thus, the respect for school education is declining, and can be characterized in Japan today as 'poverty among plenty'.

The power of business has become so strong that it dominates politics. The Japanese state is changing from a bureaucratic to an enterprise state. Here we have a new phenomenon. New liberalism of economic theory has taken the place of Keynesian theory, demanding deregulation of education in parallel with privatisation policy. Thus public education is becoming a profitable market for economic activity and education is changing into a consumer good and alienated from the concept of 'education as a fundamental human right'.

THE GOVERNMENT POSITION, SUPPORTED BY FINANCIAL AND INDUSTRIAL CIRCLES

Since the 1960s these politically powerful forces have attempted to initiate educational reform beyond modification. Meanwhile the Liberal Democratic Party has been in political control continuously. With an increase in the people's educational aspirations, the rate of high school enrolment has risen from 57 per cent in the 1960s to 94 per cent in the 1980s, and that at university level from 10 per cent to 37 per cent. Against this background of quantitative expansion in educational opportunity, the Central Council of Education, appointed by the Ministry of Education, delivered a report in 1971 on educational reform. The term 'the third period of educational reform' was coined for the plan which was then reshaping post-war educational reform. (Incidentally, the first reform refers to the period of change at the beginning of the *Meiji* era (1870s), and the second one to the reformative years soon after the Second World War.)

The report of the Central Council in 1971 was partly to confirm the changes of the 1960s, and also to enhance further reforms: the introduction of the meritocratic principle, diversifying secondary and university education and challenging the principles of equality and justice in education. Here 'diversification' referred to gradations of pupils on a single value-scale according to test marks or a score of deviation, as a result of which conformism to the unidimensional value system was heightened. Also during this period, the censorship of textbooks was tightened and great stress placed on nationalism and patriotism.

In the middle of the 1970s, however, in the aftermath of the oil price explosion, economic difficulties forced the Government to modify its policy. A policy of 'cut spending and build up defence' was implemented, and it was within this framework that the problem of education was situated. Public welfare and education both suffered from substantial cutbacks in spending while the defence budget was increased. In the 1980s, especially under Premier Nakasone, while the government campaigned for administrative reforms this trend was strengthened. As a result, large public enterprises such as the Telegraphic and Telephone Corporation have been transferred to private enterprise. Japanese National Railways was also being made the target of division and privatization, and the Government has made it clear that public education will be next. For them the words 'liberalization', 'deregulation', and 'privatization' are synonymous.

In 1984 an Ad Hoc Council on Education was organized by the Central Government, not by the Ministry of Education, but by the Prime Minister himself. Nakasone expressed his firm intention to repudiate, during his office, the post-war policy represented by the establishment of the new

Constitution and the new Education Law. He said the country should 'settle the score' on the post-war reforms of Japan. Thus we are confronted today with a crisis concerning the Fundamental Law of Education and public education generally. Concerning deregulation and privatization policy, the Government declares that once education is separated from the public sector and permitted to be free in its development, the stimulus of competition and free choice will have a positive, invigorating influence. If this line is followed through, private enterprise will be greatly stimulated. Private preparatory schools or *juku* enterprises will flourish and the public schooling will be destroyed.

The initiatives in educational reform taken by the financial and industrial groups will lead to the subordination of education to the demands of the pursuit of profit. When stress is laid on parental rights and free choice in education, this does not mean freedom of education. Here, 'free choice' by parents means no more than the opportunity of consumers to choose from among commodities produced and promoted by private enterprises in competition. The result would be the thoroughgoing commercialization and privatization of education and the end of public education.

The group advocating 'deregulation' has been strongly influenced by the American economist Milton Friedman, who espouses 'a small government and a strong America', a motto which President Reagan's government used to get powerful support. Friedman's most representative works, *Free to Choose* (1979) and *Tyranny of the Status Quo* (1984), have been translated into Japanese and have found a large audience among conservative politicians and economists. His theory of the free market and proposals to reduce the public sector comprise a strong attack against public education and promote trends toward the privatization of education. In the latter of the two books mentioned above, we find one chapter devoted to the problem of defence expenditure, where it is insisted that since security of the nation is the prerequisite of freedom, the cost of national defence is 'not expensive'. We may note incidentally just how similar are the theoretical structures and implications of the ideologies held by the Governments of the United States, Japan, and perhaps Britain.

Besides those relating to national policy, ideals held by the Ad Hoc Council concerning people also demand close examination. K. Koyama, an opinion leader in the Council, insists upon the principle of education according to 'ability' and advocates the further promotion of competition. In fact, he goes so far as to suggest that in a modern, advanced society, there is no place for people with an intelligence quotient under 110. He concludes therefore that we must turn to social engineering and education to counter the situation whereby those among the population with lower IQs tend to reproduce at a higher rate. He advocates that people with 'high quality genes' should be encouraged to have more children, and everyone else fewer. (K. Koyama 1967).

Can we find any sense of freedom or human dignity in such a view? Not only Koyama, but many of the opinion leaders of educational policy within the Liberal Democratic Party refer often to the theories of Jensen, Herstein and Burt, insisting that their opinions are supported internationally. We know, however, that the theory of the genetic determination of human ability espoused, for example, by Burt and his disciples was bitterly attacked by Simon in England, and Kamin in the United States (a comparative study of such trends would undoubtedly be useful).

Under the pressure of meritocratic competition, both in school and society, education is thus accepted as a means of career pursuit. The hierarchy of universities corresponds to that of the bureaucracy and industries. There is a rush to a few prestigious universities, and 'examination hell' and 'diploma disease' prevail. A competitive mentality and desire for upward social mobility in the value-attitude system make the situation worse. This problem of meritocracy is worth considering a little further.

CONCLUSION

In the pre-war society, where educational opportunity followed the social order, which was stabilized by status and property, the 'ability-first' principle (*meritocracy, Leistungsprinzip,* or *selon son talent*) was a revolutionary slogan against any discrimination except ability. The ability-first policy played a positive role in the democratization and modernization of society and education for a certain period, as long as it was combined with the conviction of the equality of all men as expressed in the French Revolution. But, in accordance with the development of capitalistic industrialization and bureaucratization, it has gradually shifted to overemphasizing the abilities which industries and bureaucracy needed, until at last it introduced a new discrimination based on ability, forming a 'meritocratic society'.

As Michael Young, the British sociologist, pointed out in the title of his analytical and predictive book *The Rise of the Meritocracy, 1870–2033* (Young, 1958), the problem of meritocracy or the ability-first principle is actual as well as future and universal. In a meritocratic society, 'equal opportunity according to ability' is nothing but a mechanism for alienating inferiors. In this situation, schools become a system of selecting children and youth and classifying them for each destination appointed by the demands of industry according to their 'test-mark ability', which is only a part of integral human capacity. Then, children are forced to compete with one another and kick others down with the strong guidance of self-interested parents who love their children blindly and of some teachers who believe that competition is best for learning. The ability-first policy has inevitably brought hot competition into the school system, while rejecting the principal idea of 'mutual help and respect' and excluding those who do not respond well to competition, labelling them deficient.

The principle 'each according to one's ability' can and should be understood in a different sense from the gene-determination and merit-orientation discussed above. Is it fair, for instance, to say that inferior and shorter education is adequate for handicapped or retarded children, because of their disability? On the contrary, they deserve to be treated with greater care and over a longer period, in order to overcome their difficulties. The more heavily they are handicapped, the more they need to be helped. We should thus perceive 'education according to ability' as the idea of 'education according to the particular needs for each individual's development'. This will be easy to understand if we remind ourselves that learning and education are the rights of every child. This notion can be aptly termed the 'principle of justice' in education.

Those in power have talked of 'liberalization' when they really mean 'privatization'. When we consider the meaning of the freedom of education we must accept that a person's right to learning and education is a prerequisite. This right is one of the fundamental human rights, along with the right to live and to pursue happiness. Moreover, the right to learning in the case of children is combined intrinsically with the right to develop and grow.

Children are immature, but immaturity must not be understood simply as meaning lesser capacity than adults, but as containing unpredictable possibilities for future growth. If children are deprived of their right to learning, they may grow up to be uninformed and unaware of their rights as adults. Children's right to learning and their emancipation from ignorance are preconditions to all other human rights. Moreover, in order for this right to be fulfilled there must be freedom of education and freedom of thought, otherwise the rights of children become meaningless.

A related question is: 'Who is it who holds the responsibility for a child's education?' While it is true that parents carry the heaviest responsibility of choice of education, they in the end entrust its actual carrying-out to schools and teachers, expecting them to provide quality education based on science and truth, by means of professional teaching methods. This requires then, that teachers be both earnest inquirers in the content of their teaching subject and conscientious researchers in child development and instruction theory. It is therefore essential for teachers to join closely with professional researchers and to be guaranteed freedom of research and educational practice. Educational administration should not interfere with the content of education nor with teachers' practice, but encourage educational freedom. Autonomy of teachers and schools should be guaranteed. This also can be considered a component of freedom in education.

To create education for the future, the principle of people's participation in educational reform is very important. This principle affirms people's rights not only of access to education, but also to its creation, which should not become a means of state control. What it needs is a system in which representatives from the administration, teachers, community members and parents can come together to discuss and find solutions for such problems as mentioned above.

Additionally, the term 'public' in education, first, does not mean 'of the state', as the Ministry of Education would have it, but signifies rather that which is of common concern to the individual citizens as well as to the people as a whole. Secondly, a child is not the property of its parents, but is a social being – that is, a member of the public as well as an independent person. And thirdly, culture and learning belong to all of us and should not be privatized.

Truth concerns everyone and knowledge and culture must be oriented toward the universal. A child must be taught freedom and independence of mind, not be turned by education into a link in a chain of nationalistic merchandising logic. Article 10 of the Declaration of Children's Rights states that children should be taught that culture and knowledge are not private property for the sole benefit of an individual or a country but precious possessions belonging to all and that they should be used as such.

The creation of public education in its authentic sense must begin from such a perspective.

REFERENCES

Finkelstein, B. (1991). *Transcending Stereotypes. Understanding Education in Japan.* Yarmouth, NC: Intercultural Press.

Horio, T. (1986). Towards Reform in Japanese Education, *Comparative Education*, Vol. 22, No. 1.

Horio, T. (trans. by S. Platzer). (1988). *Educational Thought and Ideology in Modern Japan – State Authority and Intellectual Freedom,* Tokyo: University Press.

Horio, T, (1990). *Problems of the Reform of Education in Japan.* Unpublished paper presented at the Annual Meeting of AREA, Boston.

Kobayashi, T. (1985). From Educational Borrowing to Educational Sharing: The Japanese Experience. In C. Brock and W. Tulasiewicz (eds), *Cultural Identity and Educational Policy.* London: Croom Helm.

Koyama, K. (1967). *Miraigaku Nyumon* (An introduction to futurology). Tokyo: Ushio Publishing Company.

Young, M. (1958) *The Rise of the Meritocracy – 1870–2033.* London: Thames & Hudson.

3 Improvements in work-force qualifications in Britain and France in the 1980s

Hilary Steedman

STOCKS OF QUALIFICATIONS: BRITAIN AND FRANCE, 1979–88

In 1979, a third of the French working population held intermediate vocational qualifications compared to just under a quarter in Britain, while a smaller proportion of the French work-force held degrees. By 1988, the French position relative to Britain had changed considerably. In Britain, numbers holding general educational qualifications, particularly at lower level (General Certificate of Education O-Level, Certificate of Secondary Education, which since 1988 have been subsumed under the General Certificate of Secondary Education), had increased by 50 per cent, while stocks of intermediate vocational qualifications in the labour force showed hardly any increase. In France, over the same period, the percentage holding vocational qualifications increased substantially from a higher base (by one quarter), while the proportion holding general educational qualifications (without vocational qualifications) remained below that of vocational qualifications. In both countries, proportions holding degrees increased with the larger increase registered in Britain (Table 3.1). In Britain, a decade which witnessed the largest number of government training initiatives, both for young people and for adults, has so far shown considerably lower growth than France of stocks of vocational qualifications in the labour force. France, on the other hand, has progressed from a level (similar to Britain in the early 1970s) of having less than half the stock of vocational qualifications of Germany to being two-thirds of the way towards the German level in 1988; France, with 40 per cent at intermediate level (1988) lies roughly half-way between Britain (26 per cent) and Germany (64 per cent).[1] (Unless otherwise stated, the term 'Britain' is used here for England, Scotland and Wales.)

These results require us to look carefully at differences between the two countries' policies towards the training of young people – an important factor contributing to changes in stocks of qualifications in the labour force.

Table 3.1 Vocational qualifications of the labour force in Britain and France 1988

	Britain %		France %	
	1979	1988	1979	1988
No vocational or educational qualifications[a]	46	30	52	37
No vocational qualifications but some educational qualifications[b]	23	34	10	16
NO VOCATIONAL QUALIFICATIONS subtotal	69	64	62	53
Lower intermediate[c]	18	20	27	33
Higher intermediate[d]	5	6	5	7
INTERMEDIATE VOCATIONAL QUALIFICATIONS subtotal	23	26	32	40
DEGREE OR ABOVE[e]	8	10	6	7
TOTAL	100	100	100	100

Sources: *Enquête-Emploi 1988*, table 01, CEREQ *Bulletin de Recherche sur l'Emploi et la Formation*, No. 42, table 3, page 3, own interpolations for 1979. Britain 1979 and 1988 Labour Force Survey unpublished tabulations prepared by the Department of Employment.

Notes:

a   In Britain, those declaring no educational or vocational qualifications. In France, those declaring no education or vocational qualifications and those holding only the CEP (Certificat d'Études Primaires), an almost superseded qualification formerly awarded to attest satisfactory completion of compulsory schooling at age 14.

b   In Britain, 0.70 of 'other qualifications', one or more Certificates of Secondary Education (CSE) below Grade I, one or more Ordinary-Level (O-Level) or equivalent, one or more Advanced-Level (A-Level) or equivalent. In France, Brevet d'Études du Premier Cycle (BEPC), awarded at the end of compulsory school (16) and of O-Level standard, Baccalauréat (Series A, B, C, D, E).

c   In Britain, all trade apprenticeships completed (1979 all uncompleted trade apprenticeships), all City and Guilds, all Business and Technician Education (BTEC) ONC/OND and equivalent, 0.13 of 'other qualifications'. In France, all Certificat d'Aptitude Professionnelle (CAP) and Brevet d'Études Professionnelles (BEP) qualifications, Baccalauréat (Series F, G).

d   In Britain, all BTEC HNC/HND qualifications, post A-Level Secondary and Primary teaching qualifications, Nursing qualifications. In France, all Brevet de Technicien Supérieur (BTS) and Diplôme Universitaire de Technologie (DUT), all other paramedical and other forms of professional education requiring 2 years higher education after Baccalauréat level.

e   In Britain, 0.17 of 'other qualifications', all degree level and postgraduate level qualifications, membership of professional institutions. In France, degree level and above.

All data taken from the *Enquête-Emploi* for France is based on the active population, including the unemployed. In Britain, Labour Force Survey tabulations are based on the population in employment. We have calculated that adjustment of the French figures accordingly would raise the percentages with degree level and intermediate level qualifications by one percentage point and lower the percentage with no qualifications by two points. As these differences are so small the figures for France used in this study have not been adjusted.

FLOWS OF VOCATIONALLY QUALIFIED YOUNG PEOPLE IN BRITAIN AND FRANCE

Patterns of flows of vocationally qualified young people in Britain relative to other advanced industrialized countries have been documented in previous work carried out by the National Institute of Economic and Social Research. In brief, over the period, under half of all of 16 year old school leavers chose to remain in full-time school or to proceed to further education. Of those who left school, few had attainments in basic subjects which could constitute the foundation for further on-the-job training to recognized skill levels, and for many in full-time employment such training was not available. Such skills as were acquired (mostly on the government-financed Youth Training Scheme) were at levels below internationally recognized minimum standards – City and Guilds Part II or Business and Technician Education Council National Level (National Vocational Qualification Level III). As a consequence, the flow of young people obtaining recognized craft qualifications in major occupations in manufacturing in Britain hardly changed in the 12-year period to 1987 while in France and Germany numbers increased by 50 per cent and 30 per cent respectively.[2]

Earlier National Institute studies have examined in detail the differences between French and British provision of initial vocational education and training.[3] The reluctance of French employers, particularly large industrial employers, to train adequate numbers of young people in general skills led the French government to provide initial vocational education and training within the public education system. The products of this system cover the whole spectrum of skill from craft-trained worker to doctoral engineer and constitute the major source of initial skill formation.

Since 1971, the law compelling firms to devote 1.1 per cent of their payroll to the training of their employees has also played a part in helping to raise qualification levels. However, in terms of formal vocational qualifications obtained, the role of *formation continué* (continuing training) remains small. In 1984 barely 5 per cent of all CAP awards were obtained by adult employees using this route rather than through full-time initial training.

During the period in question, it was clearly easier for the French government to expand the supply of training places (subject to certain rigidities such as the skills of teachers in post and infrastructure) than it was for British governments to influence the British employer-based training system to expand the training provided for young people. It was also easier to monitor and maintain an agreed standard of vocational qualification when most trainees were trained in educational institutions (as in France), than where trainees were distributed widely over a large number of work places, many with no experience of training (as in Britain for the Youth Opportunities Programme (YOP) and the Youth Training Scheme (YTS)).

PLANNING FOR SKILLS IN FRANCE

Since the 1960s, French educational policy-makers have been encouraged to develop provision for education and vocational training within the overall objectives for economic growth set out in successive economic plans. In the immediate post-war period in France a series of economic plans were drawn up to indicate the rate and type of economic growth that the government considered optimal. These plans guided the broad thrust of government legislation and investment, though at no time were they more than indicative of directions to be followed. The Fifth Plan for 1966–70 was informed by awareness of the handicap imposed on French industrial and commercial development by an education system which had evolved to meet the needs of a predominantly agricultural society (in 1966, 70 per cent of the population had no vocational qualifications, or only a primary school leaving certificate). The 1966 Plan concentrated on the need to reduce this figure and stated as its objective that no more than 20 per cent of an age cohort should leave school in 1970 with no or with low qualification levels, with 50 per cent at the next higher level (craft). Such proposals seemed ambitious at a time when over 50 per cent of a cohort left school with no recognized educational qualifications. Nevertheless, the resolve to raise qualification levels, particularly those of the least well-qualified, was reiterated in the Sixth Plan 1970–5, which stated as one of its 25 objectives that of doubling between 1970 and 1975 the extent of post-school education and that of reaching the point where no child left the educational system without sufficient general education combined with the rudiments of vocational training.[4]

A series of legislative measures were undertaken in the 1970s, including the creation of a higher qualification at craft level (the BEP), the introduction of pre-apprenticeship classes in secondary schools and the reform of apprenticeships, full recognition of the technical Baccalauréat and the creation of the University Institutes of Technology. The overriding aim was to raise numbers leaving education with some form of vocational qualification and particularly to increase the proportion with intermediate technical and commercial skills. The objective of the 1966 plan was attained in 1976 when only 19.6 per cent of school leavers left without at least completing a three-year (14–17) course of combined education and vocational training in a full-time vocational school and in 1986 the proportion was down to 15.1 per cent.[5]

THE EXPANSION OF VOCATIONAL TRAINING PLACES IN FRANCE

A combination of clear educational objectives, centralized national administration of educational resources, nationally recognized certification and the full-time provision of initial training within the education system enabled France to expand the supply of vocational training places – from 212,000 pupils in the final year of full-time craft level courses in 1971, to 281,000 in 1980 and 318,000 in 1985. However, it is obvious that no greater control could be exercised over demand from young people for vocational education and training after the completion of compulsory schooling than is the case in Britain. Nevertheless, participation rates of 16–18 year olds in full-time education (including full-time vocational education) in France were considerably higher, 71 per cent in 1987 compared to 31 per cent in Britain, in the same year.

It is beyond the scope of this article to analyse reasons for higher participation rates of young people in full-time education beyond the end of compulsory education at 16 in France. Labour market factors (relative youth wages and higher youth unemployment), demographic factors (higher post-war birth rates) and cultural factors have all played a part. However, it is important to note that the earliest age at which nationally recognized qualifications can normally be awarded in France is 17; and the course in question, the CAP (craft level) may be entered upon at age 14 or 15, before the end of compulsory education at 16.

Differences in the ages at which recognized school-leaving qualifications are awarded in the two countries help to explain differential leaving rates. In Britain the CSE and GCE 'O' level (now subsumed under the GCSE) are normally awarded at 16, and widely recognized by British employers, as it is the main indicator of employment potential; in France only a small proportion leave at 16 with the French qualification equivalent to GCSE (the BEPC); a majority of French 16 year olds are already preparing for the vocationally oriented CAP (taken at age 17) and the BEP or Baccalauréat taken at age 18 and 19 respectively and judge it worthwhile to take one or two more years to complete the course after the end of compulsory education.

Many of the French 16–18 year olds who stay on to work for these recognized vocational and educational qualifications do so because the advantages in terms of jobs and salary can be clearly judged from employers' behaviour. This first level of vocational qualification (CAP, BEP), equivalent to NVQ Level III, is widely recognized by employers to the extent that recognition of the CAP and of higher level vocational certificates and diplomas is written into Collective Agreements negotiated by employers and trade unions. Under these agreements, the holder of a relevant CAP qualification is entitled to be paid at a higher point on the agreed salary scale than an employee with no vocational qualifications.[6]

Because the CAP leads to an attestation of professional competence recognized by employers, standards are rigorously maintained. Average pass-rates remain around 60 per cent. These are 'group' examinations, rather than single-subject examinations. Many leave without the CAP certificate, because although they have passed all the practical examinations of purely professional competence, they have failed in their academic subjects. This contrasts with a British willingness to count as 'qualified' a school leaver with a single CSE or 'O' level/GCSE pass. If the rigorous criteria applied by the French were applied to British qualifications, that is if the British counted only those who had passed their written tests and excluded those who had only 'served their time', only about 19 per cent of the British active population (instead of the 26 per cent shown in Table 3.1) would be considered vocationally qualified at intermediate level.[7] This should be borne in mind when considering the higher French percentage with 'no qualifications'. Since this group contains all those who studied for but failed to obtain a CAP, many would be considered 'qualified' according to the British definition – which includes those who have completed an apprenticeship but not obtained any vocational qualifications.

THE 'RATIONING' OF GENERAL EDUCATIONAL QUALIFICATIONS: CONSEQUENCES IN FRANCE AND BRITAIN

How does the pattern of growth in qualifications in France compare with that in Britain? This question can be better understood by examining average annual percentage growth rates of the different categories of qualifications obtained by French school leavers aged 16 and over during the ten-year period 1976–86. While numbers obtaining general educational qualifications grew by only 1 per cent per annum in this period, numbers obtaining the lower level vocational qualification (CAP) increased by 4 per cent and higher level technical qualifications by 6 per cent. (It should be noted that these growth rates relate to increases in flows of young people with vocational qualifications and not to the growth of stocks of qualifications in the labour force. Flows contribute to the growth of stocks but are not the sole determinant.)

Are these differences in growth rates the result of greater popularity of vocational and technical courses among French 16 year olds or has the French educational structure played a part in the differential growth in numbers? There is no doubt that places in the traditionally more prestigious 16–19 secondary education courses leading to the general or technical Baccalauréat have been 'rationed' on the basis of attainments. Demand for places on these courses at the guidance point at the end of compulsory schooling invariably exceeds supply. Those pupils who have not been allowed to continue on to Baccalauréat courses may enter the lower level vocational courses (CAP, BEP), entry to which is open to all.[8] Within the group which proceeds to Baccalauréat courses, a similar process operates, whereby access to the more prestigious general Baccalauréat courses is restricted to the more able; most growth has actually taken place in the newer technical Baccalauréat options.

By restricting the expansion of general educational courses in a period of steeply rising demand for post-compulsory secondary education and providing alternative vocational and technical routes, the French government has ensured that most of this growth has been directed into technical and vocational education. Lack of parity of esteem for the three routes open to 16 year olds (General Baccalauréat, Technical Baccalauréat and CAP/BEP) has been a source of unease on the part of educationalists, and in particular the vocational route with its more limited possibilities of progression to higher level qualifications has been criticized. Although a 'common core' of mathematics, French and a foreign language is stipulated for all qualifications offered to 16–19 year olds and routes for transfer from CAP/BEP to Baccalauréat courses are available, the standard required is very demanding and no more than 10 per cent of CAP/BEP students normally make the transfer to the higher level Baccalauréat courses. Dissatisfaction among employers with the narrow scope of the CAP, and the need to provide realistic progression opportunities led to the introduction in 1986 of the Vocational Baccalauréat taken in the vocational lycée two years after the BEP, which gives access both to employment and to technical courses within higher education.

Access to higher secondary school examination courses in Britain ('A' levels and the equivalent Scottish examinations) has been restricted in ways similar to those in France by the widely applied prescription of higher grades of the Ordinary Level of the GCE achievement as a condition of access. As in France, the proportion of the age group taking a range of the academically orientated 'A' level courses hardly expanded over the period under study. The difference between the two countries lies in the contrast between the post-compulsory school careers of 80 per cent of the age group for whom satisfactory achievement at 'A' level (as presently constituted) is not an appropriate target.

In France, almost all of this group, including those with no record of success at secondary school, enrol in a range of full-time technical or vocational courses whose structure and labour-market value is widely recognized and understood. In Britain, offers of apprenticeships normally target the same restricted pool of leavers with 'good' 'O' levels/CSE/GCSEs as do 'A' level courses. Further Education Colleges offering full-time vocational and educational courses might, at first sight, appear to offer suitable provision and opportunity for those with few educational qualifications to move from school on to vocational courses. However, initial evidence from the Youth Cohort Survey indicates that 16 year olds with no or low-level educational attainments are unlikely to choose this route.

A clearer and more coherent system combining general education with vocational and technical qualifications and offering courses appropriate for nearly all levels of attainment at ages 15–16 has been an important factor in enabling France to enrol the 80 per cent of all pupils who are not selected for entry to an academic Baccalauréat course. The success of this 80 per cent in gaining a range of technical and vocational qualifications has made a substantial contribution to France's recent progress in increasing stocks of vocational and technical qualifications in the labour force.

In England and Wales, over the period 1979–88, the greatest growth occurred in qualifications obtained at school and in further education, i.e. in general educational qualifications ('O' level and CSE grades 2–5).[9] Stocks of 'O' level and CSE qualifications in the labour force increased by 4 per cent per annum between 1979 and 1988 while stocks of individuals holding vocational qualifications increased by less than 1 per cent per annum over the same period. These calculations are based on analysis of 16–24 year olds in employment taken from special tabulations of the Labour Force Survey 1979 and 1988. In the absence of adequate national statistics on vocational qualifications gained in Britain at levels comparable to other European countries we have had to rely on the measure of 16–24 year olds in the labour force holding vocational qualifications at two different dates in order to try to judge whether there has been any growth. Detailed analysis distinguishing City and Guilds Part II from, for example, trade apprenticeships completed is not possible because of the reordering of qualifications in the Labour Force Survey analysis between 1979 and 1988.

CONCLUSIONS

Britain's policies to improve educational and vocational qualifications has increased the numbers in employment holding lower level general educational qualifications but has failed to increase stocks of intermediate vocational qualifications, in the nine years to 1988. France has registered a 25 per cent increase in numbers with vocational qualifications over the same period.

Policies of setting educational goals in terms of proportions qualified to different levels with strong emphasis on the upgrading of skills have served France well in the period 1960–88, to the extent that from a position of relative disadvantage France has now 'overtaken' Britain in all but graduate-level qualifications. The British effort has also been considerable but has failed to provide a satisfactory basis for progression for more than a small proportion of leavers. The school-leaving qualification attesting general educational attainment awarded at 16 has been extended to include virtually the whole age group but expansion has been mainly in lower grade passes and with no increase in the tendency to continue with training to recognized levels of vocational qualification. In France, a commitment to staying-on in full-time education beyond the minimum school-leaving age to at least age 17 or 18 is necessary to obtain any vocational or general educational qualification that is recognized and accepted by employers. Employment of 16 year olds without training or apprenticeship is now almost unheard of in France.[10]

Damaging gaps are most apparent in Britain at the lowest level of internationally recognized qualification (NVQ Level II) and Britain's priority should be the promotion of a broadly based Level III vocational education and training to the age of 18 for most young people, giving access to the workplace or to higher education. National Curriculum provision 14–16 should, therefore, as a first priority lay the foundations for such courses, for example by preparing pupils for BTEC First certificates or modules, in order to provide continuity and a sense of progression through to post-compulsory education or training.

The French have already set their target for the year 2000 – 75 per cent of young people to the equivalent of 'A' level – and intend to achieve this aim principally by expanding technical and vocational courses of an 'A' level standard.[11] In Britain, despite the lead given by the Confederation of British Industry and Trades Union Congress there is no sign of a nationally coordinated response from those responsible for education and training policy.[12]

Changes in courses and provision for 16–19 year olds initiated by the Department For Education currently address only the issue of changing

GCE Advanced Level courses in order to bring their standards and methods of assessment more into line with those of the GCSE. These initiatives seem inadequate in two respects; first, 'A' level will remain an academic course of study without the practical vocational dimension found in both the French technical and vocational Baccalauréat courses. Secondly, and more importantly, it seems doubtful whether – even in greatly revised form – it will provide an appropriate aim for more than 40 per cent of the age group. These efforts attempt to offer a strictly education-based solution to less than half the 16–19 population.

In its own and artificially segregated context, the Department of Employment is promoting and financing training for young people in employment through locally based Training and Enterprise Councils (TECs). In comparison with French initiatives, two points are noteworthy here. First, the stated aim for most trainees in these two-year programmes is NVQ Level II while the minimum level attained in France is the equivalent of NVQ III; secondly, the routes followed by trainees are not part of the same system of qualifications available within the education system and with opportunities for transfer between different routes as is the case in France. It seems clear that great benefits derive both to employers and young people from the clarity and coherence of the 16–19 framework of qualifications in France and from the deliberate efforts to provide within such a framework for virtually the whole ability range – and that in an education system which maintains rigorous and high academic standards. If the French system can overcome the handicap of an élitist academic tradition and firmly establish that educational goals must be compatible with national economic growth, Britain should be capable of doing the same.

ACKNOWLEDGEMENTS

A fuller version of this chapter appeared in the *National Institute Economic Review*, No. 133, August 1990 under the title, 'Improvements in Workforce Qualifications: Britain and France 1979–88'.

NOTES

1 The German figure is taken from work in progress at the National Institute and is based upon unpublished tabulations from the 1987 Mikrozensus for Germany.
2 H. Steedman, Vocational training in France and Britain: mechanical and electrical craftsmen, *National Institute Economic Review*, No. 126, November 1988, table 6.
3 S.J. Prais and H. Steedman, Vocational training in France and Britain: the building trades, *National Institute Economic Review*, No. 116, May 1986. H.

Steedman, Vocational training in France and Britain: office work, *National Institute Economic Review*, No. 120, May 1987. H. Steedman, Vocational training in France and Britain: mechanical and electrical craftsmen, *National Institute Economic Review*, No. 126, November 1988. V. Jarvis and S.J. Prais, Two nations of shopkeepers: training for retailing in France and Britain, *National Institute Economic Review*, No. 128, May 1989.

4 This account draws heavily on W.D. Halls, *Education, Culture and Politics in Modern France* ch. 5, Pergamon 1976 and on OECD, *Reviews of National Policies for Education: France*, pp. 133–7, Paris 1971.

5 Ministère de l'Éducation Nationale, Note d'Information No. 86–18, Table 1; Note d'Information No. 89–33, Table 1. In both these tables young people entering apprenticeship are counted as staying within the education system.

6 Agreements covering metal-working, the chemical industry, pharmaceuticals and the building industry are documented and analysed in F. Eyraud, A. Jobert, P. Rozenblatt and M. Tallard, *Les classifications dans l'Entreprise*, Ministère du Travail, de l'Emploi et de la Formation Professionnelle, June 1989.

7 The figure of 19 per cent comprises all higher education below degree level, all Ordinary National Certificate (ONC) certificates, all City and Guilds (C & G) passes.

8 M. Duthoit, 'Le processus d'orientation en fin de troisième', in *Éducation et Formation* 1987 (11). Ministère de l'Éducation Nationale, Duthoit divides his sample into three groups. In Group I (pupils who have not repeated a school year, i.e. average and above average ability), 78 per cent opt for the Baccalauréat course and 60 per cent are successful. In Group II (pupils who have repeated the last year of compulsory schooling), 48 per cent apply and 29 per cent are successful (fig. 1, p. 40).

9 Department of Education and Science Statistical Bulletin 13/88, table 3, December 1988.

10 Some 165,000 pupils aged 16 or 17 left the education system in 1985 without obtaining recognized qualifications. Six months later, only 13,000 were in paid employment, the rest were in apprenticeship or other training schemes. (*Note d'information*, No. 87–34 Ministère de l'Éducation Nationale.)

11 The complete plan for leavers from education in the year 2000 is 5 per cent without qualifications, 20 per cent with a CAP or BEP, 30 per cent with a Baccalauréat, 20 per cent with BAC plus 2 years of higher education and 25 per cent at degree level. Haut Comité Éducation-Économie, *Éducation-Économie: Quel système éducatif pour la société de l'an 2000?* Documentation française, 1988, p. 30.

12 The Confederation of British Industry (CBI) set a target for the year 2000 of NVQ Level III or its academic equivalent achieved by 50 per cent of young people. *Towards a skills revolution – a youth charter*, Confederation of British Industry, July 1989. Trades Union Congress, *Skills 2000*, 1989.

4 Law and vocational education and training of 16–19 year olds: the English experience since 1979

Gerald Strowbridge

INTRODUCTION

If Lord David Eccles was right when he described the education curriculum as a 'secret garden' then Further Education (FE) would probably be best described as the 'kitchen plot' in its most hidden corner. Very few legislators will have had first-hand experience of its culture and purpose and seem to view it as only marginally changed from its forebears, the trade schools and Mechanics Institutes of the last century. The fact that over two million people in 1990 enrolled in FE classes might come as a surprise to some.

This chapter examines the legal framework under which further education has operated in Britain since 1979 when a Conservative Government came into office and three general elections later remains in power. It then goes on to consider the development of FE during this period of political continuity up to the passing of the 1992 Further and Higher Education Act, as well as responses by the Departments of Employment and Education and Science (now the Department For Education) to alleged shortcomings of FE. It concludes with a brief examination of the current situation and prospects. It is worth bearing in mind that it has been a unique opportunity this century for one political party to have had the opportunity to legislate in order to shape and develop education and training over a period of fourteen years according to its priorities.

THE LEGAL FRAMEWORK OF FURTHER EDUCATION, 1979–88

When the Conservative Party under Mrs Margaret Thatcher came to power in the United Kingdom in 1979 the essential primary legislation governing all sectors of education had been in force for thirty-five years. The secondary sector had had its upheavals as over Circular 10/65 requesting Local Education Authorities' plans for comprehensive reorganization, and the Higher Education (HE) sector had its post-Robbins expansion, but apart from the training changes following the creation of the Industrial Training Boards in 1964 and the Manpower Services Commission (MSC) in 1973 the FE sector had not been seriously disturbed. Prior to the 1944 Act there had been no legal duty for Local Education Authorities (LEAs) to supply any further education, but under Section 41 local authorities were placed under a general duty 'to secure the provision for their area of adequate facilities for further education'. Further education was defined as 'Full-time and part-time education for persons over compulsory school leaving age; and leisure time occupation in such organised training and recreative activities as are suited to their requirements for any persons over compulsory school age who are willing to profit by the facilities provided for that purpose.' It was no longer a power to be exercised at LEAs' discretion as had been the case before the Act. In practice the term 'further education' covered what later became to be referred to as non-advanced and advanced further education. The LEAs could, should they so wish, provide higher as well as further education in what was often referred to as a 'seamless robe'.

However, the imprecise wording of the clauses and the lapsing of the requirement to prepare and submit schemes of further education to the Secretary of State allowed LEAs to act somewhat independently. This meant that a variety of FE provision grew up across the country. Some of the provisions of the 1944 Act, such as the introduction of universal part-time education for all young people in employment and the creation of 'county colleges', suffered the same fate as their predecessor clauses in the 1918 Education Act – they were never carried out. The state of the economy after both World Wars was blamed by governments for these failures.

The 1944 Act vested powers in the Secretary of State to 'secure the effective execution by local authorities, under his control and direction, of the national policy for providing a varied and comprehensive education service in every area'. Thus the Secretary of State set the powers and duties for the LEAs to carry out the educational service, and began the 'partnership' between central and local government, in which each depended on the other. In reality since LEAs were not held to the regular monitoring of their schemes of further education provision some of their activities in this area were later deemed *ultra vires* (Joint DES/LEA Working Party, 1981; Liell and Saunders, 1987). The imprecise nature of the 1944 Act had allowed LEAs to develop their colleges as they saw fit, but the students' needs for nationally recognized educational and vocational qualifications meant that they were not as dissimilar as might have been expected. It simply meant that each college would first try to meet the needs of industry and commerce as its employers' advisory panels, board of governors and local authority perceived them and then attempt to satisfy student needs. Critics would later claim that colleges were too complacent during this period to want to involve more than token numbers of local employers and ascertain gaps in their course provision. And the steady flow of students into FE resulting from high birth rates during the 1960s and rising youth unemployment in the late 1970s could also, perhaps, be held partly responsible for a largely uncritical acceptance of the *status quo*.

THE DEVELOPMENT OF FURTHER EDUCATION SINCE 1979

As has been pointed out by investigators in this area of education and training there are problems in classification and therefore some confusion over the picture the statistics paint (Smithers and Robinson, 1991). However, the broad canvas shows a sector of education which grew from just under 1.5 million in 1980 to almost 2 million students in 1989. The percentage of full-time and 'sandwich' students aged over 18 (that is, on courses which combine training in industry with periods of study averaging more than 19 weeks in an academic year) went up by 34 per cent, and by 24 per cent for 16 and 17 year olds. These increases were taking place while 16 and 17 year olds declined in the general population by 20 and 13 per cent respectively.

In 1980 men outnumbered women in FE by 8 per cent. By the end of the decade women outnumbered men by almost 10 per cent. In 1980 the most popular area of study taking full- and part-time students together was Engineering. By 1989 this had been replaced by Business, Professional and Management. Another area of growth over this period was Mathematics and Computing.

Table 4.1 Enrolments on Further Education courses in FE colleges and related LEA maintained institutions (in '000s)

	1980–1	1987–8	1989–90
Full-time and sandwich			
Full-time	290	339	366
Sandwich	6	15	10
Total	296	354	376
Part-time			
Part-time day	585	702	783
Evening only	573	726	826
Total	1158	1428	1609
Total FT and PT	1454	1782	1985

Source: Statistics of Education, London DFE.

The figures exclude those students attending adult education institutes even though some authorities administer the two services together. Adult education has been characterized by being part-time and the courses offered being of general and recreational interest and usually not certificated. But this picture, too, is changing as Adult Education Principals have sought out new areas such as adult basic literacy and involvement in post-16 education in schools. The term 'community college' is often used to describe institutions which provide both further and adult education and training.

One area of FE work which has severely declined over this period has been providing the off-the-job training for apprentices. The numbers have fallen from nearly a quarter of a million in the 1960s to under 100,000 today. This parallels the fall in the work done for the Industrial Training Boards which have now disappeared. The one to survive longest was the Construction Industry Training Board.

In 1989 the number of 16 and 17 year olds remaining in schools was 28.8 per cent of the age group, while the number in FE was 18 per cent full-time and 16.5 per cent part-time. The percentage in sixth-form colleges was 5.1 per cent. (These were institutions usually formed by combining a number of 'sixth-forms' (Years 12 and 13) leaving the affected schools catering for only the 11 to 16 year olds.) Forty-one per cent of all Advanced Level full-time and part-time students were in FE in 1989. Nearly one-third of the full-time students were studying for a Business and Technology Education Council (BTEC) qualification, 20 per cent for GCE Advanced Levels, and 30 per cent for other vocational qualifications, such as those of the City and Guilds of London Institute, and the Royal Society of Arts. The most popular courses in FE for men of all ages in 1989 were in Engineering and Technology, General Education mainly to GCSE, 'A' and 'A/S' Levels, and Architecture, Building and Planning, while for women it was Business and Administration, General Education, Creative Arts and Design, and Modern Languages.

The current scene shows that over a third of those in post-16 education are in FE establishments in England and Wales, while in Scotland over 90 per cent remain in schools. Local unemployment rates are influential in staying-on rates, yet interestingly in Scotland poor employment prospects have persuaded young people to stay on in education, it is not yet so evident in England and Wales (Scottish Young Peoples' Survey, 1990).

Some LEAs have not treated same age pupils from schools and students in FE colleges equally. For example, in some authorities those that remain in schools will have their examination fees paid for them while if they come to college, which may involve added expense through travelling, they will have to pay their own. In addition there will be considerable expense to purchase protective clothing and tools or other items. LEAs have differing policies over the 'discretionary' awards made to FE students. And those young people that choose to join the Youth Training programme (now the Training Credits Scheme) will find these items paid for, and receive the trainee allowance in addition. Participation rates can be distorted by such policies – the 'uneven playing field'.

FE provides a very wide range of short courses. The most popular courses in 1989 were in Business and Administration, General Education, Engineering and Technology, and Mathematics and Computing. Some of these are arranged with local employers for their own staff which are charged at 'full cost' (without local authority subsidy). FE has provided linked courses for schools (including Special schools) in vocational areas, such as Office Practice, Catering, Engineering and Building Studies.

PICKUP or Professional, Industrial and Commercial Updating was a scheme set up in 1982 to provide flexible, part-time education and training in the latest skills, knowledge and techniques to workers in companies. With a budget of just £13 million in 1989 it assisted nearly one million adults. It operates through FE colleges as well as the universities, the Open University, the Open College and 'in-house' in industry.

Another service which is provided by some FE colleges has been managing education in prisons. The Home Office invited LEAs with penal establishments in their areas to provide this service, and most of them in turn passed the responsibility to local colleges. Prison Education Officers were, therefore, under their local college for professional purposes although operationally they came under the Prison Governor. This service is now provided by contractors who were successful in tendering for this work from the Home Office and is done by a variety of organizations, private as well as public training establishments.

FE employs significant numbers of part-time staff on short-term contracts. These are often workers or professionals who pass on their skills and knowledge of their industry or business. It also allows colleges the flexibility to introduce new or discontinue old courses. Although such staff will be qualified in their specialism there is no legal requirement to be a qualified teacher but many will take a part-time course such as that leading to the City and Guilds' Further and Adult Education Teachers Certificate or the FE Certificate in Education.

THE PRESSURE FOR CHANGE IN FURTHER EDUCATION

The view from industry

During the first few years after 1979 both schools and colleges had received a great deal of criticism for apparently failing to prepare young people adequately for work and in some cases creating an anti-work ethos. 'Employers therefore strongly suggest the case for vocational elements within the school curriculum in the later years of compulsory education' (CBI, 1981). There was also the view that the education and training were not amenable to radical change because of the vested interests of teachers and lecturers and their professional associations, and the 'educational establishment' in administration at all levels in maintaining existing practices.

Surveys of employers had found that FE was not sufficiently flexible in its provision, that its training was not always appropriate to the workplace setting, and that colleges were not always as sufficiently responsive to industry's needs; lecturers were not always as well informed and as up to date as they should be, and colleges were not good at marketing courses and keeping employers informed (Labour Market Studies Group, 1990). It was certainly true that colleges were uneven in their provision being influenced by the educational and training needs of their locality and the entrepreneurial skills of their senior management. Certainly there was no central mechanism to remedy national skill shortages which were contributing to Britain's economic difficulties.

There was criticism, too, of the most common organizational model in colleges of FE in the early 1980s, which was one of strong and rather independent vocational departments with (usually) a department of general education. Colleges were accused of being slow to react to the changing needs of students, such as those wishing to delay choice of vocational specialism, and potential students, such as women wishing to return to work after bringing up a family.

International comparisons

International comparisons of UK education and training of young people were being made in the early 1980s which were also a source of disquiet. One of the most influential was the study 'Competence and Competition' (National Economic Development Council, 1984) which indicated that on many counts, such as numbers entering higher education, days released for off-the-job training by employers, and numbers of students reaching the equivalent of a grade C pass in mother tongue, mathematics and a foreign language the UK was falling behind. This study examined education and training in the US, Japan, Germany as well as Britain.

Other investigators were also examining the skill levels and quality of training offered by foreign vocational education systems and links with industrial productivity. Various studies by the National Institute for Economic and Social Research were focused on specific vocational areas such as mechanical and electrical craftsmen (Steedman, 1983). The researchers noted the apparent lower level of general education of those entering training, and the narrower view of the skills and knowledge necessary in vocational subjects in the UK. The 'inchoate state of British vocational qualifications' (Prais, 1989) was cited frequently as a weakness in training, as was the depth of the divide in English and Welsh education between the esteemed academic and the lower status vocational qualification (Fatchett, 1991). An OECD study of fifteen countries put the UK next to last in the numbers of 18 year olds participating in education and training, although its figures did not count those on Youth Training (OECD, 1990).

THE GOVERNMENT'S RESPONSE

Job creation and training programmes

After the Conservative Government came to power in 1979 its major preoccupations were less with the supposed failings of education and training but more directly with the economy and unemployment ('Labour is not working' had been a potent and successful election slogan). It was, however, particularly sensitive to the pressure of youth unemployment which was increasing. A Conservative administration under Edward Heath had set up in 1973 the Manpower Services Commission to run public employment and training programmes. It had started a variety of schemes to assist through training and work experience the unemployed and those receiving little or no training in their employment. The Job Creation Programme was begun in 1975, the Work Experience on Employers' Premises (WEEP) Programme for 16–18 year olds in 1976, the Unified Vocation Preparation Programme (UVP), the Training for Skills Programme, the Training Opportunities Programme (TOPS), and the Youth Opportunities Programme (YOP) in 1977 and the Special Temporary Programme (STEP) to take over the Job Creation and Work Experience Programmes in 1978.

The new (1979) administration was to continue the policy of these *ad hoc* measures by replacing STEP with the Community Enterprise Programme in 1981 which became the Community Programme in 1982. The FE sector was involved in delivering much of the off-the-job training for these schemes, as it had earlier assisted the Industrial Training Boards to provide specific industrial training.

The Youth Training Scheme

The application of the policy of opening up vocational education to market forces by the Government and involving employers more directly in training became clearer with the publication of a White Paper 'A New Training Initiative: a Programme for Action' (Department of Employment, 1981). This paper proposed to open up training opportunities to adults, employed or not; to move away from the idea of time serving in apprenticeships and other forms of training to that of reaching agreed standards; and to aim towards giving the opportunity to all young people under 18 of either continuing in full-time education or receiving a combination of work experience and training. The Youth Task Group Report recommendations on the latter were accepted and formed the basis of the Youth Training Scheme (YTS). This was introduced in April 1983, and was welcomed by those involved such as the Confederation of British Industry as a 'New deal on training' (CBI, 1982).

YTS took over the role of Unified Vocational Preparation and the Youth Opportunities Programme – to provide 'a permanent bridge between school and work. It is not about unemployment' (Manpower Services Commission, 1982). Trainees were now to be paid an allowance (£25 to 16 year olds in 1983). FE would have an important role to play in providing the training and education to trainees in the scheme, most of whom would not normally have considered going on to college. Although the MSC wanted employers to take on the role of 'managing agents' for the YTS where this did not happen colleges were allowed to run programmes, albeit reluctantly, just as they had been permitted to run training and work programmes for the unemployed. Colleges, therefore, provided much of the off-the-job training while local companies provided the work experience element. Private trainers, though, were warmly welcomed to contribute to the off-the-job training. The Scheme was extended to two years in April 1986, and trainees received a basic allowance of £27.30 in the first year and £35 in the second. (This figure remains the same today.)

The YTS was replaced by Youth Training (YT) in May 1990 and by the Training Credits Scheme in 1993, and responsibility for its operation passed to the Training and Enterprise Councils (see below) and out of the hands of the Training Agency, descendant of the former MSC. In 1990 the percentage of young people 16–18 on YT schemes was 15 per cent (23 per cent of 16 year olds, 21 per cent of 17 year olds and 2 per cent of 18 year olds).

Vocational qualifications

The 1981 White Paper had listed a 10–point programme for action of which the creation of the Youth Training Scheme was the first to be put in place. It also wanted to see recognized standards set for all the main craft, technician and professional skills to replace time-serving and age-restricted apprenticeships. This was further developed in the 1986 White Paper 'Working Together – Education and Training' (DES, 1986) and by the Review of Vocational Qualifications Working Group. As seen above the qualifications system, or lack of it, had been a recurring criticism of English and Welsh education and training. Over 400 autonomous bodies were able to certificate students at a variety of levels resulting in confusion over standards and progression. The contrast with academic education was stark – from success in the General Certificate in Secondary Education (GCSE) a student could move on to Advanced Level, and then smoothly on to grant-supported Higher Education. Employers may not know the content or the assessment methods used in courses but they all understood what a GCSE, 'A' Level or a degree represented in level of attainment. Outside the relevant commercial or industrial setting most vocational qualifications were valueless, and those who wished to change from one occupational area to another had in most cases to start again at the beginning.

Those involved in training, therefore, welcomed the setting-up by the Government of the National Council for Vocational Qualifications (NCVQ) in 1986. This established a ladder of certification with rungs on to which all awards (including academic eventually) would fit. An awarding body could submit existing programmes or proposals to the National Council for approval. When it met the criteria (the standards of competence demanded by the 'industry lead-body') the programme would be approved at one of four levels (eventually five) of a National Vocational Qualification (NVQ). Thus the Government sought to bring order into an area of confusion for students, their parents and employers.

Progress has been slower than anticipated with difficulties experienced in bringing some well-established programmes of study, such as those of BTEC, into the 'competence-based' format. Broad-based vocational courses are now running in schools and colleges and receive accreditation at appropriate levels of the General National Vocational Qualification (GNVQ). Just as the test of acceptability of certification for the academic route lies with the universities, those for the vocational must lie with both higher education institutions and employers. This must remain in doubt until the evidence is there. The Further Education Unit still needed to say recently that it is necessary 'to take UK qualifications and awards away from the current divisions and confusion . . . and towards greater rationality and coherence'. Should there fail to be a rationalization of the qualifications' system which is broadly in line with standards in the European Community then students and workers from England and Wales will be at a distinct disadvantage.

It is worth noting the contrast in this respect with the Scottish education and training system. Here the award of the National Certificate is made by the Scottish Vocational Education Council (SCOTVEC) established by the Secretary of State for Scotland in 1985 as a national examining and validating body.

The management of vocational education and training

The Technical and Vocational Education Initiative (TVEI) was a scheme designed to influence both the content and the delivery of education to pupils and students in the age range 14–18. Both it and the YTS were managed through the Manpower Services Commission which was an agency of the Department of Employment and not through the Department of Education and Science. Pilot consortia (groups of schools and an FE college) for TVEI were established in 1983 and schemes were introduced by all LEAs that wished to be involved during the subsequent five years. Over this period LEAs and colleges got accustomed to the procedures of bidding for financial support for education and training from the allocated funds. A sum of £900 million was set aside for the scheme over the period 1983–93. Although the MSC has been replaced the extension of TVEI to all schools and colleges is still managed by the Department of Employment via the Training, Enterprise and Education Directorate (TEED).

The Manpower Services Commission and the LEAs

To remedy the perceived weakness of excessive dependence on the LEA in the structure of Further Education the Government steadily increased the role of the Manpower Services Commission in its funding. The 1984 White Paper 'Training for Jobs' (Department of Education, 1984) announced the way in which the MSC would hold one-quarter of the grant made by central government to local authorities for their expenditure on further education. The MSC then examined the authorities' three-year development plans and annual programmes of 'work-related further education' in their areas to see if in its view they met the needs of local industry and commerce. It would approve them, reject them or request changes. The practice also underlined the Government's belief that only wholesale adoption of sound business principles to educational administration would make for effective and accountable management. The language of the world of business and management consultancy became familiar to LEAs and colleges: terms like 'strategic planning', 'rolling three-year development plans', 'franchising', 'quality assurance', 'performance indicators', 'client-centred approaches', 'staff and curriculum audits', 'staff appraisal' though not as yet 'the bottom line' since they were not to have full responsibility for their own budgets until incorporation under a funding council in 1993.

Curbing the powers of the LEAs

In 1984 an Act had been passed [Education (Grants and Awards)] which circumscribed the discretion that Local Authorities had over the way central block grants could be used. Moneys were now 'targeted' or 'ring-fenced' to ensure that the funds could only be used for the purposes intended by the Department of Education and Science. When applied to education it meant, for example, that if central funds had been allocated to Staff Development then national priorities were to be dealt with first and then local. This was to widen further the rift between central and local government over education and training, which had been proudly referred to after the 1944 Act as a 'partnership', 'a national service locally administered'. There was an unmistakable ideological dislike of the public service model of management with control exercised by local politicians whether they were in County Hall or on the boards of governors of schools or colleges. As we shall see later this rift was to widen further.

'The responsive college'

To stimulate entrepreneurial activity by colleges the Conservative Government passed the 1985 Further Education Act which allowed LEAs to conduct commercial activities. Their colleges could now set up companies to engage in business such as providing training for employers. College staff could now find themselves with a commercial as well as a teaching role. The report of Her Majesty's Inspectors 'Further Education in Practice' (HMI, 1989) concluded that generally FE had become responsive to client needs, were marketing courses more efficiently, and the quality of teaching had improved by becoming more student- instead of lecturer-centred. It would thus appear that the changes were having the results the Government intended.

The TECs/LECs

The 1988 White Paper 'Employment for the 1990s' had announced the creation of the Training and Enterprise Councils (known as Local Enterprise Councils in Scotland). It said they were 'to plan and deliver training and to promote and support the development of small businesses and self-employment within their area'. They were also to be asked to develop links with education in their areas.

   The stimulus for their development has partly come from the Private Industry Councils (PICs) in the USA (Norman Fowler's key adviser at the Department of Employment was Catherine Stratton who was involved in establishing the PICs in the United States), and from the Chambers of

Trade and Commerce of France and Germany, regional labour boards of Sweden and Japanese government-industry relations (Bennett *et al.*, 1989).

They were to have an incorporated structure which means that they are independent companies, limited by guarantee and subject to company law. The TECs would have performance contracts with the government from whom the financial resources would come. The bulk of their work would be arranging adult Employment Training (ET) and Youth Training (formerly the YTS) for the 16–18 age range, and the drawing-up of training contracts for these trainees with such providers as companies with in-house training facilities, private training companies or FE colleges.

The TECs would also have responsibility for the Training Credits scheme for employed young people who would be given vouchers which could be exchanged for training when matched by a contribution from their employer. The FE colleges would have to bid for this work and it is possible that some schools would also be able to provide training.

There are now 82 TECs in England and Wales, and the Training Credits scheme was introduced on a pilot basis in 1991.

Links with business

Pursuing its consistent theme that education and industry must form stronger links the Department of Employment has supported school-business compacts since November 1989. It has financed the appointment of link staff by LEAs, and the secondment of teachers and lecturers to industry for short periods, and people from industry to work in schools. Business-Education Partnerships are now widely established with the assistance of the TECs and the LEAs. Their purpose is to foster links between schools, colleges and local industry. Since 1990 the DES (now the Department For Education – DFE) has allowed BTEC First and National vocational courses to be offered in schools. This is consistent with Conservative philosophy of providing the 'client' with greater choice.

Other changes

Some changes over the period were caused by factors beyond government control. Changing demographic patterns in various parts of Britain forced LEAs to reorganize their provision for the post-16 age range. The drop in the numbers staying on in the sixth forms of individual schools persuaded some authorities to adopt the 'sixth form college' solution and others to form 'tertiary colleges'. The former maintained a broadly academic education while the latter provided the full range of academic and vocational programmes in a locality where the LEA had only 11–16 age range maintained schools. The 1980s saw a large number of tertiary colleges open so that today there are nearly sixty.

CURRICULAR CHANGES

The Technical and Vocational Education Initiative (TVEI) and the curriculum

Although past Governments had been anxious to avoid entering into the 'secret garden' to remedy what they considered were the curricular weaknesses in Secondary and Further Education this one was prepared to do so. It 'was the latest phase in an unprecedented strategy, in the recent history of British educational policy implementation, of government interventionism in the curriculum of British schools' (Saunders, 1988). With Mrs Thatcher's personal endorsement the TVEI was launched with the specific aim of making education broader and more vocationally relevant. Fourteen pilot schemes were started in September 1983, extended to almost all LEAs by 1986 and from 1987 to all secondary schools. It looked for coherence over the 14–18 age range, and therefore stressed progression to other educational and training opportunities, a curriculum designed as a preparation for adult life in a society experiencing rapid change, with vocational elements, planned work experience, opportunities for showing initiative, problem solving ability and personal development, as well as core elements of numeracy, communication skills and information technology. As mentioned above it was an agency from outside the DES to influence the development of education and training. The hope was that the lessons learned through TVEI by schools and colleges would be embedded in their curricula even when the funding ran out.

Pre-vocational education

In 1979 the Further Education Unit had published 'A Basis for Choice' (ABC) which recommended a broadly based, general education for the increasing numbers staying in full-time education after the age of 16, but who were undecided over their precise vocational direction. It had suggested that curriculum objectives could be negotiated between tutor and student, that learning should be experience-led, and that guidance and counselling were fundamental. Programmes were developed which became the Certificate of Pre-Vocational Education for the 16+ student and the Foundation Programme of the Joint Board for the 14–16 age group. The MSC accepted the underlying principles of 'ABC' and encouraged their incorporation into YTS as well as TVEI courses.

Other curricular changes

Colleges had been involved for many years with distance learning, often providing the local tutorial base for Open University students. In collaboration with the National Extension College students have been able to study independently but have access to local tutorial support at their college via Flexistudy. Support for more development of open learning came with MSC providing pump-priming finance to FE. The early learning packages were originally aimed at the training and retraining of adults in technician and advisory level skills. This was supported by the Open College. Flexible learning has now become established including its use by full-time students and by others on an informal basis. Colleges now have 'drop-in' workshops with facilities for study in Information Technology, Mathematics and Communications (including Modern Languages).

The work on the Accreditation of Prior Learning (APL) which had begun in the UK in 1981–2 grew during this period but would require new flexible mechanisms to allow it to operate and develop in FE. A Credit Accumulation and Transfer System (CATS) has been operating in the polytechnics and universities since 1986.

FE was tapping a potentially rich seam when it participated with higher education setting up Access and Return to Study courses based on the APL principle that life experiences are valuable and can be recognized as such to enable adults to enter Higher Education (HE) although they may lack the traditional entry qualifications. Students enter a participating HE institution after successfully completing an Access programme.

THE RESORT TO MAJOR LEGISLATION – 1988 ONWARDS

The 1988 Act

Despite all the changes it was clearly the Government's belief that only a major new enactment could push education into the direction it wished it to take in a society whose attitudes had profoundly changed since the 1944 Act was passed. The Conservative Party had been returned to office in 1987 for a third consecutive term and educational reform had been an important issue in its manifesto. The 1988 Education Reform Act or ERA, though mainly concerned with schools, affected both Further and Higher Education. To schools (except the private ones) the 1988 Act meant the introduction of the National Curriculum, open enrolment, local financial management, and the opportunity to choose grant maintained status ('opting-out'). For universities the Act meant the replacement of the University Grants Committees by the University Funding Council with between six and nine of its fifteen members to have 'experience of, and to have shown capacity in, industrial, commercial or financial matters', again making it clear that it looked outside education for its stimulus and direction.

For Further Education it took the opportunity to clarify the legal basis by replacing or repealing sections of the 1944 Act. Section 41 was replaced by Section 120 (2):

1 'It shall be the duty of every local education authority to secure the provision for their area of adequate facilities for further education.
2 'Subject to the following provision of this section, in this Act 'further education' means:

   (a) full-time and part-time education for persons over compulsory school age (including vocational, social, physical and recreational training); and
   (b) organised leisure-time occupation provided in connection with the provision of such education'.

In this Act, 'further education' does not include higher education, so clearly distinguishing between the two.

'Public sector' Higher Education, such as the polytechnics and certain other colleges which had been provided by most LEAs in that 'seamless robe' with its further education, was now to be placed under the Polytechnics and Colleges Funding Council. The PCFC could, however, contract with LEAs to provide certain higher education courses. Higher Education was defined by type of course leading to degrees, diplomas and professional qualifications. The institutions under the PCFC were to become corporations with autonomy limited by centrally allocated resources and the conditions under which they would be released.

Further Education was similarly defined by the level of course it could offer, being at or below the GCE Advanced Level, or the Higher Grade of the Scottish Certificate of Education, or the Business and Technology Education Council National awards or the SCOTVEC National awards. The LEAs were to delegate responsibility for financial management and the appointment and dismissal of staff to the governing bodies of colleges remaining under its control. The colleges' governing bodies were to have a majority of members drawn from 'business, industry or any profession'.

No standard title was proposed so colleges have continued to use a variety of names which has done nothing to assist students, parents or employers, e.g. Technical College, College of Technology, College of Further Education, Community College or simply College. Those that are provided by the LEA were to be referred to as 'maintained' to distinguish them from those under the Polytechnics and Colleges Funding Council, or under the Education Department in Scotland or private establishments. The 1989 Self-Governing Schools, etc. (Scotland) Act allows Scottish LEAs the option of establishing management companies to run further education. These companies operate in similar ways to other corporate status institutions in that they have considerable autonomy, but depend on the authorities for the annual grant allocation.

The 1988 Act gave the LEAs a strategic planning role of the FE provision in their area. They also had the duty to provide education and training (or as the Act terms it 'further education of a vocational kind') for those already in employment as well as those preparing for it.

The Further and Higher Education Act 1992

It was an obvious inconsistency to allow schools to opt out and the higher education institutions to have corporate status under a separate funding body, yet still keep FE under LEA control. Reports such as 'Managing Colleges Efficiently' (DES and LAA, 1987) and 'Further Education in Practice' (HMI, 1989) had commented favourably on colleges and their ability to plan and deliver the work-related further education, their increased responsiveness to client needs and quality of teaching. Increasing the powers of governors and diminishing the influence of the LEAs on the colleges' governing bodies, together with delegated budgets were bound to have significant effects on the way colleges perceived themselves. It was obvious that the anomaly in the position of FE would need to be re-examined. That opportunity came in 1992.

The Further and Higher Education Act 1992 established a Further Education Funding Council (FEFC), which receives funds from the Secretary of State and then allocates these to various institutions. From April 1993 colleges became incorporated under the FEFC, which has a duty to secure the provision of full-time education for 16–19 year olds having regard to that already provided by the LEA. In practice this means that students in the sixth form (Years 12 and 13 in schools) which have decided not to 'opt out' will remain under the control of the LEAs, schools which have chosen to 'opt out' (have grant maintained status) will be funded directly by the DFE, while Sixth-Form Colleges, and the 385 or so Tertiary and FE Colleges will be under the Funding Council. This excludes the private providers of vocational education and training which number about 130.

FE college and sixth-form college staff are now employed by their governing bodies and not the LEA. Staff in the sixth-form colleges have moved from school to FE conditions of service. There are bound to be

changes in the power and influence of the national organizations representing teachers and lecturers as the LEAs cease to be their employers.

Schools are able to admit and charge adults for joining the courses of
their 16+ students.

CONCLUSIONS

Market-led vocational education and training

The period since1979 might have been considered for Further Education a
period in which change was entirely uni-direction under an Administration
committed to an ideology of free-market principles in most areas of social
and economic life. Its policies would obviously be buffeted by forces, some
beyond its control, such as demographic change and world economic
conditions, and incidentally by the side-effects of its other legislation, such
as Employment Law and Social Security provision. One might have
expected a period of steady development. Instead it appeared to make
policy in the early 1980s based on assumptions rather than research
evidence that FE itself was failing, and not perhaps the environment in
which it operated. It listened to certain voices notably employer organizations, and its agents acted on those assumptions. One result was a youth
training programme which is considered second-rate by most people
eligible to take part in it; it borrows heavily in part from European practice
but omits a few vital elements, such as the wholehearted participation of
employers, the backing of legislation, a linking of training qualifications
and experience to remuneration, and adequate resourcing.

The anxiety now is the decision to look to the United States for market-
led practices such as competition between education and training
providers, located, however, in a different social culture. The premise is
that competition equals quality: that local management and competition
between providers will improve quality and widen, not narrow, choice in
the long term. Competition will go on increasing as institutions compete for
students and the funding policy remains that of 'money following the
student'. To be borne in mind is the fact that the number of 16–19 leavers
will drop from 911,000 in 1982–3 to an estimated 613,000 in 1993–4 which
means an almost 33 per cent fall in numbers (*Employment Gazette*, October
1991).

LEAs may well choose to reopen their remaining maintained school
sixth forms where they had been previously closed on grounds of cost in
order to now compete with their former colleges. In the anxiety to increase
numbers it may well be that minority courses will be sacrificed for the
popular and cheaper, unless funding weighting mechanisms take this into

account. Some traditional academic Sixth-Form Colleges will wish to develop vocational courses despite high costs, higher than for the FE and Tertiary colleges already better equipped to do so. Collaboration between colleges to provide specialist courses may be a better alternative.

The policy of 'franchising' courses to other institutions is now established. It is driven by a funding policy which encourages institutions to cater for as large a number as possible. If courses cannot be accommodated on the home institution's premises then it can be contracted out to another on a franchised basis. Funding passes to the home institution that 'pays' for the service of the other. Higher Education is franchising FE colleges to provide courses while colleges franchise their own to schools. Quality could be elusive under these conditions.

The involvement of employers in FE

The involvement of committed employers can be beneficial to vocational education and training. Employers are now in the majority on college governing bodies, they form the 'lead-bodies' which advise the National Council for Vocational Qualifications, they advise awarding bodies, and they direct the work of the Training and Enterprise Councils. The Government attaches great importance to their presence and is expecting inspiration, efficiency and leadership from them. 'But it provokes scepticism among historians of Britain's attempts to raise vocational training standards, on which employers have placed all too little emphasis in the past' (Gapper, 1989). How committed are they, for example, to develop the skills and knowledge that will allow British students to take full advantage of the mobility of labour from 1993 onwards? By their very nature (annual accounts notwithstanding) can they take the long view about the quality and quantity of skills needed by society?

The awarding bodies

Like other parts of the English and Welsh vocational education system the influence of the certifying or awarding bodies has been crucial. With the employers and others who sit on their advisory panels they have maintained high standards of training. They have been innovative and prepared to accept challenges from Government when asked to monitor and evaluate new programmes, such as the Pre-Vocational Certificate and competence-based courses. Yet it must be remembered that they, too, are commercial organizations. They find themselves in a highly competitive situation with the diminishing number of 16–19 students – their traditional business – and are looking for alternative markets, such as in the schools and mature students, and through providing more attractive programmes. They will be under some pressure to relax standards.

Another question must be, how determined is the National Council for Vocational Qualifications to pursue its objective of an easily comprehended award system? Is competency, albeit under certain conditions, sufficient to underpin the skill and allow flexibility in a changing industrial and commercial world? Will these levels and the awards tied to them be equally valued throughout the European Community?

Despite the uncertainties education seems to be becoming a more attractive alternative to young people. More students are entering further and higher education. The low prospects of employment during the recession since 1990 is one factor, but there is also a genuine demand for more academic and vocational education. For example, since 1988 the national percentage increase in the numbers of 16–18 year olds in full-time education rose from 32 to 36 per cent of the age group. Where further and adult education are still administered separately they will almost certainly come together. Alternatively, the incorporated colleges will become community institutions providing the full range of programmes.

The criticism over the narrowness of the curriculum for the 16+ will be partly allayed by the inclusion of 'core skills' into the General National Vocational Qualification-approved courses. Voices such as the CBI and the National Curriculum Council are firmly in support. 'Indeed their incorporation should be a requirement for all post-16 qualifications. Such a step would contribute towards parity of esteem' is the view from the Business and Technology Education Council.

The resort of the Government to law has been to now attach FE firmly to the centre for resourcing and general direction, yet give the individual institutions more autonomy if they have a governing body willing to use their new powers. Most 'horticulturalists' in the kitchen plot of Further Education will look forward to the new arrangements, recognizing the opportunities and the responsibilities. They have adapted to the changing economic and social conditions since 1979 and will respond as positively as possible to the increasingly competitive situation, in which recent legislation has put them. They will continue to develop new areas of work, particularly the training and retraining of adults and those with special needs. Gardeners have problems enough battling with the soil and the elements so that guidance rather than direction from the foremen is more likely to deliver better produce.

REFERENCES

Bennett, R., McCoshan, A., and Sellgren, J. (1989). *TECs and VET: The practical*

requirements: organisation, geography and international comparison with the
USA and Germany. Research Papers (Department of Geography, London School
of Economics).

Confederation of British Industry (1981). *Education and Training Bulletin*, Vol. 12,
No. 1. London, Confederation of British Industry.

Confederation of British Industry (1982). New Deal on Training. *Education and
Training Bulletin*, Vol. 12, No. 2, London, Confederation of British Industry.

Department of Education (DES) (1984). *Training for Jobs*. Cmnd 9135, London,
HMSO.

Department of Education (DES) (1986). *Working Together – Education and
Training*. Cmnd 9823, London, HMSO.

Department of Education and Science and Local Authorities Association (1987).
Managing Colleges Efficiently. London, HMSO.

Department of Employment (1981). *A New Training Initiative: A Programme for
Action*. Cmnd 8455, London, HMSO.

Education Statistics for the United Kingdom (1991). DES Education Statistics,
London, HMSO.

Employment Gazette (October 1991).

Fatchett, D. (1991). *Removing the Academic–Vocational Divide*. Interim Report of
the European Inquiry Team, London.

Further Education Funding Council (1993). *Statistics Bulletin*.

Further Education Unit (FEU) (1979). *A Basis for Choice*. Further Education
Curriculum and Development Unit, London.

Gapper, J. (1989). A Late Starter in the Race. *Financial Times*, 21.11.89.

Her Majesty's Inspectorate (HMI) (1989). *Further Education in Practice: Tertiary
Colleges*. London, HMSO.

Joint DES/LEA Working Party (1981). *The Legal Basis of Further Education*.
London: HMSO.

Labour Market Studies Group (1990). *Employers' Views of Work Related Further
Education*, University of Leicester.

Liell, P. and Saunders, J.B. (1987). *The Law of Education*. London, Butterworths.

Manpower Services Commission (1982). Youth Task Group Report. MSC,
London.

National Economic Development Council (1984). *Competence and Competition*.

Organization for European Economic Cooperation (OECD) (1990). *Education in
OECD Countries 1987–88*. OECD, Paris.

Prais, S.J. (1989) in 'Productivity, Education and Training'. Reprints of studies
published in the *National Institute Economic Review*. London, National Institute
of Economic and Social Research.

Saunders, M. (1988). The Technical and Vocational Education Initiative: Enclaves
in British Schools in J. Lauglo and K. Lillis (eds) *Vocationalizing Education*,
Pergamon, Oxford.

Scottish Young Peoples' Survey (1990). Centre for Education Sociology,
University of Edinburgh.

Smithers, A. and Robinson, P. (1991). *Beyond Compulsory Schooling – a
Numerical Picture*. London, Council for Industry and Higher Education.

Statistical Bulletin 9/91 – *Statistics of Schools in England – January 1990*. London,
DES.

Statistical Bulletin 13/91 – *Educational Activities of 16–18 year olds in England*.
London, DES.

Steedman, H. (1983) *Mechanical and Electrical Craftsmen*. London, National Institute of Economics and Social Research.

Treasury (1979). *The Government's Expenditure Plans, 1980–81*. Cmnd 7746, London, HMSO.

5 Legislation, university education and economic performance: the Nigerian experience

Peter Ezeh

For the purposes of this chapter, three periods may be identified in the development of Western-type education in Nigeria: the colonial period (from 1842 to 1959), the early independent period (from 1960 to 1970), and the post-civil war period (from 1970 until the present). It can also be established that education in the two earlier periods was more functional and made more positive contributions to the economy and public affairs of those periods. Writers fired by certain anthropological considerations, which are outside the scope of this chapter, prefer to include a period earlier than the country's contact with the missionaries to recount certain practices in traditional society through which young people were integrated into their various communities (Fafunwa, 1974 and Ojike, n.d.). Nevertheless, there appears to be little or no argument about the complementary nature of the Western-type education and such practices to each other. For obvious reasons, neither system could have served the purpose of the other. The fact that the two have continued to coexist most harmoniously in many parts of the country testifies further to the difference in their functions.

Writers who discuss Nigerian education exclusively from pragmatic perspectives begin with the efforts of the missionaries of the two main foreign religions – Christianity and Islam. The two are similar only to the extent that each is more cosmopolitan than folk initiation procedures, which usually are village- or town-specific. But again, even between the Western-type education and Muslim education, it is the former that has had a greater impact on Nigerian public institutions.

THE COLONIAL PERIOD

Although nationalists were vehement in their opposition to foreign rule, the one thing they never objected to was the introduction of Western-type education. They were guided by the logic that if a people must perform well politically, economically or otherwise in a world that has become irreversibly interdependent, they should rise above wasteful parochialism and adopt and adapt systems which had proved to be effective in the new era. Mbonu Ojike, one of the most committed of the pre-Independence Nigerian nationalists, was at once a redoubtable advocate of the preservation of whatever is good in Africa's ways of life and unbudging critic of blind nationalism. He would always say, 'There is no race but mankind' (Ojike, n.d., p. 95).

One of the foremost innovations of the Western-type education was the introduction of English language. One has to be familiar with the language situation in most parts of Africa to appreciate why. In some areas, there are as many languages as there are towns. Within Nigeria's present 923,768 square-kilometre territory, for instance, there are some 300 distinct languages. Linguists profess an inability to establish exactly how many languages there really are. So, any system that ameliorated the problem by introducing a neutral compromise language should have been jumped at. The Nigerian-born world-famous novelist Chinua Achebe believes that even the nationalists' anti-foreign rule agitations would have been more difficult without the introduction of English language among Nigerians (Achebe, 1990).

Nigeria in its present form is a creation of British colonial policy. Those parts of Africa which were not previously under one government were brought together under the same economic and political structures. And Western-type education was used to sell the new system to the indigenes.

Writers on Nigeria do not agree on who were the first – Methodists or Presbyterians – to arrive in Nigeria. There is no dispute, though, about the enormous pioneering roles of either group in the introduction of education in Nigeria. Also writers tend to be unanimous in their view that Nigerian indigenes recognized the usefulness of Western-type education rather quickly. Even in cases where locals rejected Christianity parents soon aspired to send their children (usually boys) to school for the attendant socioeconomic advantages (Fajana, 1976; Comhaire, 1981). Those who acquired proficiency in the English language and the basic skills of reading, writing and arithmetic would trade much more easily with Europeans (and to that extent, the outside world) and with larger areas of Africa than could otherwise be possible. May we stress here, however, that although some historians have shown that economic contacts between inhabitants of parts of present-day Nigeria and other parts of the world pre-date the coming of the Europeans there is no gainsaying the improvements the Europeans brought in (Ifemesia, 1979).

People trained in informal literacy classes and later in primary schools by the missionaries soon began to help both in the church and colonial secular services. They acquired enviable positions, in the eyes of the local people, as interpreters, clerks, catechists, teachers, parsons, and so on. Never mind that they were not exactly the best posts a person could get in any of those fields. The problems which both parties encountered in such intercultural activities have inspired some of the best works of fiction and nonfiction set in the region (Cary, 1962; Basden, 1982).

By 1855, the Baptists had built the first postprimary institution. Other churches did the same afterwards. Such names as CMS Grammar School, Lagos; Hope Waddel Institute, Calabar; Annunciation School, Ikere-Ekiti; the Methodist Boys' High School and so on still ring a bell. Those post-primary institutions imparted increased skills to future teachers in mission schools and workers in the colonial service, mission health institutions and big foreign business organizations. Usually a place was waiting for anyone who was trained in those schools. So employment was the next logical and sure stage after graduation.

Even now, the word for a paid permanent job in some of the indigenous languages translates literally *White man's work* apparently as a result of the experience of that time. Such jobs are called *olu bekee* (or, *olu oyibo*) in Igbo and *utom mbakara* in Ibibio and Efik. People strove to send their children to school so that they could acquire such new socioeconomic status.

Unfortunately, this pristine view of education outlived its usefulness yet it continued up until the present when it has become clearly counter-productive as we shall establish presently. By the 1920s, students who passed through the postprimary schools were beginning to agitate for tertiary education. There was none in Nigeria at that time. Those who were lucky went overseas. One easily remembers Nnamdi Azikiwe who later became the first President of independent Nigeria besides other distinguished posts; Obafemi Awolowo, eventually the first Leader of Opposition in the federal parliament; Akanu Ibiam, eventually the first Governor of the then-Eastern Nigeria (now the seven states of Abia, Akwa Ibom, Anambra, Cross River, Enugu, Imo and Rivers) and so on.

It is remarkable that some writers on Nigeria link the formation of Lagos Youth Movement, the precursor of Nigeria's first political party, to the clamour for the introduction of Western-type higher education (Sklar, 1983). In 1948 the University of London opened one of its colleges at Ibadan. That college ultimately became a fully-fledged university. Western-type education first became popular in the southern part of Nigeria. Muslim proselytizers introduced an educational system based on that religion. But it did not include English language in its curriculum nor did it teach those subjects which would open up economic or political opportunities. One educationist has observed: 'People educated in the Koranic schools found themselves inferior in their roles compared with those educated in the Western schools' (Fajana, 1976). Opinion leaders in that part of Nigeria realized this flaw and began planning for a change. Barewa College, one of Nigeria's best-known private schools, was established to impart Western-type education (Williams, 1982). Many people from that part of the country who later played important roles in Nigerian public affairs passed through that school. A few examples: Shehu Shagari, President of the Second Republic; Yakubu Gowon, the army general who ruled as the Head of State from 1966 to 1975; Kashim Ibrahim, first Governor of the then-Northern Region; Ahmadu Bello, first Premier of the same region and Abubakar Tafawa Balewa, the first Prime Minister of the Federation.

In general, there are examples of eminent people in Nigerian public affairs who had only passed through the primary or secondary schools of that period for their regular education. They include the first Minister of Education Aja Nwachukwu, Prime Minister Tafawa Balewa, the renowned poet/novelist Gabriel Okara, Secretary to then-Eastern Nigeria (later Biafra) Government N.U. Akpan, former president Shehu Shagari, and a host of others. When they left public office many of them made, and have continued to make, significant contributions to the economic development of the country. If the effectiveness of an educational system is measured by the inputs of its products to the development of the society, then the period under discussion is unrivalled.

THE EARLY INDEPENDENT PERIOD

At Nigeria's Independence in 1960 education had already evolved to a stage where the church no longer retained a seeming monopoly over it. Besides mission schools, there were also those established by private investors. Among the privately run schools such names as Barewa College in the north, Mayflower in the west, Awomamma Secondary School in the east were quite famous. Fees charged at government schools were frequently lower, and in some cases no fees were charged at all. Before Independence, the government of the then-Western Region introduced universal Primary Education under which pupils studied free of charge. Nevertheless, people believed that private and mission schools offered better quality education. Many decades afterwards, in a different setting, this view is still popular according to a widespread survey carried out by a Lagos news magazine (Oloyede *et al.*, 1990). Not much changed in the Nigerian educational system until the beginning of the civil war in 1967. We may only add that universities and polytechnics had by then been established to provide those levels of education to students who wanted to continue after their secondary education. University of Nigeria Nsukka, the first autonomous indigenous institution at its level in Nigeria, was opened by Princess Alexandra of Kent on 7 October 1960, the very first week of the country's Independence.

THE POST-CIVIL WAR PERIOD

Perhaps the most significant development in the Nigerian educational system after the civil war in that country was the takeover of mission and most private schools by the government. The takeover of schools by the government has produced some advantages and disadvantages. Among the former is uniformity in the system and increased pay for teachers. But it now appears impossible to deny that the quality of education has declined. Graduates of even university-level centres or polytechnics appear less able to help themselves outside school. There are no examples of the equivalents of Okara, Balewa, Shagari or Aja Nwachukwu at the present. Some local writers on this issue believe that mission and private investor schools performed better in instilling discipline into students (Ogazimorah, 1990; Oloyede, 1990). Nigeria's high unemployment rate can, at least in part, be explained by the quality of education given to students. Usually students aspiring to higher education do this with the hope that they will acquire the certificates which will earn them a place in government establishments or the existing big businesses. Times have changed, but the initial orientation which Nigerians got on education has scarcely changed. In some places in 1989, unemployment was nearly 11 per cent according to government statistics which independent economic sources dispute as an underestimation of the true position (unnamed reporter, *Nigerian Economist*, 1990). Secondary school leavers constitute nearly 65 per cent of that number in the average city. Graduate unemployment is rising. Many are now being compelled by the hard economic realities to retrain in occupations not related to the fields they graduated in.

The number of indigenous universities has, of course, grown from zero at Independence to thirty-one at present, although all of them combined are only able to admit a small percentage, some 20 per cent, of high school leavers wishing to continue to that level. Admissions to most tertiary schools, in fact to all the thirty-one universities, are through a central body known as Joint Admissions and Matriculation Board (JAMB) which was created by a military government in 1978. In 1990/91 session there were 290,296 candidates for places in all the universities, of which only 16.78 per cent or 48,726 were successful. In 1984, 193,107 candidates had applied, and 23,557 got placements; and in 1989, 214,000 applied for a little over 30,000 places. JAMB (a favourite acronym in Nigeria for the admission board) frequently resorts to extra-academic considerations to tackle this unenviable task. It uses a method which it calls 'cut-off points' to reduce the number of otherwise qualified candidates, in a manner which many an adversely affected Nigerian criticizes. Abioye Alabi, Head of JAMB's Information and Publications Unit, has said that the percentage of students admitted strictly on the basis of their brilliant performance in matriculation examinations is really as little as between 30 and 40 per cent (Alabi, 1990). Sociopolitical considerations are used to distribute the remaining places among students from particular localities who may not necessarily have scored as highly as rejected candidates in the matriculation examinations. The students so patronized come from either the Nigerian districts technically designated educationally less developed states, or from localities where the universities are sited; but much more so the former. For the latter, each Nigerian state which is considered to be in the catchment area of a university usually fills only two vacancies on account of such a position (Alabi, 1990). It is in fact the so-called educationally less developed states that are mostly favoured by the extra-academic considerations.

One of Nigeria's best-known academics, Professor Chimere Ikoku, the Vice-Chancellor of the University of Nigeria, has been reported as recommending the abrogation of such a favour, saying it might be counter-productive, for obvious reasons, in the end (unnamed reporter, *Lagos Daily Times*, 19.12.90). There are no indications that this method of admission is about to change, though polytechnics and subdegree teacher training colleges are even more in number than the universities but this growth in number is not a reliable measure of the contribution of the Nigerian post-civil war educational system to the country's economic development.

Overall, the government has several new policies that tend to pass a vote of no confidence, as it were, on the old system. So far, in practice, there has only been a continuation of the colonial-type curriculum (which was excellent for its time and purpose but whose effectiveness now is highly doubtful). Students went to school to obtain credentials and return to the labour market. There has been no serious effort to impart self-reliant training that could enable students to get along on their own after their education. For example, although government statisticians claimed there was a decline in unemployment in 1990, fresh school leavers still constitute the bulk of the unemployed. One analyst has calculated that earnings from non-oil sectors actually accounted for only 4.2 per cent of the country's total export revenue for 1990 (Efunwoye, 1990). The persistent problem with the economy for the past two decades has been how to restimulate interest in the non-oil sectors. Hence discerning analysts are not excited that the year's estimated 39 billion earnings from crude oil was actually exceeded. It is easy to trace the increase in earnings to the last four months of the year, the peak of the so-called Gulf boom. More than 12 billion Naira

(£1 =17 Naira, 1990) were earned in September alone from oil. Compare this to a little more than 6 billion in January.

When there is a major instance of budget indiscipline as there was in 1991 – in spite of the much-talked about 'gravies' from the Gulf War-related oil sales – economists put a large part of the blame on the government's attitude of assuming more roles than it can practically play in a modern free-market economy. The Nigerian official figures for the unexpected earnings from the oil sales of the Gulf War period are 2.1 billion US dollars, although independent journalistic investigations by the then Lagos-based William Keeling of the London *Financial Times* put the figure at 5.2 billion US dollars, which revelation, alas!, earned the British reporter arbitrary deportation (Ezenwelu *et al.*, 1991). The government, nevertheless, ended up recording an unanticipated budget deficit of 19.56 billion Naira, according to the figures released by the Nigerian Central Bank and published in September the same year, instead of the expected 50 million Naira surplus which it announced in the beginning of the year (Ikediala, 1991, p. 92). There was a retained revenue of 14.056 billion Naira, and expenditure of 33.61 billion. Only 5.7 per cent of the expenditure was on productive activities. Nearly 72 per cent, or a little less than 34 billion Naira, was spent on such subheadings as pensions and gratuities, debt servicing and the like.

It was the same year the Manufacturers' Association of Nigeria – a private investment-promoting body – reckoned that unutilized industrial capacity for the organized private sector was as much as 121 billion Naira. Opportunities abound, too, in other spheres open to private entrepreneurs.

Naturally, continuous growth is rare in an economy where there is high unemployment. A major local newspaper quoting World Bank statistics reported a negative annual growth rate of 15.8 per cent for the country's gross national product for the seven years 1982–9. Per capita consumption dropped by 3.9 per cent per annum (unnamed reporter, *The Punch*, Lagos, 21.12.90). Per capita income is 300 US dollars according to another writer (Akpan, 1990). A liberal military government introduced various pro-free market policies since 1986, and has been grappling with 33 billion US dollars foreign debts accumulated mainly by its predecessors. In 1989 alone it spent 1.3 billion dollars servicing those loans (unnamed reporter, *The Punch*, Lagos, 21.12.90). For a country whose budget for 1990 was but 39.7 billion (1 dollar = 9 Naira in 1990), those debts are no peanuts. The author suggests that when the effects of Gulf crisis-generated unexpected earnings from the crude oil trade are subtracted, the economic situation even for 1990 was not really so good. And there will not always be Gulf crises. So, one has a lot of sympathy for the principle underlying the government's present efforts to restructure the educational system to stress the type of training that equips willing benefi- ciaries for self-employment. Colonial and immediate post-Independence mission schools tried to do this at a stage when they began to train more students than the labour market could take. Curricula of that time had subjects which trained students on various self-employment oriented activities.

Nigeria has now introduced a new education policy – commonly known here as the 6-3-3-4 system – in which emphasis is put evenly on both the skill-cultivating and academic subjects in order to give students economic opportunities after their training. But it is still too early to predict how successful this will be. Even states that began the policy earlier than others have run it for less than ten years.

There is also the much-criticized policy of replacing English with indigenous languages as the media of instruction in schools. One immediately obvious disadvantage is that monolingual literacy in an indigenous language hardly spoken outside one geographical area of Nigeria itself will circum-scribe the student's chances in today's world. What a huge irony that Nigerian education policy-makers seem bent on introducing a system for the likes of which our Bantustan brothers in South Africa are putting in every bit of their energy to resist. In a different context the novelist Chinua Achebe was surprised at the inability of some of his colleagues to see the enormous advantage of English in the multilingual environments of Africa. 'For me it is not either English or Igbo [one of Nigeria's major languages which is his mother tongue], it is both' (Achebe, 1990, p. 42).

But perhaps the single most important step Nigeria should take to revitalize its educational system is to encourage competition among proprietors as was the case up until the recent past. In some states, governments already encourage the establishment of new mission and private-investor schools but big investors, apparently conscious of previous experiences, are reluctant to come in. Where such schools are opened, many are easily more sought-after than government-run schools (Oloyede et al., 1990). A previous civilian government even allowed private ownership of universities but the succeeding junta in 1984 decreed against that (Ezeh, 1984). Many of those still-born institutions showed signs of being substandard, of course, but the same remark cannot be made of all of them. One of them was set up by a proprietor who has one of the most com-mended secondary schools in the country.

It is remarkable that in the last three months of 1990 there was a renewed clamour for the repeal of the 1984 decree (Ifredi, 1990, p. 5; *Lagos Daily Times*, Editorial, 1990, p. 18; and *Lagos National Concord*, 1990, p. 6). Advocates of private universities believe that such institutions could make up for the lapses in the present admission and instructional methods. Minister of Education Babs Fafunwa, a Professor of Education, was quoted as supporting private ownership in principle, but saying that very extensive spadework was necessary before the government might review its present position (unnamed reporter, *Sunday Concord*, 23.9.90).

At present all universities are owned by governments which finance them with their lean resources. Apparently afraid of possible adverse reactions, the Federal Government chooses to continue with a policy which began during the oil sales boom years when tuition was free in all its universities. Only some universities belonging to the coordinate states charge tuition fees. This arrangement has the obvious consequences of tying the fortunes of the universities to those of the government. In 1990 the government borrowed 120 million US dollars overseas to bail out the universities which were in serious economic trouble, as was the government itself. Some frequently owe their staff arrears of salaries. The University of Nigeria Nsukka owed indigenous banks 4 million Naira in the last quarter of 1989 in overdrafts alone, in addition to a separate 8 million Naira previously being owed to diverse creditors (unnamed reporter, *Enugu Daily Star*, 19.9.89). And, of course, the Federal Government had to cut down its subventions to the University because it, too, was hard up. The country relies heavily on crude oil for its revenues and is still suffering from the effects of the slump of the pre-Gulf crisis days. Universities are generally poorly equipped and staff there are comparatively poorly paid.

CONCLUSION

Being neither an educationist by profession, nor a lawyer, nor a government official, the writer has simply examined this issue from the point of view of a journalist who has covered Nigerian affairs, including of course Education, for the past twelve years. From that perspective it seems that only one thing needs to be done to put the Nigerian educational system on the path to increased contribution to the economy and that is the demonopolization of school proprietorship at all levels. This will encourage competition of methods and ideas among institutions. Such a system has worked before, and no doubt, can work again.

This now seems to have been accepted since the federal government-run *Daily Times* newspaper reported that the Nigerian authorities had finally agreed in principle to permit private investors to establish tertiary institutions, including universities (Obi, 1992, pp. 1, 20). The fact that the decision is based on the report of a commission headed by Gray Longe, one of the most experienced members of the bureaucracy in Nigeria who was Head of the Federal Civil Service in the previous junta which outlawed private-investor participation makes this *volte-face* even more interesting.

Nigerians still await the enabling law on this decision. However, there appears to be no reason not to be hopeful. Even if the military government is not able to issue any of those quasi-arbitrary decrees on the matter before it hands power over to an elected government, hopefully earlier rather than later in 1993, still one can only but expect the elected lawmakers to finish the job. More than soldiers, many a regular politician appreciates the great need for demono- polization of the management of education.

REFERENCES

Achebe, C. (1990). African Literature as Restoration of Celebration. London: *New African*, 270.
Akpan, D. (1990). The Economics of Per Capita Income. Lagos: *Guardian Financial Weekly*, 17.12.90.
Alabi, A.E. (1990). Students, JAMB vs Cut-off Points. Lagos: *Daily Champion*, 12.11.90.
Basden, G.T. (1982). *Among the Ibos of Nigeria*. Onitsha: University Publishing.
Cary, Joyce (1962). *Mister Johnson*. London: Harmondsworth Penguin Books.
Comhaire, J. (1981). *Le Nigeria et ses Populations*. Brussels: Editions Complex.
Editorial (1990). For Private Universities. Lagos: *Daily Times*, 7.11.90.
Editorial (1990). The Return of Private Universities. Lagos: *National Concord*, 21.10.90.
Efunwoye, B. (1990). Budget Statement Still Gaps Implementation. Lagos: *Guardian Financial Weekly*, 4.9.90.
Ezeh, P. (1984). Banning of Private Universities. London: *New African*, 201.
Ezenwelu, E. *et al.* (1991). On the Trail of the Billions. Lagos: *African Concord*, 15.7.91.
Fafunwa, B. (1974). *History of Education in Nigeria*. London: George Allen and Unwin.
Fajana, A. (1976). U.P.E. – Issues, Prospects and Problems, in N.A. Nwagwu (ed.) *Universal Primary Education in Nigeria*. Benin City: Ethiope Publishing.
Ifedi, C. (1990). Need for Private Universities. Lagos: *Sunday Concord*, 23.9.90.
Ifemesia, C. (1979). *Traditional Humane Living Among the Igbo – an Historical Perspective*. Enugu: Fourth Dimension Publishers.
Ikediala, A. (1991). That CBN Half Year Report. Lagos: *Business Times*, 9.9.91.
Obi, F. (1992). Individuals Can Now Establish Varsities – White Paper on Longe Commission Out. Lagos: *Daily Times*, 18.5.92.
Ogazimorah, I. (1990). Government Urged to Hand Back Schools to Missions. Enugu: *Daily Star*, 9.8.90.
Ojike, M. (n.d.). *My Africa*. Lagos: Stevebond Press.
Oloyede, D. (1990). Breeding Super Elite. Lagos: *The Nigerian Economist*, 6, 22.
Sklar, R. (1983). *Nigeria Political Parties – Power in an Emergent African Nation*. New York: Nok Publishers International in arrangement with Princeton University Press.
Unnamed reporter (1989). Economic Indicators. Lagos: *The Nigerian Economist*, 2, 25.
Unnamed reporter (1990). Review Quota System of Admissions. Lagos: *Daily Times*, 19.12.90.

Unnamed reporter (1990). Nigeria's External Debt now 262.4 Billion. Lagos: *The Punch*, 21.12.90.

Unnamed reporter (1990). Our Enthusiasm is Bigger than Our Pockets. Lagos: *Sunday Concord*, 23.9.90.

Unnamed reporter (1990). UNN Owes Four Million. Enugu: *Daily Star*, 1.9.89.

Williams, D. (1982). *President and Power in Nigeria – the Life of Shehu Shagari*. London: Frank Cass.

6 Constraints on female participation in education in developing countries

Colin Brock and *Nadine Cammish*

'Si les filles fréquentent l'école au même titre que les garçons, le rapport de féminité est généralement faible. Les filles sont régies par les normes coutumières.'

(Koloko, 1990, p. 157)

In her comment on the participation of girls in education in Cameroon, Marie-Yvette Koloko pin-points the dichotomy between the theoretical legal position and the everyday reality of traditional sociocultural norms.

The recent research project *Factors Affecting Female Participation in Education in Six Developing Countries*[1] examined a range of factors, with a focus on primary education. Fieldwork was done in Sierra Leone, Cameroon, India, Bangladesh, Jamaica and Vanuatu and included a survey of attitudes covering 1,200 pupils in upper primary classes in urban and rural locations in the six countries, and further surveys among students in teacher-training institutions. In none of the project countries are there gender specific admissions policies at primary level, or at the secondary and tertiary stages either, but this does not prevent there being a widespread divergence of opportunity between the sexes, as evidenced in the wider literature and in the research findings of the project.

We view the 'legal factor', therefore, more in terms of the regulation of female opportunity at three different levels:

1 The general laws of the country or state/province and their observance/ enforcement.
2 The educational laws regulating the systems of provision and delivery and their observance/enforcement.
3 The sociocultural norms of groups of people in terms of their behaviour, which may have to do with whole groups such as tribes or sub-groups such as religious affiliates, age sets and social classes within and between which the sex factor is a *de facto* regulator.

We will consider, therefore, the factors which affect female participation in education with the legal dimension in this regulatory sense, but a sense which does have strong repercussions.

Legislation at a national level may appear not to discriminate against females but the implementation of legislation and educational reform is another matter especially when the socioeconomic and sociocultural structures remain unaffected. It suffices perhaps to examine the statistics for girls' education in five regions of India (see Tables 6.1 and 6.2) to appreciate the possible disparities in the implementation of female educational opportunity. The figures for women teachers in the same regions (Table 6.3) reflect the same disparities.

FACTORS AFFECTING FEMALE PARTICIPATION IN EDUCATION

Separation of factors into groups is necessarily artificial and there are many areas of overlap, as there are in respect of the disciplines constructed to examine and explain them. In our work we have generally recognized the following: economic; sociocultural; religious; geographical; political; and educational.

Table 6.1 Percentage of girls' enrolment to total enrolment, 1986

	Classes I–V	Classes VI–VIII	Classes IX–X	Classes XI–XII
Gujarat	43.18	38.82	36.23	37.52
Kerala	48.79	49.12	49.63	43.00
Orissa	42.10	36.32	32.41	35.51
Rajasthan	28.02	19.75	16.82	16.42
Delhi	45.56	45.32	43.07	44.76

Table 6.2 Enrolment in classes II–VIII as percentage of enrolment in class I (boys and girls)

	Class 1	Class 2	Class 3	Class 4	Class 5	Class 6	Class 7	Class 8
Gujarat	100	73.04	69.48	57.35	50.61	41.29	34.82	30.03
Kerala	100	106.10	103.16	97.45	98.84	92.18	84.73	81.31
Orissa	100	80.15	74.60	56.48	47.10	35.15	31.01	27.92
Rajasthan	100	47.61	35.38	33.25	27.55	27.19	20.87	18.50
Delhi	100	92.58	83.10	77.51	70.51	79.56	72.00	64.37

Table 6.3 Percentage of women teachers

	Primary stage	Upper primary	Secondary	Higher secondary
Gujarat	44.81	41.17	21.25	22.67
Kerala	61.20	57.34	60.51	45.69
Orissa	16.08	13.14	16.13	45.94
Rajasthan	23.07	22.99	19.37	18.98
Delhi	66.11	54.88	49.34	48.41

Source: NCERT *Fifth All-India Educational Survey – selected statistics*, Delhi, 1989 (extracts from various tables).

The economic factor

Throughout our study we have found this to be the single most important influence on the differential participation of males and females in formal education. This factor operates in a number of ways:

1 The *direct cost* of tuition and attendance, including in some cases books, uniforms and transport; although not normally different as between boys and girls, in most families where funds are insufficient preference will be given to males despite the fact that non-attendance or non-enrolment may be against the general/educational law.

2 The *opportunity cost*, meaning the cost of work 'lost' to the family or community if children are withdrawn to go to school; inability or unwillingness to meet this cost is normally found to affect female participation in schooling more than male and may also be regulated by some sort of cycle such as sowing, harvesting and marketing schedules.

   Even when girls are enrolled at school, they may attend irregularly or drop out as is often the case in Bangladesh – 'The mostly common but less acknowledged phenomenon behind the non-attendance of village girls is the fact that they are indispensable household assets to a traditional large family' (Islam, 1982, p. 36). Child labour in the rural household is both directly and indirectly productive. As Salahuddin points out, again in the case of Bangladesh, 'the introduction of compulsory primary education without raising the standard of living of rural households and bringing about appropriate socio-economic changes may not achieve any meaningful results' (Salahuddin, 1981, p. 102).

   The results of the Primary 6 questionnaire surveys in the Project reflect the amount of help children contribute at home and in the fields, even when enrolled at school. It was alarming to see that 27 per cent of the pupils surveyed in the six countries had been absent from school some time in the week preceding the survey. Indeed 45 per cent overall said that they sometimes could not come to school because they had jobs to do for their mother or father. In rural Sierra Leone, this figure rises to 86 per cent. In Vanuatu only 5 per cent of the pupils surveyed said that they 'never' helped in the 'gardens' (subsistence farms).

3 The *cultural cost* of going against society's norms may not favour equality of educational opportunity or practice as between the sexes and may lead to the under-utilisation of knowledge and training by overt or covert discrimination against females in respect of employment and promotion.

> Because of cultural and labour market restrictions on women's work in many poor countries, the private benefits to the family that pays for a daughter's education are often not large enough to off-set the costs. Unless parents see and appreciate all of the benefits of educating daughters, they will not be willing to pay the economic costs or the costs of defying cultural norms.
>
> (King, 1990, p. 2)

The cultural cost is particularly severe in parents' eyes when a few years of primary education are insufficient to open up jobs for their daughters in the modern sector but make it difficult for the girls to reintegrate into traditional village life.

> En l'absence d'une possibilité de mobilité sociale l'éducation ne servirait, selon les parents, qu' à aliéner leur fille aux valeurs socio-culturelles et aux normes de comportement qui prévalent dans le village.
>
> (Bagla-Gökalp, 1990, p. 102)

It is clear that implementation of universal primary education, especially in the case of girls, is not a matter of simple legal enforcement: it has to contend with strong socioeconomic and sociocultural forces

> to cut across the hurdles of the very roles that girls perform in the parents' households, the very socialization process that prepares a girl for her expected adult role, the prolonged family cycle of child rearing which engages a girl in the family, the values that are attached to a girl's overall status.
>
> (Islam, 1982, p. 114)

Another aspect of the economic problem is that the majority of women in developing countries do not have access to income-generation opportunities which in turn provide a degree of independence and power, which might *inter alia* enable them to challenge discrimination through the legal system. This normally requires at least basic literacy and numeracy to make it operational and effective. Some of the best work observed during this project has been that of non-governmental organizations (NGOs) working with rural women to provide not only a degree of economic independence but also particular skills which safeguard against illegal practice, such as the writing and interpreting of official letters and contracts and basic accountancy skills.

As with developed countries, a major factor is that the economic contribution of the majority of women is 'invisible', i.e. in the home/family and places them in a position of dependence: 'women, the last colony'. In Vanuatu, for instance, women have a highly significant role in subsistence agriculture but rights over the resources used (including land) and the products of work generally rest with the men (UNICEF, 1990, Part C, Section 1).

Sociocultural factors

A range of factors interrelate here, but have to do with society's views of women and girls. These views become instrumental through pressures perhaps even regulated through social structures, for example of kinship and marriage. These may link with economic considerations such as dowry and bride-price (see for example Rarua, 1988). Depending on the system operating in any particular social group the acquisition of formal education may be advantageous or otherwise. Consequently girls may be deterred from enrolling, attending or succeeding in school by social pressures, emanating from whether or not money or goods are to be given or received in marriage contracts. Such practices are now illegal in most countries, but they operate freely nonetheless.

There is also the question of the effect of the attitude of males, especially young males, to educated females. This often manifests itself in insecurity and a preference for a less educated partner. Girls may then make a conscious choice to drop out of school or at least moderate their performance in order to increase their eligibility for marriage.

The form of marriage and kinship is also significant. As the majority of forms are patrilocal, the girl is lost to her family, becoming an asset to her husband's family. For the majority of the population of the countries concerned – the rural peasantry – this means that investment in a boy's schooling may be worth while, while support of daughters is investing in the well-being of another family. Anti-educational pressures from senior female in-laws can also be a deterrent against the educational advancement of younger women, even in the more affluent strata, that is to say the urban elites, of developing countries. Some forms of marriage provide for rights in the female issue, that is they may be retained by the giver, and this may bring influence of one sort or another to bear on their education. This clearly links with the economic factor, as expressed by the Bangwa tribal group 'Women are a scarce resource . . . given in marriage to the highest bidder' (Brain, 1972, p. 119).

The age of marriage has obvious implications for the education of girls and is also normally a legal matter. It tends to be linked with other social factors such as early pregnancy and the security of females. In many developing countries the minimum legal age of marriage for girls is lower than that for boys. The legal age may often in any case, especially in rural areas, be ignored when both sets of parents are willing. In discussing the ignorance or indifference about child marriage laws, Ushar Nayar (1989, p. 10) points out that in Rajasthan more than 18 per cent of girls are married between 10 and 14 years of age. The Child Marriage Restraint Act is obviously not always enforced.

Even if observed, the minimum legal age of marriage has a disadvantageous effect on female education, but it is often disregarded with early pregnancy being a major cause for withdrawal from education in some countries. Such pregnancies may not even lead to the degree of security that may be provided by marriage. Pregnant girls may well be rejected by schools as well as by their families and society in general (see Jackson, 1979, p. 200; May-Parker, 1987). Consequently, some of the most enterprising initiatives observed by the writers in respect of compensatory education for disadvantaged females were to do with maintaining the schooling of pregnant teenagers (McNeil, 1989; Dash, 1987). It was interesting to note the liberalizing of the rules for readmission to school after pregnancy in, for example, Cameroon (Ministère de la Condition Féminine, 1987, p. 7).

The issue of security may take different forms. For example, in some places economic security might be sought by a young girl through marriage of some sort to an older man (the 'sugar-daddy syndrome'). This often includes the funding of the girl's education. In other places the issue is one of physical security, especially in societies where abuse of females of all ages is endemic. Social norms such as confinement of, especially young, females to the home or village are in part purely practical measures to minimize the incidence of abuse, and they may result in girls not attending school. Indeed male teachers were occasionally found in some countries to be perpetrators of such criminal acts, but due to the remoteness of rural locations and the fact that officers of the law would also use their privileged position in this way, the legal sanctions failed to operate (see for example, Akanda and Shamin, 1985). In such circumstances there is, not surprisingly, a dearth of female teachers in rural primary schools. In any case the majority of female teachers in developing countries, as perhaps elsewhere, come from more affluent, usually urban social classes. They prefer urban locations for a number of reasons in addition to that of security, and if also married will have family ties and responsibilities in the town/city. This leads us on to the next factor.

Geographical considerations

Although universal primary educational provision as well as attendance is a policy, if not a legal requirement, in most countries, the geographical accessibility of schooling is frequently a problem. This mal-distribution of schooling has a variety of causes ranging from difficulties in the physical environment to differential patterns of mission activity and ethnic bias on the part of secular administrations, but it tends to disadvantage females more than males, combining with the issues of economy and security.

Urban/rural dichotomy is well illustrated by the relative situations of equality of educational opportunity as between the sexes as well as by some of the related factors and effects (see Fyle, 1988). For example, the enrolment rate of girls in urban schools is higher than in rural ones, and there is less wastage. Figure 6.1 shows the contrast between urban and rural enrolments in Vanuatu, where there is also a core/periphery syndrome.

The ambitions of girls tend to be more developed in the towns where there are successful female role models in greater evidence and information is available. The Project Survey found that rural children operated with a far smaller range of choices than did urban children and this was particularly noticeable in the case of girls where sometimes only 'teacher' and 'nurse' represented the aspirations of a whole class (Brock and Cammish, 1991, p. 16).

There are more single-sex institutions in urban areas, due to the concentration of population, providing the critical mass for such provision at secondary level (see Islam 1982, p. 60) and in such institutions girls tend to achieve more than in co-educational schools. Accessibility to, and choice of, schools is much less a problem in towns, though public transport is important for those girls who cannot be transported by parents. The lack of such a facility in Freetown for example, and its inadequacy in Kingston, serve to disadvantage poorer pupils and especially girls. Indeed the urban poor can easily be overlooked in a simple urban/rural contrast, especially if they are illegal settlers with no rights to social facilities such as education.

Migration of population has both educational causes and effects, and it also seems to vary according to gender. In Jamaica, at least in recent decades, women have migrated more than men from rural to urban areas and even beyond the country (Brodber, 1986; Morrissey, n.d.). In Bangladesh it is the reverse. This contrast is due in part to social and to

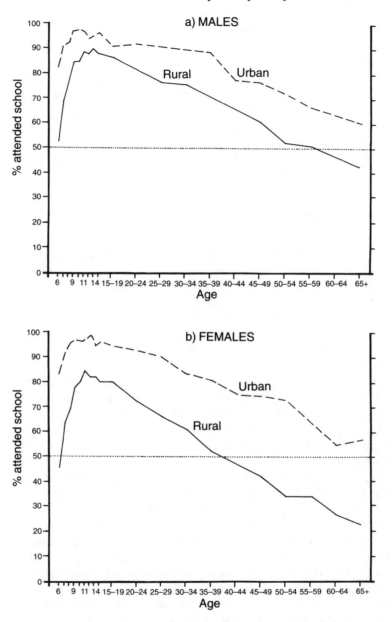

Figure 6.1 Percentage of ni-Vanuatu aged 6 years and over in rural and urban areas who have attended school.

Source: Bedford 1989, p. 93.

educational reasons. The place and role of Jamaican females is prominent and positive, as a result of the particular social structure developed in the island over centuries. One of the outcomes is a relatively strong educational profile with related opportunities for employment (Hamilton and Leo-Rhynie, 1984; Leo-Rhynie, 1989). In Bangladesh, for reasons of custom and security, the majority of rural females are hardly mobile even within the countryside and have few credentials for urban schooling or employment (Islam, 1983; Huq and Islam, 1988, p. 38). This may change in view of the large scale and effective work of NGOs on behalf of rural females and their education, such as the initiatives of the Bangladesh Rural Advancement Committee (BRAC) (Lovell and Fatema, 1989).

The political factor

NGOs are only able to be effective in this way if the holders of real political power in a country choose to allow them to be. Governments make educational policy and enact the necessary legislation to give legal status to their policies. Whether they can, or wish to, provide the necessary resources to give effect to their educational laws and regulations is another matter (see for example Elliott, 1984, p. 253). If, as is often the case in developing countries, the economy cannot support a complete education system, even at primary level, then it is the females who are normally disadvantaged. Indeed the funding regulations operated by most governments in respect of their sectors of education, primary, secondary and tertiary, clearly favour higher education the most and primary education the least. This can have divisive gender effects, for example, the majority of primary sector teachers being female will enjoy relatively low incomes as compared to their secondary and tertiary counterparts, the majority of whom are likely to be male. It is also normally the case that the majority of students at university level are male, enjoying facilities paid for by the total population, about half of whom are female. However, with the advances made by middle- and upper-class women in terms of emancipation, the enrolment and the achievement of female undergraduate and graduate students is fast catching up with their male counterparts and indeed 'invading' so-called 'male' subject areas such as engineering. This trend is quite marked in India for example, and though mainly a phenomenon of the urban elite is nonetheless bringing women into contention with men for positions of responsibility and power in the various professions, and providing the all-important role models for younger females.

Elite females may or may not support the cause of their sisters in the urban and rural masses; there are examples of both real efforts to improve the lot of the majority as well as of posturing. The decision taken by some countries to establish 'Women's Ministries' does not seem to help. It merely means that the male dominated government can shunt the gender issue, that is the problems of half the population, into a low status, under-funded ministry. Even in Jamaica where female educational profiles at all levels are superior to those of males (Leo-Rhynie, 1989), in the political arena the men hold sway and use their power to maintain their position. Unlike many professional occupations, politics does not require certification.

Official regulations can sometimes have curious consequences. For example, one of the legacies of French colonial rule in Cameroon is that wives of government employees who are teachers have a right to employ-ment in the locations where their husbands are required to be. This means the urban areas, and especially the capital city, Yaoundé. In consequence the schools of Yaoundé are grossly overstaffed by affluent females who cannot be given many classes but are able to draw a full salary: an inter-esting aspect of the sociopolitical geography of education.

Religion as a factor

One might have expected religion to be placed in, or close to, the socio-cultural discussion above, but the writers have found that where there appears to be a discrimination against females in societies with a strong religious identity, it is usually the social norms that are the cause rather than the religion *per se*. For example, some of the most impressive initiatives on behalf of the education of girls at secondary level observed by the writers have been in Islamic societies. The Christian denominations, too, have been prominent in promoting education for all, and therefore supporting equality of opportunity as between the sexes.

So we must view the religious bodies as part of the political factor as providers of education, working according to the laws and regulations of the Government of their particular country as well as those of their own organization.

Such regulations include those governing the content and structure of the curriculum and in this area the writers found, even in those places strongly promoting the education of girls, that gender-based curricular stereotypes often prevailed.

CONCLUSION

An attempt has been made to illustrate some of the main factors responsible for the constraints on female participation in education in developing countries, and to show connections with legal dimensions whether they be general, educational or customary forms of regulation.

As Koloko indicates in the opening quotation of this chapter, it is often the customary forms of regulation which operate most powerfully against increased female participation in education. When in northern Sierra Leone, 77 per cent of the pupils surveyed agree that 'Girls don't really need to go to school' and when this result is not statistically significant by sex, the majority of the girls agreeing with the boys (Brock and Cammish, 1991, p. 89), we can see local custom operating as a strong regulator of female enrolment and attendance at school.

Failure to implement or enforce existing legislation continues to disadvantage females in many countries, and the education system is itself part of the system of social regulations and control that continues to permit a situation of gender bias.

NOTE

1 This chapter arises from a funded research project (1989–91) undertaken by the writers at the invitation of the *Overseas Development Administration* (ODA) into factors affecting female participation in education. (The full report on this project is listed in the Bibliography.) We are grateful for the help and support of ODA and of our assistants in each of the project countries.

REFERENCES

Akanda, L. and Shamin, I. (1985). *Women and Violence: a comparative study of rural and urban violence against women in Bangladesh.* Women for Women, Dhaka.

Bagkla-Gökalp, L. (1990). *Les Femmes et l'Éducation de Base. Etude spéciale pour la conférence mondiale sur l'éducation pour tous.* Thaïlande, mars 1990, UNESCO.

Bedford, R. (ed.) (1989). *Population of Vanuatu: an analysis of the 1979 Census,* Population Monograph No. 2, South Pacific Commission, Nouméa.

Brain, R. (1972). *Bangwa Kinship and Marriage,* Cambridge University Press, Cambridge.

Brock, C. and Cammish, N.K. (1991). *Factors Affecting Female Participation in Education in Six Developing Countries.* Report to ODA (mimeograph) London.

Brodber, E. (1986). *Rural Urban Migration and the Jamaican Child,* UNESCO Report 11-02122STG, (mimeograph).

Dash, C.M.L. (1987). Some population problems in the anglophone Caribbean and initiatives towards their solution: an example from Jamaica. *Présence Africaine,* No. 141, pp. 29–36.

Elliott, C. (1984). Women's education and development in India. *World Year Book of Education,* p. 243 ff.

Fyle, Magbaily (1988). *History and Socio-Economic Development in Sierra Leone.* SLADEA, Freetown, ch. 10.

Hamilton, M. and Leo-Rhynie, E. (1984). Sex roles and secondary education in Jamaica. *World Year Book of Education,* p. 123 ff.

Huq, J. and Islam, M. (1988). *Women, Development and Technology*. Women for Women, Dhaka.

Islam, M. (1983). 'Impact of male migration on rural housewives', in Huq, J. *et al.* (eds) *Women in Bangladesh: some socio-economic issues*. Women for Women, Dhaka, pp. 46–53.

Islam, S. (1982). *Women's Education in Bangladesh: needs and issues*. FREDP, Dhaka.

Jackson, J.V. (1979). *An Exploratory Study of Achievement Need Among Girls Attending Secondary Schools in Jamaica*. Unpublished MA(Ed) thesis, University of the West Indies, Jamaica.

King, E.M. (1990). *Educating Girls and Women: Investing in Development*. World Bank, Washington, DC.

Koloko, M.-Y. (1990). *La Décennie des Nations Unies pour la Femme et la Condition de la Femme Camerounaise – aspects politique, économique et social*. Thèse de doctorat 3e cycle, IRIC, Yaoundé.

Leo-Rhynie, E. (1989). 'Gender issues in education and implications for labour force participation', in K. Hart (ed.) *Women and the Sexual Division of Labour in the Caribbean*, University of the West Indies, Jamaica.

Lovell, C.H. and Fatema, K. (1989). *Assignment Children – the BRAC non-formal primary education programme in Bangladesh*. UNICEF.

McNeil, P. (1989). *Women's Centre: Programme for Adolescent Mothers* (mimeograph), Jamaica.

May-Parker, J. (1987). *Counselling to Prevent Pregnancy Among Schoolgirls*. Report on a project by the Planned Parenthood Association of Sierra Leone (mimeograph), Freetown.

Ministère de la Condition Féminine (1987). *Possibilités de Formation Ouvertes à la Femme Camerounaise*. MICOF, Yaoundé.

Morrissey, M. (n.d.). *Women in Jamaica*. Dept. of Statistics, Jamaica.

Nayar, Ushar (1989). *Hamari Betiyan – Rajasthan: a situational analysis of the girl child*. Paper presented at UNESCO sponsored National Training Workshop on UPE for Girls. NCERT, Delhi.

Rarua, K. (1988). 'Vanuatu', in Taiamoui Tongamoa (ed.), *Pacific Women – roles and status of Women in Pacific Societies*. USP, pp. 76–87.

Salahuddin, K. (1981). 'Aspects of child labour in Bangladesh', in P. Ahmad *et al.* (eds) *Disadvantaged Children in Bangladesh: some reflections*. Women for Women, Dhaka, pp. 85–119.

UNICEF (1990). *Draft of Situation Analysis of Children and Women in Vanuatu*. Joint Vanuatu Government and UNICEF Project (mimeograph).

7   Greek education and its legislative framework

Mihalis Kassotakis and *Alexandra Lambrakis-Paganos*

Introduction

Since 1834, the year in which the first educational enactment appeared in the newly independent Greek state, more than 150 years of educational history have passed. This long period is generally characterized by a painful effort by both the state and other educational authorities to establish and organize a national education system in the face of the enormous difficulties involved in its development.

The glorious past of Ancient Greece and the Western cultural tradition were the main sources of the values and ideals which permeated educational theory and practice in Modern Greece. The Greek Orthodox Church also played a significant role in the formation of the Greek educational system.

The development of education in Greece during the nineteenth and the first half of the twentieth centuries was slow, with the socioeconomic conditions of the new state, its lack of an infrastructure, buildings as well as teaching staff, the diversionary efforts relating to the consolidation of the country preventing rapid educational expansion. By the early 1950s Greece was still a developing agricultural country, but from then on the rate of economic growth increased. Greece gradually became a developed European country, and a full member of the European Community despite the problems and structural weaknesses of its economic system, which still beset her (Kassotakis, 1991, pp. 309–23; Massialas *et al.*, 1988, pp. 479–507).

The delayed socioeconomic development of the country and its dependency on Western capitalist countries had an impact on the educational system as well as on educational theory and thought in Modern Greece. The evolution of its educational legislation reflects the development of Greek education with its inconsistencies, contradictions and regressions, between conservatism and liberalism and between attachment to the civilization of Ancient Greece and the modern orientation towards the educational practice of Western capitalist countries (Koutalos, 1968, pp. 415–19; Dimaras, 1973; Saitis, 1992).

This study aims to examine the evolution of the legislative framework of Greek education and analyse its present structure.

BASIC CHARACTERISTICS

Education in Greece is the responsibility of the state. It is offered completely free of charge in state educational institutions at all levels. Private primary and secondary schools are allowed to operate and do so under the supervision of the Ministry of Education and Religion. They are obliged to follow the national curriculum of studies and operate according to the legislative framework which is valid for all publicly maintained schools. The number of independent schools is relatively small (in 1990 it was about 4–5 per cent of the total number of schools), while the establishment of private universities is prohibited by the Constitution.

The Greek educational system has from the start been very centralized. This has imposed a latent uniformity on the curriculum, syllabuses, teaching materials, the appointment and promotion of teachers, and the funding and administration of schools. The Government through the Ministry of Education and the central educational authorities controls and regulates all matters pertaining to the organization and functioning of the educational system. Educational bills are drawn up by the Ministry of Education and then submitted to Parliament to be voted on. Furthermore, the presidential decrees and ministerial decisions needed to allow most of the educational acts to be introduced give the central educational authorities the powers to rigidly control the entire educational system. Regional authorities have only limited capacity for making decisions even on local educational matters.

The complicated legislative system which requires that the whole area of education should comply with it, has led to the central bureaucracy and formalism which characterize education in Modern Greece. It is a factor in the low efficiency of the system and its inertia despite successive attempts at modernization. Recent governments, both socialist (PASOK) and conservative (ND), have attempted to increase social participation in the processes involved in the formulation of basic educational measures by setting up the so-called 'Democratic Planning of Education' (PASOK) or the 'National Dialogue about Education' (PASOK and ND). Both parties when in government had determined that educational bills should be studied by all political parties and others who are concerned in order to formulate possible counter-proposals before being passed through Parliament. In reality, the proposals made by the government are seldom altered and in cases where they are the changes are usually in matters of minor importance.

THE EVOLUTION OF GREEK EDUCATIONAL LEGISLATION: A BRIEF OUTLINE

Greece became an independent state in 1827 after the victorious revolution of 1821 against the Turks. The Turkish occupation combined with the various difficulties arising from sociopolitical and economic upheavals delayed modernization. The new Greek state depended on the powerful countries of that time and especially on the so-called Protecting Powers (Great Britain, France and Russia) which played an important role in its independence. The establishment of the political and cultural influence of the Protecting Powers and the absolute monarchy under King Otto of Bavaria (1835–65) overturned the ideals of the Greek Revolution for a democratic structure for the new state.

From independence until the decade of the 1980s

Primary and secondary education

The educational system was initially designed by a foreign lawyer, the Bavarian Mauer, and organized in line with legislative measures which were taken during the period 1834–56. It was a modern state system, but not a natural outcome of Greek historical, social, cultural and economic development, adjusted to the peculiarities of the newly created state (Glinos, 1925, p. 4). It was modelled after foreign educational patterns (e.g. the Guizot law for French elementary education and the Bavarian system of secondary education) without taking into account the ideals of the Greek Revolution and the socioeconomic situation of the country.

According to the law of 1834 the state, the communities and the citizens were able to establish primary schools, called *Demotic Schools*. Attendance at these primary schools was compulsory and free of charge for all children who started at the age of six and went on through to the age of ten. Funding was provided by the communities, but economic support was occasionally also given by the state. By the enactment of a law in 1836 secondary education was established and comprised the so-called *Hellenic School* which had three grades and the *Gymnasium* which had four.

Despite changes to the Greek constitution in 1844, the legislative framework introduced by the Bavarian officers remained valid with minor modifications until 1929. The inadequate educational system based upon it, however, could not satisfy the needs of a developing country. Its dual character, favouring academic learning, and its hierarchical and central-ized structure contributed to the persistence of illiteracy among the rural masses, and failed both to reinforce autonomous economic growth and to spread a type of culture and social life based on national tradition and suited to the characteristics of modern Greek society (Dendrinou-Antonakaki, 1955, p. 20). This was revealed especially at the beginning of the twentieth century, after the victorious Balkan wars, which brought in new socioeconomic and demographic conditions, such as the doubling of the country's territory and a significant increase in the urban population. There were moves to re-orientate the system, widely believed to be an anachronism.[1]

Demands for reducing the classical component in the curriculum, for the development of practical and vocational education, the introduction into schools of the 'demotic' language (the popular form of modern Greek), the creation of a six-year elementary school, and for measures encouraging the access of the female population to higher educational institutions gained ground, all of which required an appropriate legal framework.

In 1913 an unsuccessful attempt was made towards satisfying the above demands. In the coming years, however, changes made were successful, the most important being those of the years 1929–32, 1964–5, 1976–7 and 1982–5. It can be said, therefore, that the existing educational legislation derives many elements from the nomothetic work of the years 1929–32, 1964 and 1976–7.

The nomothetic work of the years 1929–32[2] was the first important step for a democratic organization and a modern orientation of the educational system. According to the laws 4375/1929, 5045/1930, and 4397/1929 a six-year elementary school with a practical bias was established. The *Hellenic School* was abolished, and a six-year *Gymnasium* created. The teaching of the demotic language was introduced in the elementary and lower vocational schools. Unfortunately, the modernization process then stood still for about thirty years (Kazamias, 1983, pp. 415–67; Kazamias and Kassotakis, 1986; Charalambous, 1990). New laws superseded earlier ones without succeeding in satisfying the existing demands (Kazamias, 1990, pp. 33–53).

Since 1950, there have been resurgent demands to adapt the educational system to present-day socioeconomic needs. Responding to these the Conservative government of the ERE (National Radical Union) passed the 3971/1959 law for technical and vocational education, although it did not dare to introduce the additional measures needed to upgrade the educational system to make it truly efficient.

In contrast, the legislative work of the years 1964–5, introduced by the government of the Liberal Centre Union, was marked by a new reformist spirit. Many measures which came into force at that time showed a social sensitivity and reflected a political will for modernizing and democratizing the system.[3] According to the 4379/1964 law, secondary education was divided into two cycles of three years each: the *Gymnasium* (lower cycle) and the *Lyceum* (upper cycle). Compulsory education was extended from six to nine years thus encompassing the six-year elementary school and the three-year *Gymnasium*. Enrolment in the *Gymnasium* did not require an entrance examination. The same law also made education free of charge and confirmed the use and teaching of the 'demotic' language throughout the school. Furthermore, it introduced the teaching of classical Greek texts through modern translation into the *Gymnasium*.

The *Junta* regime (1967–74) abolished the 1964 and 1965 reforms and brought the educational system back to the form it had before 1964. However, the reaction of all political parties to these measures combined with the new socioeconomic and political climate which prevailed after the fall of the *Junta* (1974) favoured the ideological convergence of the two major political parties (New Democracy and the Liberal Centre Union) on educational matters. As a result, both political parties supported the educational reform of 1976–7 based on the 309/1976 and 576/1977 laws which re-established and indeed extended the reforms of 1964–5. The nine years of compulsory education now became a reality. Technical and vocational *Lycea* and new types of technical and vocational schools were created. The examination system for entrance to higher education was revised. Special institutions for the in-service training of teachers were established. A Centre for Educational Research and In-Service Training of Teachers, KEME, was founded and several other educational innovations were introduced into the educational system.

THE PRESENT FORM OF THE EDUCATIONAL SYSTEM AND ITS LEGAL BASIS

The current educational system, especially that of the primary and secondary sectors, owes its formulation mainly to measures taken by the PASOK governments (1981–9) which made remarkable efforts to modernize the whole legislative framework of Greek education and harmonize it with European educational reality. Changes which were legislated during this period and beyond are dealt with in more detail below. The modifications which the present New Democracy government has carried out from 1990 to 1992 do not substantially alter the framework set up during the years 1982–5.

The PASOK government (1982–3) broadened the educational goals and completed the reform of 1976–7. The presidential decree 297/1982 established the *Monotonic System* of pronunciation (a simplification of accentuation with the use of just one stress), while the 1232/1982 and 1304/1982 laws abolished School Inspectors who were replaced by Counsellors and Provincial Directors, providing a more devolved dual system of supervision and control as well as consultation.

In 1983 the state proceeded to:

(a) establish 220 post-*Lyceum* centres for students who had not succeeded in entering university and wished to try again;
(b) abolish the National Entrance Examination from *Gymnasium* to *Lyceum*;
(c) modify the system of entrance examinations to institutions of higher education.

The most important law in the 1980s was 1566/1985, which designated the structure and the functioning of primary and secondary education.[4]

A brief analysis of the 1566/1985 law

The aim of the new legislated framework for primary and secondary education was to provide an integral network of new educational institutions, which through a democratic administrative policy and social involvement sought to improve the quality of Greek education. It sought to connect it with the wider policy for the development of the country as a whole and its adaptation to the demands of the European Community. According to the ideology which supported this act of legislation, education and culture were seen not only as a means for development but a goal in itself, in the sense that they constituted a system of values which should be adopted by everybody for their personal development and social integration.

The first article of this law defined the goals of Greek education and emphasized that education should mould and prepare Greek citizens to meet the constantly emerging social and economic demands. Further, articles included novel values and ideals with the goals of education as they were defined in the 1566/1985 law. For the first time, special emphasis was given on respect for the environment, the recognition that intellectual and manual activities should have the same status in society and in the school curriculum, and the cultivation of friendly and peaceful cooperation with others (individuals and nations). These goals were expected to be fulfilled through the new curriculum, the new institutions, the updated teaching methods and materials and the reorganization of school life, all of which were legislated for by various articles of school and administrative laws and regulations.

The framework of the educational system, as presented by the 1566/1985 law, is based on three functionally interrelated axes:

1 administration;
2 popular participation;
3 scientific and pedagogical counselling.

The administrative services were to have a decentralized character, vested in the Prefectural, Municipal and Community Councils. Administration was to function separately from the scientific-pedagogical counselling which became the responsibility of the School Counsellors. The 1304/1982 law stated that the duties of the School Counsellors were to:

1   provide scientific-pedagogical counselling;
2   take part in the evaluation and in-service training of teachers;
3   encourage every effort on behalf of educational research.

In particular School Counsellors were to cooperate with teaching staff on planning, implementing educational innovations and improving teaching methods. The institution of School Counsellors constituted an important innovation within the educational system.

The funds for the day-to-day running of schools as well as the management and maintenance of school property were transferred to local government authorities following further legislation.

The participation of various social groups ('popular participation') in decision-making by elected representatives was another major innovation introduced by the 1566/1985 law in the context of the democratization of education. For example, the Municipal or Community Education Council (*Dimotiki i Kinotiki Epitropi Paideias*) was to recommend to the local government authorities matters pertaining to education and the distribution of funds in that area. Members of this Council were to include the mayor, president or representatives of the community, parent representatives, representatives of the local education authorities, and representatives of the various social groups. The Council was to be linked with the schools through the School Board (*Scholiki Epitropi*) and the School Committee (*Scholiko Symvoulio*). The School Board was to comprise representatives of the municipality or community, the president of the parents' association and the principal of the school. They were to have the authority to deal with any educational problem and provide the link with the local authorities. The School Committee was to be the agency which directly supports the schools. It consisted of the teaching staff of the school and the executive board of the parents' association.

Each prefecture (*nomos*) was to have a Prefectural Board of Education (*Nomarchiaki Epitropi Paideias*) which would study and refer to the Prefectural Council educational issues and recommendations from Municipal or Community Education Councils. On the national level, a National Council on Education, called ESYP (*Ethniko Symvoulio Paideias*), was expected to provide overall guidance on educational matters. The Council was to be composed of representatives of the Central Government, political parties with representatives in Parliament, local communities, social groups, educators, parents and local councils and committees.

All the above committees and councils should have facilitated cooperation and interaction so that local social needs could be met more easily. In reality the above structural innovations did not substantially change the centralized nature of the decision-making process in matters of education. The power and the actual role of all the above councils have remained marginal, their role consisting mainly of passing on decisions from the centre. Nevertheless the law provides for local institutions such as the Regional Centres for In-Service Teacher Training (*Periferiaka Epimorfotika Kentra* – PEK) which came into existence in September 1992.

Among the institutions whose aim was to improve the quality of education was the Pedagogical Institute (PI), an Educational Research Centre which replaced the KEME. The PI was to assist the Minister of Education by advising on policy issues. It was also charged with developing the school curriculum and the production of teaching materials. It was to supervise in-service teacher training activities. A number of counsellors and specialist teachers from a variety of areas of education were to be included on the professional staff. What has happened here is that the number of central bodies was increased providing a plural administration. In reality educational bills are very seldom based upon proposals made by the PI. Usually the Minister consults it before legislative proposals are made by the central services of the Ministry.

Types of schools

The *Gymnasium,* the lower grades of secondary education, together with the primary school (*Demotikon*) form the nine years of compulsory schooling (six for the primary school and three for the *Gymnasium).* At the age of 14¼–15, Greek pupils enter the upper secondary school into one of four streams: the General Lyceum, the Technical and Vocational Lyceum, the Compre- hensive Lyceum or the Technical and Vocational School. Education in all Lycea lasts three years and in Technical and Vocational Schools two years. All the above type of Lycea operated before the 1566/1985 law, except for the *Comprehensive Lyceum* (*Polykladiko*), which began in 1984.

The *Comprehensive Lyceum,* which sought to bridge the gap between general and technical-vocational education, started functioning on an ex- perimental trial basis. Its creation is considered one of the most important innovations instituted while PASOK was in government.

The New Democracy government (1990–2) did not propose a new legislative framework for primary and secondary education. It retained that of the PASOK administration, with just a few modifications in line with its more conservative policy. Specifically, it re-established the examination system for the last classes of primary schools and for all classes of the *Gymnasium*. It decided to bring back the teaching of older forms of the Greek language (ancient Greek, Medieval, *Katharevousa*) in the *Gymnasium* and it abolished the post-*Lyceum* centres.

RECENT DEVELOPMENTS IN THE NATIONAL SYSTEM FOR VOCATIONAL EDUCATION AND TRAINING

Greek education, especially at the secondary level, has to a great extent been oriented towards offering general education with an emphasis on classical studies, and preparing students to enter higher education rather than helping them to acquire marketable skills. Technical and vocational education was poorly developed until the mid-1970s, when efforts aimed at its renewal were made (law 576/1977). Even after that period it made but slow progress. Thus, a great demand for higher education had been created. However, the limited educational efficacy of the existing institutions and the inability of the economy of the country to absorb large numbers of highly educated workers have never managed entirely to satisfy the social demand for higher education. For this reason about two-thirds of *Lyceum* graduates remain outside the institutions of higher education without any kind of preparation for working life.

This shortage restricts the chances of Greek employees to respond to the international competition with the completion of the European integrated market, and it remains one of the most important problems facing education and the labour market. In addition, the professional rights of graduates of the different kinds of technical and vocational schools are not legally defined, something which will cause problems with the recognition of their diplomas in the context of the European Community. A new law (2009/1992) for vocational education and training promulgated under the pressure of the challenge of the European market, seeks to cope with the above problems.[5] It provides for the establishment of a National System of Vocational Education and Training (ESEEK), which aims to establish:

(a) the organization and development of vocational training outside formal education;
(b) the credentialling of vocational training;
(c) the creation of links between formal education and informal vocational institutions;

(d) participation in various national or European projects for vocational training.

According to the above law the national system of ESEEK identifies the constantly changing needs of the labour market, and monitors economic and social changes at national and international levels as well as scientific and technological progress. The development of cooperation with public and private agents and organizations in the rest of Europe and especially in the European Community is included among the major objectives of this law, which allows for the creation of Greek state maintained and private institutes for vocational training (IEKs) which operate outside the formal educational system.

The same law goes on to define the various qualifications, titles and degrees awarded in vocational education and training and determines the procedure for the recognition of the job rights of each. A special Commission (OEEK), which includes several state officers and representatives of social groups, has been set up by the same law in order to supervise the above institutes, to handle any problems relating to vocational training, and to foster cooperation with the rest of Europe.

The implementation of the 2009/1992 law has been greeted by attacks by students of technical and vocational *Lycea* and also by the students of the comprehensive *Lycea* because they believe that their certificates will be devalued, their difficulties in finding jobs will be increased and professional training will eventually become mainly a matter for the private sector.

HIGHER EDUCATION

A historical review

Efforts to establish higher education began soon after the independence of Modern Greece. The first Greek University was founded in Athens in 1837 under the auspices of King Otto and was named after him. Later it was renamed the National and Kapodistrian University of Athens.

During the same period a school called the *'Polytechnic'* was established in Athens, which was granted University status in 1914 and developed later into the Metsovio National Technical University of Athens. New higher education institutions appeared in the period 1920–30 and some others already functioning were given legal status. The establishment of the University of Thessaloniki in 1925 was the most important event during this period. But the need for a substantial development of higher education became more imperative after the 1950s, when an acceleration in the economic growth of the country began. Between 1964 and 1985 50 per cent of existing Greek university level institutions were established.

In 1970 Centres for Technical and Vocational Education, the so-called KATEE were approved. These Centres, which were later converted into Technical Educational Institutions (TEI), plus the schools for the training of pre-primary and primary teachers constituted the non-university higher education sector. The latter were abolished in 1988–9 since they were replaced by corresponding university-level institutions.

As regards the evolution of the legislative framework for higher education it has been characterized by an immobility over a long period (Vrichea and Gavroglou, 1982; Papaspiropoulou, 1968, pp. 396–8). Until 1911 the University of Athens operated according to regulations which had first been introduced in April 1837. In 1911 a new legislative framework was approved by Parliament from proposals drawn up by the Venizelos government. This remained in force until 1932, the year in which it was replaced by law 5343/1932. This law reflected a conservative ideology with regard to the role and function of higher education which determined the way higher education operated until 1982.

The need to update the legislative context of higher education was being felt in the early 1950s and it increased significantly in the following years. Many efforts were made and several proposals were submitted by different committees of experts, prominent politicians and academics none of which managed to bring about substantial and radical reforms for higher education, so that only partial changes of minor importance had taken place before the 1980s.

The recent reforms of higher education

During the autumn of 1981, the Socialist Party (PASOK) was returned to power. Parliament approved the laws 1268/1982 and 1404/1983 subject to which higher educational institutions were governed until the academic year 1992–3. These laws provided for important changes in Greek higher education and aimed at the modernization of the structure of institutions, the democratization of their administration and the upgrading of programmes of study.

The main innovations brought about by the 1268/1982 law which only affected the universities [6] were as follows:

1 The old faculties to be divided into departments, each of which corresponds to a university discipline area.
2 The chair system, which was the focus of the past organization of universities, to be replaced by a scientific sector (*tomeas*). The *tomeas* is responsible to a General Assembly in each Department.

3 All policy decisions related to the various levels to be taken in the appropriate General Assemblies which consist of all members of the teaching staff and a considerable number of undergraduate and some postgraduate students.

4 As electors who choose the administrative heads of the University, undergraduates to have the same representation in the electoral bodies as members of the academic staff.

5 Teaching staff members to form a single body with four grades: (i) lecturer, (ii) assistant professor, (iii) associate professor and (iv) professor. Only those belonging to the two upper ranks of the academic hierarchy to possess permanent positions. Appointments and promotion of all teaching staff to be made by special electoral bodies, who meet together with the General Assemblies of the departments, and are approved by the Ministry of Education. New categories of auxiliary teacher, technical and administrative personnel to be created.

6 Each university to be administered by: (i) the president who is supported by two vice-presidents, elected for a period of three years by the General Assembly of the whole University, (ii) the Chancellors' Council, which consists of the president, the two vice-presidents, one representative of the students and one representative of the administrative personnel and (iii) the Senate consisting of the president and the vice-presidents, the deans of the university faculties, the heads of the autonomous departments, one representative of the teaching staff and one representative of undergraduate students from each department, one representative of the administrative personnel and a number of representatives of the postgraduates. All representatives to be elected. The Senate to be regarded as the top administrative agent of the University.

Each faculty consisting of relevant departments to be administered by: (a) the Dean, who is elected for three years by the General Assembly of the faculty, (b) a Council which comprises the dean, heads of the departments and one undergraduate student from each department and (c) the General Assembly of the faculty which consists of the General Assemblies of the departments.

Each department to be administered by: (a) the head, who is elected for two years, (b) the Administrative Council which comprises the head, the directors of departmental sections and representatives of the students and of the technical or administrative personnel, and (c) the General Assembly of the department. The director of each sector, who is elected for one year, and the General Assembly of the sector are to be its administrative agents.

7 The undergraduate studies to be reorganized into 'semester courses' and a basic structure for the promotion of graduate programmes to be set up.

Both the organization and the functioning of the Technical Education Institutions (TEIs) are based on the 1404/1983 law, and the Presidential decrees and Ministerial decisions issued in connection with this law. The TEIs are distinguished from the Science Education Institutions, the AEIs, in terms of their purpose and function which concerns certain administrative details and also in terms of staff qualifications in the hierarchy, the length of programmes and the fact that they offer no postgraduate courses.

However, their organization and operation are similar to those of the AEIs. TEIs are oriented towards the application of recent technological knowledge and practice, while AEIs are more applied-science and research-based institutions. Thus the TEIs have direct links with various productive enterprises where most of the practical work of the students is carried out.

TEIs are self-governing bodies enjoying academic freedom and freedom of teaching and research. They are divided into schools and departments similar to those of AEIs. Each TEI together with its schools and departments is administered by members elected by the General Assemblies in which the teaching staff, an important number of students' representatives and a number of representatives of support personnel participate.

The permanent teaching staff are grouped into three scales: suppliants, assistant professors and professors. Possession of a doctorate is a necessary prerequisite for appointment to the rank of professor.

The new law for TEIs provides for the establishment of two Advisory Services at the Ministry of Education to offer TEIs advisory support. They are: (a) the Council for Technological Education (*Symboulio Technologikis Ekpedefsis* – STE), (b) the Institute for Technological Education (ITE). Regional Technological Councils also operate. Their role is to facilitate the formation of links between TEIs and productive units for economic and any other support.

Despite the above changes brought about in the structure of the higher institutions and in the democratization of their administration, the reform which took place in 1982–3 does not seem to have improved substantially the socioeconomic efficiency of the tertiary education sector and its quality of studies. Neither had it solved most of its major problems. It is a general belief that the new system has become more bureaucratic, that too many privileges have been given to undergraduate students and that interference by political parties in university life has increased. This led to proposals to reconsider some of the innovations introduced by the reforms of 1982–3.[7]

The new Conservative government replaced the 1282/1982 by its 2083/1992 law.[8] While the general structure and the administration of higher institutions remain as provided by the earlier law, a number of changes concerning the functioning of the above institutions was introduced by the new law. These changes may be summarized as follows:

1 The participation of students in the procedures for the selection of administrative bodies of higher institutions and in decision-making bodies has been reduced.

2 The election of the Vice-Rectors has become a separate procedure from that of Rectors.

3 A four-year plan for the creation and advertisement of teaching staff positions has been established.

4 The role of the administrative councils with a small number of members has been strengthened.

5 Members of the teaching staff are ranked according to the service they provide (full-time or part-time employment).

6 Two cycles of graduate studies have been established, the first has four semesters. Success in the examination in all subjects taught during the first cycle is a condition for the continuation of studies in the second cycle.

7 Students who fail to complete their studies within the prescribed time, which this law has extended to two extra years, are not entitled to any kind of financial help awarded by the university.

8 Postgraduate studies and the functioning of research programmes have been reorganized.

9 Free distribution of academic textbooks is permitted to students with low annual income.

10 New academic institutions such as the Centre for the Greek Language, the Open University and the Committee for Evaluation of Higher Education have been created.

Special regulations concerning 'guest' students and the mobility of teaching staff and students were also introduced by the new law. This is an attempt to adjust the legal framework of Greek higher education to the context of a united Europe and to promote cooperation with other countries.

Despite the above innovations the new law has failed to receive the general approval of students. Negative reactions have also come from a number of teaching staff especially those coming from the lower academic ranks as the law does not guarantee job security and teaching autonomy for them. This is a fate often reserved for legislation, proposals for which had not received sufficient popular support before being passed.

NOTES

1 See: *Ekpedeftika Nomoschedia Ipovlithenta kata tin B Sinodon tis I9 periodou is tin Voulin ipo I. D. Tsirimokou* (Educational Legislative Proposals Submitted to Parliament during its 19th Session by I. D. Tsirimokos), Athens, National Printing Office, 1913.

2 See: *Geniki Isigitiki Ekthesi ke Ekpedeftika Nomoschedia Katatethenta is tin Voulin Kata tin Synedrian this 2as Apriliou 1929 ipo tou Ipourgou K. B. Gontika* (General Introductory Statement and Educational Law Plans Submitted to Parliament during the session of 2 April 1929 by the Minister K. B. Gontika).

3 See: *Isigitiki Ekthesi sto Nomo 4379/1964 'Peri organoseos ke Diikiseos tis Genikis (Stichiodous ke Mesis) Ekpedefsis'* (Introductory Statement to the 4379/1964 law concerning the Organization and Administration of General (Primary and Secondary) Education).

4 See: *Ipourgio Ethnikis Paidias ke Thriskevmaton, Nomos Plesio 1566/1985* (Ministry of Education and Religion, The 1566/1985 blueprint law), Athens, Organization for the Printing of Educational Textbooks (OEDV), 1985.

5 See the 2009/1992 law concerning the National System of Vocational Education and Training, in Government Gazette No. 18/1992 of 2 February.

6 For more details see: Kladis D. and Panoussis G., *O nomos plesio gia ta Anotata Ekpedeftika Idrimata* (the blueprint law for the Higher Educational Institutions), Komotini, Sakoulas, 1989.

7 Articles concerning this issue appear quite often in Greek newspapers. For instance, see a series of articles published in *To Vima* (5 and 12 March, 1989) under the general title: Universities or What happens at the Universities. See also the following publications: (a) Tsaoussis, D. (ed.) *He Evropaiki Proklisi stin Tritovathmia Ekpedefsi (The European Challenge to Higher Education),* Athens, Gutenberg, 1990, and (b) *Ta Elinika Panepistimia stin Evropi tou 2.000 (Greek Universities in the Europe of 2000),* Athens, University Rectors' Committee Synod on European Affairs, 1992.

8 See the 2083/1992 law entitled: Modernization of Higher Education Institutions, Government Gazette No. 159, 1992, of 21 September.

REFERENCES

Charalambous, D. (1990). *Ekpedeftiki Politiki ke Ekpedeftiki Metarrithmisi sti Meta- polemiki Ellada (1950–1974)* (Educational Reform and Politics of Education in post-World War II Greece 1950–1974). University of Thessaloniki.

Dendrinou-Antonakaki, K. (1955). *Greek Education.* New York, Teachers College, Columbia University.

Dimaras, A. (1973). *I metarrithmisi pou den egine (The Reform which Never Happened),* Athens, Ermis. (This gives extensive quotations from a number of legal texts.)

Glinos, D. (1925). *Enas atafos nekros: Meletes gia to ekpedeftiko mas systima* (An Unburied Dead: Studies about our Educational System). Athens, Ed. Rallis.

Kassotakis, M. (1991). Higher Education Reform in Greece, in Wickremasinghe, W. (ed.) *Handbook of World Education,* Houston, American Collegiate Service.

Kazamias, A. (1983). I Ekpedeftiki Krisi stin Ellada ke ta Paradoxa tis: Mia Istoriki Sigkritiki Theorisi (The Educational Crisis in Greece and its peculiarities: A Historical Comparative Analysis), in *The Proceedings of the Academy of Athens,* Vol. 58.

Kazamias, A. (1990). The Curse of Sisyphus in Greek Educational Reform: A Sociopolitical and Cultural Interpretation, in *Modern Greek Studies Yearbook,* Vol. 6.

Kazamias, A. and Kassotakis, M. (eds) (1986). *I ekpedeftikes metarrithmisis stin Ellada: Prospathies, adieksoda, prooptikes* (The Educational Reforms in Greece: Attempts, Impasses and Perspectives), Athens, Rethymnon.

Koutalos, D. (1968). Ekpedeftiki Nomothesia (Educational Legislation) in *Megali Pedagogiki Egkiklopedia* (Educational Encyclopedia). Athens, Ellinika Grammata (Greek Letters), Vol. 2.

Massialas, B., Flouris, G. and Kassotakis, M. (1988). The educational system of Greece, in *World Education Encyclopedia*, New York, Files and Fact publication.

Papaspiropoulou S. (1968). To Panepistimio Athinon (The University of Athens) in: *Megali Pedagogiki Egkiklopedia* (Educational Encyclopedia), Athens, Ellinika, Grammata, Vol. 4, pp. 396–8.

Saitis, C. (1992) *Organosi ke Diikisi tis Ekpedefsis: Theoria ke Praxi* (Organization and Administration of Education: Theory and Practice), Athens, published privately.

Vrichea, A. and Gavroglou, K. (1982). *Apopires metarithmisis tis Anotatis Ekpedefsis 1911–1981* (Attempts for Reforming Higher Education 1911–81), Athens, Ed. Sinchrona Themata.

8 Education laws and schooling: the case of the German Democratic Republic

Eberhard Meumann

Three laws determined the development of all areas of education affecting policies and pedagogy over the four decades of existence of the German Democratic Republic (GDR) as an independent state: the *Law for the Democratization of German Schools* (1946), the *Law for a Socialist Development of Educational Institutions in the GDR* (1959) and the *Law for a Uniform, Socialist Educational System* (1965). What follows is a critical historical account of these laws and the impact of their implementation.

The development of the educational system in East Germany between the capitulation in the east on 8 May 1945 and the political and economic changes which began in the autumn of 1989 was inextricably linked with the overall social development of creating a socialist system of government in that part of Germany. Its educational system, it may now be argued, has failed, although in its structure and content it contained important pointers towards the future. It was bound to fail as a part of an ideologically encrusted and economically inflexible superstructure despite the undoubted commitment of a great number of educationists to the educational reforms it promised.

1945 – A NEW BEGINNING?

The year 1945 marked a deep incision in German educational policy. In the east of Germany, the then Soviet sector of occupation, a radical change in the educational system was underway. It was made in accordance with the sociopolitical, economic and philosophical ideas of the occupying power, and in an ongoing dialogue with a contradictory, historical inheritance. On the one hand Germany, as one of the West's most industrialized countries, had established a well-developed educational system; on the other hand this system, and in particular its schools, had been increasingly undermined by the spread of anti-humanist ideals, for example the fascist racial theories during the nationalist-socialist period.

Since the seventeenth and eighteenth centuries elementary schools had been established in most German territories, attendance at which was made compulsory during the nineteenth century. These schools provided an elementary education for most children. This education was necessary first, for the economic development of the country within the capitalist system, and second because it enabled children to receive a basic general, albeit elementary, education.

At the beginning of the twentieth century elementary schools were intended to provide an eight-year basic education for all future workers. In the event they offered varying levels of instruction, in terms of both quality and quantity. Some schools were well equipped while others suffered from a lack of teachers, the necessary teaching aids, or because they were housed in unsuitable, unhygienic buildings. It was possible to find schools where several forms, consisting of all age groups, were taught together in cramped conditions in one classroom (*Mehrstufenunterricht*). Schools in rural areas, attended by the children of poor peasants, were particularly underfunded, because most of the *Junker* landowners were opposed to educating the rural population. Educational opportunities in the countryside had remained minimal – 40.7 per cent of all elementary schools, particularly those in the country and in the provinces which were to become the Soviet sector of Germany, were one-class schools housed in old unsanitary buildings. At all levels of access to education, girls were at a disadvantage compared with boys.

Even so, as a consequence of industrialization an efficient basic vocational training programme and a well-planned vocational further education system had been put in place, aimed at providing vocational qualifications, instilling skills of precision, and fostering attitudes of industry, professional pride and a willingness to work among the workers. These qualities can be counted among the specific traditions of German educational history.

The educational institutions, on the other hand – which were intended to prepare the new generation of professional cadres and managers in both state and industry, the junior high, general and technical schools, like the *Realschulen* at the intermediate level, the various secondary level schools, in particular the grammar schools (*Gymnasien*), as well as the universities and institutions with university status at the tertiary level – provided good quality education. Apart from numerous private schools with different starting ages, secondary education usually began after four years of elementary schooling, the future cadres attending preparatory schools in lieu, and was concluded for those still at school after nine (or since the 1930s after eight) years, with a school-leaving examination qualifying for university entrance (*Abitur*).

This structural development of the educational system, the introduction of compulsory school attendance and the tradition of training for a profession, resulted in a comparatively high general level of education, despite serious differences which existed, for example those between elementary and secondary schools, between schools in town and country, and between educational opportunities for girls and for boys.

In 1933 at the beginning of the national socialist dictatorship German education experienced a radical break with all progressive German educational traditions. Social democratic, communist and progressive bourgeois teachers were dismissed, Jewish and other ethnic educators were subjected to racial discrimination. Elementary education programmes were deformed by fascist ideology. Children and adolescents were indoctrinated with racism, anti-communism and the spirit of an extreme nationalism and chauvinism. The German educational system and the Hitler youth organization, made compulsory for all youth in 1936, were fashioned into a tool for the physical and psychological preparation of school children for war. The curriculum of the junior high schools (*Realschulen*) and secondary schools was changed to serve the priorities of national socialist power interests. In newly created boarding institutions the elite of the National Socialist German Workers' Party (NSDAP) was to be raised. Specially established programmes in vocational and professional training colleges were designed to meet demands resulting from the development of new aggressive priorities in industrial production.

The Second World War had a decisive effect on the entire educational system and the situation of all children and young people. In the course of it most school buildings had been destroyed. There was an acute shortage of teachers. In many regions no regular teaching could take place. Many thousands of school children had been conscripted into military service; many thousands of older pupils were killed in battle. Paradoxically, in 1945 it was possible to see both the utter devastation caused by German fascism as well as the chance for the great achievements of progressive German educational and political traditions, part of German historical inheritance, to re-emerge.

Between May and June 1946 the *Law for the Democratization of German Schools* was passed in the provinces and districts of the Soviet sector.[1] It came into force on 12 June 1946 in the whole of the future German Democratic Republic, fundamentally changing the character of all schooling, after Thuringia, the last province to do so, had finally voted for the new law. Five years later this day was proclaimed the 'Day of the Teacher'. Because of the special conditions prevailing in Berlin, a separate democratic educational law came into force for all sectors of the city in 1948, the result of efforts in particular of Max Kreuziger, Otto Winzer and Ernst Wildangel.[2]

The law enshrined, for the first time in German history, the bourgeois-democratic demands for a uniform, secular and free school system for all children in compulsory education. It guaranteed an education free of fascist and militaristic ideas; fostering the spirit of international understanding and peaceful cooperation among all peoples, and dedicated to establishing genuine democracy and humanity. Education for peace, in agreement with the democratic school reform, was supported by legally enforced school rules. Indeed peace education became an integral part of the most valuable school traditions of the German Democratic Republic.

The dual structure of the old system, which envisaged a different education route for children after the age of ten according to a variety of criteria, was replaced by a common eight-year first school (*Grundschule*) for all children as the cornerstone of a uniform system intended to enable 'each child and youth to receive a complete education according to their inclinations and abilities, irrespective of wealth, faith or ancestry'. [3] Based on well-tried historical experiences, the first school led to either two- or three-year courses in vocational training colleges or to four years of secondary schooling. Whether in secondary schools, technical training colleges, in evening classes for workers or in so-called 'preliminary training institutions' founded in 1946 (which in 1949 became the higher education faculties for workers and peasants), everyone who had the ability could gain the university entrance qualification necessary for further study. Educational cul-de-sacs had become things of the past. Of course the law could not solve all outstanding problems. For example, demands for a one- or two-year compulsory kindergarten could not be met because of the parlous state of the economy. Nevertheless the kindergarten was from the beginning regarded as an integral part of the general educational system. In the early years, too, it was necessary to charge means tested fees for secondary and university education. Another point of debate was whether to reintroduce the thirteenth year of schooling traditional in Germany until 1933. Mainly economic reasons also led to the decision to establish a separate four-year secondary school after the first school. The two types of school combined later to provide twelve years of compulsory schooling for all. On the other hand, despite reservations against compulsory vocational schools, these were not abolished because historically it would have meant a step backwards. It was also felt their abolition might have had negative repercussions on the economy.

On 1 July 1946 the first curricula for elementary and secondary schools were published by the German *Central Administration of People's Education*. They were developed by experienced teachers and qualified educationists in a relatively short period. The curricula formulated the specific contribution of each school subject to the realization of the aims of basic general education and the inculcation of anti-fascist, democratic ideals. They provided a sound education with a leaving point guaranteeing a finishing level recognized as fully comparable and equal chances for all, allowing for the possibility of transfer between all school types at all stages of the system. This provided a high scientific and systematic level of instruction and was available to all pupils. In the senior forms of the first school they were to receive specialist instruction in mathematics, physics, chemistry, biology, German, art and other subjects. The study of a foreign language was made compulsory.

Much effort was made to secure equal chances for children of the rural population. First of all the 4,114 one-class-schools had to be abolished. Common initiatives of the rural population and the school administration managed to reduce the number of one-class rural schools to 3,142 by March 1946. The *Regulations for School Reforms in Rural Areas*, issued on 21 July 1946, showed that improvement of rural schools was to be one of the main tasks of the government.

The final break with the fascist, militaristic past could only be achieved by the efforts of a new, democratically oriented body of teachers with firm roots among the people and close ties with them. This was difficult in view of the fact that before 1945 70 per cent of teachers living on the territory of the GDR had been members of the NSDAP or other fascist organizations, and totally unsuitable to work for a new, anti-fascist start. An overwhelming majority were in fact dismissed before the autumn of 1945, others had to leave the schools in the course of the following months.

The dismissal of around 20,000 Nazi teachers within a few months made the existing shortage of teachers, owing to war losses, worse. More than 40,000 teachers were needed to staff a normally functioning school system. The problem was solved with the help of a dedicated, hardworking, courageous, democratically minded cohort of young men and women, most of them from the working class, who started teaching after only a short period of training, which in most cases lasted only for a few weeks or months. They ensured, often under the most difficult circumstances, a successful school start and continuation of lessons, determined as they were to fulfil the educational mission of the schools which was to remove the spiritual debris of the fascist inheritance and to bring about social progress. They not only had to fight against economic hardship but had to put up, at first, with the mockery and hostility of reactionaries. They gained authority and trust through their social commitment and their growing pedagogical achievements. Together with the 'old teachers', the communist and social-democratic teachers persecuted under the fascists, they secured the new democratic education, based on new curricula and new teaching materials. They began, step by step, to introduce the system of specialist teaching in all classes to improve the scientific quality of education, a process which continued right into the 1950s, in particular in rural areas. In the first full year 15,000 new teachers, mainly former workers, trained in the academic year 1945–6 were prepared for their new career. A further 25,000 were trained in the following year. The political, subject specialist and pedagogical demands made on them were great.

A new pedagogy was needed gradually to realize the high policy aims of the anti-fascist, democratic educational reform. This had to reflect the historical prerequisites of the time, working from national pedagogical traditions and international influences, in particular those of the Soviet school. It also had to include the perspective of the current educational reform programme, to enable teachers to work successfully to construct a new relationship between cultural policy and education. The new pedagogical theory would have to promote the humanist, anti-fascist character of culture and education in schools and contribute to a spiritual rebirth of society. This was not an easy task, since educational thinking could not simply continue from where it had stopped in 1933. It was necessary consciously to link up with the progressive tendencies of German education, for example those of the Weimar Republic, and to make productive use of them in the struggle for the new democratic school reform.

Especially complicated for the socialist reforms were the relations with the educational legacy of the reformist movement of the *Reformpaedagogik* [4] developed at the beginning of the twentieth century. Its educational theory included important pedagogical insights, such as respect for each pupil's individuality and autonomy, the concept of the school as a community and a social organism, its curriculum incorporating the ideals of manual work and preparation for employment, the importance of aesthetic training, and the development of pupils' independent and creative thinking. At the same time it contained a number of anarchistic trends which underestimated the importance of systematic study and the leading role of the teacher. It had also established elements set up as methodological absolutes in opposition to aims and content. Clearly, none of these, nor the tendency of separating politics and education could serve the newly formulated aims and targets of schooling.

Even so, many teachers tried to enlist the theories of the *Reformpaedagogik* to achieve the new, post-1945, educational aims by combining the earlier reformist programmes with the principles of the anti-fascist, democratic school of East Germany. This did represent progress. The authoritarian and militant Nazi teacher, who had succeeded the Prussian teacher equipped with cane, was in turn replaced by a democratic teacher who tried to establish a teacher–pupil relationship based on mutual respect and who encouraged creative and joyful study methods. A new understanding of the child and a new conception of the teaching profession became possible, introduced by teachers influenced by the reformist trends in teacher training, the current pedagogical ethos and their personal experiences of fascist rule and the ravages of war. The 'work school' (*Arbeitsschule*), a Froebel-type institution which had introduced manual work and work preparation methods,[5] supplied many didactic and methodological stimuli which were of great help to the new teachers, who otherwise might have gone back to the formal teaching approaches of the Herbart-Ziller school.[6]

The extremely complex political and ideological situation of those years led to exaggerations and distortions in both theory and practice. These arose not only in the tendency to copy Soviet experiences wholesale, without sufficient evaluation, but also in the ready rejection of reformist models, despite the fact that they constituted an important part of the national educational tradition. This had long-term effects leading to a new series of vigorous debates, in particular during the 1950s, about what should be the sources and impulses for education and schooling in the German Democratic Republic.

By the autumn of 1949, the year of the foundation of the German Democratic Republic, the anti-fascist, democratic restructuring of the educational system was, in a sense, complete. Within a short historic period thousands of anti-fascists managed fundamentally to change the aims, the contents and the structures of all educational institutions.

In January 1949 the first Conference of the Socialist Unity Party (SED) had decided to make raising the educational and cultural levels of the people, on the the basis of the four-year economic plan, its top priority. In August 1949 the Fourth Pedagogical Congress took stock of this process of change and considered the future likely consequences for work in education, now freed from the negative influences of fascist ideology, militarism and other reactionary theories, in the German Democratic Republic.

The new body of teachers started work educating the young in the spirit of democracy, in a school system which had abolished the traditional dualism, and where the secondary school (forms 9 to 12) had acquired a new political, scientific and social character. By 1948/49 the number of one-class schools had been further reduced to 1,407 and the material and personnel conditions of country schools considerably improved. The number of vocational schools had grown from 673 in 1945/46 to 888 in 1948/49, with an increasing number of young people attending. Some 98,000 more children could be accommodated in kindergarten by the end of 1948 compared with the autumn of 1946. Although this was not enough, an important step had been taken to allow more women to use their right to employment and to play an active part in building the new society.

While the academic quality of education had improved considerably, schools had also made it their task to prepare young people for their future occupations in industry or farming and to provide a sound basis for their personal development. The ideological education of young people in the spirit of Marxism-Leninism increasingly came to the fore.

THE INTRODUCTION OF POLYTECHNICAL EDUCATION IN THE 1950s

The high level of political and academic standards of the newly created eight-form first schools must be seen as a particular achievement of this period. This development continued throughout the 1950s. The rural schools improved so as to make a meaningful contribution to the equal right to education for people in both town and country. They also made an impact as cultural and political centres in the country decisively supporting the policy of restructuring the agricultural industry. The number of one-form country schools went down from 668 in 1949/50 to 236 in 1951/52. During the same period the number of central schools (fully developed schools for pupils from several villages) was doubled, reaching a total of 1402 in 1952. At the same time much consideration continued to be given to improving teaching methods and developing new approaches to teaching in schools where children of two, three or more age groups were still taught together. Since 1949, with the introduction of an extended testing and examination system, the satisfactory completion of the teaching syllabus and the level of achievement reached by each first school pupil could be reliably assessed and recorded. The intention of the tests was for educators to be able to learn conclusively how to impart knowledge systematically. Particular attention was paid to ways of improving the educational chances of the children of workers and peasants. The number of school teachers began to stabilize. At the beginning of the 1950s more than 65,000 teachers were employed of whom 70 per cent were new recruits.

In 1951 began the gradual introduction of a new curriculum for schools in the GDR based on the methodological principles of Marxism-Leninism and on Soviet practical experiences. Its main objectives were to obtain a marked improvement in pupils' performance and to increase the peda-gogical effectiveness of instruction in the spirit of socialist ideology. The dynamics of social development and the rapidly changing demands of society upon schools, the contradictions between the demands of the curric-ulum and both the existing and the newly developing ways of achieving them in the schools, led to significant curriculum changes as early as the following year, starting a process which continued until 1955/56. Despite its relative instability, the 1951 curriculum constituted an important basis for developing a new quality in the teaching of a many-sided, comprehensive, and systematic knowledge and skills and ensuring their acquisition by the pupils.

Polytechnical education and training in the GDR in the 1950s established one of the main characteristic features of socialist schooling. In the curriculum reform plan of 1951 the demand for 'a polytechnical education for all pupils' achieved by rigorous subject teaching, close to real-life experience and directed towards the production process, was made for the first time. The achievements in science education of school pupils since 1946 provided an important precondition for this in spite of complex problems to do with the contents, the personnel and the materials required. At the start of the 1950s many schools still had the workshops and school gardens created in the 1920s in response to the ideas of the *Arbeitsschule* with its emphasis on manual training and preparation for work. The earlier ideas of work education had been taken up with great interest by many of the new teachers. It was important, therefore, that polytechnical education and training should now be reorientated firmly towards the Marxist education demand for work experience in socialist production and for the study of production processes in industry and agriculture.

Interpreting this link with production, which at first had been seen exclusively as imparting the relevant knowledge and so-called 'application skills' in lessons as a task for scientific experiments in school on the one hand, and visits made by pupils to firms and factories outside on the other, led to the conviction held well beyond the mid-1950s that productive work by pupils constituted part of their extra-curricular commitment. Indeed in 1951 manual training in school was abolished, the result of both a one-sided interpretation of what constitutes reformist pedagogy and a rigid adherence to Soviet educational models of the 1930s and 1940s. For example, school gardens were used exclusively as an out of school activity lying outside the formal curriculum.

The 1952 resolution which demanded the creation of a firm basis on which to establish socialism in the GDR, identified polytechnical education and training in school, as an essential trait of socialist education. Its introduction at the start of the school year 1958/59, based on entirely revised curriculum schedules, was a revolutionary step in the development of socialist education. For the first time in German educational history a start was made to provide a polytechnical general education combining education and productive work for all young people. An important sphere of life, namely technology, production and work-practice thus became part of general education. This opened up new approaches for pupils' personal development, at the same time new educational measures were put to use in schooling, which required the introduction of new organizational structures in general education. Because staff were prepared to do all they could to help, the necessary conditions in respect of personnel and material were created in schools and factories to help bring all this about. The academic year 1958/59 was marked by the enormous effort of teachers, representatives of parents, factory workers and management, researchers and politicians of education as well as by the release of resources to schools to secure the system of polytechnical education and training. At the same time it sought to create the necessary political, scientific, manpower and material preconditions for the introduction of the ten-form, compulsory polytechnical school. This meant that individuals had to be convinced of the usefulness of a ten-form polytechnical general education for themselves as well as the need of one for society as a whole.

During the academic year 1958/59, 43 per cent of all pupils, including those attending the twelve-form secondary schools, were already in receipt of a general education which went beyond the usual eight forms of schooling. About 400,000 pupils aged between 13 and 18 spent one day a week working in state-owned enterprises, in factories and on the land. In the following decades polytechnical education and training in the GDR was implemented and developed with the full support of specialist vocational trainers and ordinary workers. During the second half of the 1950s this support became particularly important when decisions had to be made about the syllabus of polytechnical subjects. Right from the start it led to specific solutions of problems concerning the exact relation between general education, polytechnical education and vocational preparation and training. Arising from the initiatives of schools, factories and local organizations, various forms of socially relevant and productive work done by pupils outside school hours were developed. An important source of information for the realization of polytechnical education and training, especially in respect of pupils' productive work, were school experiments carried out in the mid-1950s which linked elements of vocational training viewed from a polytechnical angle with the curriculum in forms 9 and 10 of the intermediate schools, *Mittelschulen,* then still in existence. Pupils of an eighth form who had applied to be trained as mechanics at the state-owned bookkeeping-machinery factory in Karl-Marx-Stadt were, with the consent of their parents, transferred in September 1956 to form 9 of the Comenius intermediate school to enable them to complete their training. Once a week they were given polytechnical training in a factory. In rural areas, for example in Golzow, Wesenberg, Haubinda and Herbsleben, the so-called pupil-production brigades were formed for similar reasons.

The close ties between schools and industrial enterprises, partly consisting of partnerships formed at the start of the 1950s, played an important role in guaranteeing the necessary personnel and material resources for the teaching of craft, wood and metal work. Manual training had been reinstated as a school subject in 1956/57 in forms 1 to 10 as the first polytechnical subject in the school curriculum. Lessons were, in most cases, taught in workshops in factories partnered with the school. Many factory workers decided to become craft teachers. Some intermediate schools (*Mittelschulen*) began to combine craft lessons in the upper forms with lessons in physics, chemistry and biology, in order to provide, in cooperation with factories and local organizations, weekly lessons in production and work experience for their pupils. It became clear that the growth of factories and agricultural cooperatives organized on socialist economic principles was a necessary precondition for the introduction throughout the system of polytechnical subjects and in particular for training days in production. The various forms of productive or socially useful work carried out by pupils in their spare time, which were developed in the main between the years 1955/56 and 1957/58, contributed general support at focal points for industry and agriculture and helped secure economic needs. Most of all, however, this enabled young people to gain an insight into the complex problems associated with building socialism in the country.

The cooperation of educationists and professional pedagogues responsible for the theoretical side of general education in schools, and factories responsible for the practical testing of different forms of polytechnical education and training, were of great significance for solving specific problems arising from the introduction of polytechnical general education in the GDR, where from early on the polytechnical principle was fully accepted as a component part of general education and training. The relation between polytechnical general education and professional training increasingly moved into the centre of pedagogical debate from the mid-1950s onwards. This led eventually to the designation of the ten-form general education, polytechnical high school (*Allgemeinbildende Polytechnische Oberschule*) as the centre-piece of socialist education whose task it was to teach the foundations indispensable for all professional training and all forms of further education.

Meanwhile, teachers' qualifications and preparation had consistently improved helping to speed up the emergence of a socialist school system. In 1950, the twelve-months emergency training scheme was phased out, replaced in 1951/52 by various distance education courses which led to a professional qualification for teachers of elementary and secondary schools. During the early 1950s the first graduates reached the schools who had been trained at the pedagogical faculties set up at universities since 1946, and at the pedagogical institute in Potsdam, founded in 1948. In 1950/51 several teacher training colleges were established in which teachers for forms 1 to 4 and teachers of Russian were trained. From 1953 onwards pedagogical institutes with university status were created. In 1955 the *Central Institute for the Further Education of Teachers* was founded. Thus, by the mid-1950s an integrated system for teacher training had been established with teachers for the lower forms of schools being prepared at teacher training institutes, so-called middle-school teachers (forms 5 to 8 or 5 to 10) at pedagogical institutes which had been granted higher education status, and teachers for senior forms (forms 5 to 12) in universities and other institutes of higher education. By the mid-1950s all teachers in employment had completed their professional training.

THE DEVELOPMENT OF A SOCIALIST EDUCATION SYSTEM

The legal recognition in the 1959 Law *(Developing a Socialist Education System)* of the socialist character of the compulsory 10-form *Allgemeinbildende Polytechnische Oberschule* was the necessary precondition for a comprehensive restructuring of the entire education system on lines demanded by society after intense debates involving educational politics and pedagogy. The polytechnical school itself was the object of discussions. It would provide a polytechnical general education of the highest quality, combining theoretical with practical concerns, and preparing its pupils for a life of activity useful for society. At one end this school had to be linked with a pre-school education, at its other end it would lead to professional training and preparation for university entrance in the extended high school *(Erweiterte Oberschule)*. Detailed work on establishing such a school was carried out by experts, mostly but not exclusively educationists, at every level.

CONCEPT AND ORGANIZATION OF A UNIFORM EDUCATION SYSTEM

The uniform socialist education system was developed by representatives of all spheres of social life between 1963 and 1965.[7] The law *Introducing a Uniform Socialist Education System* was formulated under the guidance of a Commission, convened by the Council of Ministers of the GDR for the establishment of a uniform socialist education system. Members were appointed under the chairmanship of Alexander Abusch, deputy chairman of the GDR Council of Ministers. His deputies were Margot Honecker, Minister of Education and Prof. Dr Ernst-Joachim Gießmann, Undersecretary of State for higher and professional education. The Commission consisted of a further 62 members and two secretaries representing all political parties in the Democratic Assembly *(Demokratischer Block)*, mass organizations like the Free German Trade Union (FDGB) and the Free German Youth (FDJ), as well as state and economic institutions. Chemists, historians, mathematicians, medical doctors, military specialists, economists, musicologists, educationists of all levels, philosophers, physicists, psychologists, lawyers, sociologists and linguists were all members of the State Commission. In collaboration with governmental organizations and institutions of the state, social and scientific institutes, such as the Science Council of the Ministry for Education, the Central German Pedagogical Institute, the German Academy of Sciences and the Research Council for the Encouragement of Research set themselves the following tasks:

1   To determine the aims of and demands made on the content of education and training at all levels of the uniform socialist education system.
2   To decide the place and function of all educational establishments within the uniform education system.
3   To draft guidelines for the systematic development of a curriculum for the training professions, vocational profiles, study programmes, teaching materials, guidelines for further education – including higher academic and higher professional education – requirements, the pre- and in-service education of teachers at all levels. The findings of a number of research projects on specific problems within the uniform socialist education system helped the Commission to define the aims and contents of education. [8]

A year or so later the State Commission published its draft of a discussion paper, *Basic Principles for the Establishment of a Uniform Socialist Education System*. In the public debates which ensued, on a scale never before seen in the GDR, virtually everyone, especially if a member of an organization, was invited to give an opinion about education and its problems. Government institutions, political parties, mass organizations, professional associations and educational institutions organized discussion groups, conferences and other events throughout the GDR. Thousands of articles on the formation of a uniform socialist education system were published in national and local newspapers, as well as in professional journals. Special radio and television programmes were broadcast, the Commission receiving thousands of letters from all sections of the population. Of particular importance for the development of this debate was the decision of the executive committee of the FDGB (Free German Trade Union) to arrange discussions of the draft paper in all trade union groups.

Members of the Commission and leading representatives of the state, the economy, science and culture spoke at these meetings and explained the possibilities (*Perspektive*) offered by the proposed education system to the work-force. Increasing numbers of workers realized, perhaps for the first time, that educational concerns were part of their personal development and that they themselves had a responsibility to realize the aims contained in the *Basic principles*. Until July 1964 in the district of Schwerin alone some 15,000 citizens at more than 1,000 separate events had discussed the draft paper. By September 1964 in the city of Meißen (district of Dresden) more than 14,500 workers had done so, from the city of Weimar 19 amendments had been sent to the Commission by the end of June. Nearly 1300 parents' and work-force meetings were held in the northern town of Guestrow.

Interest centred in particular on problems concerning contents of the curriculum, the relation between general and specialist education, uniformity and diversity in socialist education, further education, initial and in-service vocational preparation, and what makes for effective pedagogy in the classroom. People seemed to have grasped that the character of education was determined by the conditions and perspectives reached in social development, and that a solid general education must form the basis for any specialist training. There were different opinions on the precise contribution of each individual general education subject in the curriculum to pupils' further educational and professional development.

In the foreground of the discussions were contributions on how to bring about an improvement of polytechnical education. The importance of polytechnical training for an all round and harmonious personal development was stressed. Besides the improvement of mathematical and science teaching, better quality in the teaching of fine arts subjects and languages was considered to be of great importance.

On 25 February 1965 the People's Chamber of the GDR passed the law *Introducing a Uniform Socialist Education System* and thus gave the force of law to a document which had been produced with the active support of society, and which determined the general direction which the development of the education system would take.

The educational policy and pedagogical objectives of the law *Introducing a Uniform Socialist Education System* had been to achieve 'a high level of education for the nation, ensuring an all-sided and harmonious development of socialist personalities, capable of consciously shaping their social lives, harnessing natural resources in the service of mankind, leading a fulfilled and happy life worthy of a human being'.[9]

The basic components of the uniform socialist education system were:

– centres for pre-school education;
– the ten-form general polytechnical high school;
– institutions for vocational training;
– educational establishments leading to university entrance;

- high-level qualifications;
- engineering and other specialist professional colleges;
- universities and institutions of university status;
- establishments for the training and further education of the working population.

Physically and mentally handicapped children were to be cared for in special schools. Children and young people whose education and development, even with community support, could not be assured by their natural parents, were to be cared for in youth welfare centres (homes, young people's working communities) for shorter periods or until attaining their majority.

For the first time in German educational history this law applied to all educational institutions.

The law laid down the following fundamental principles governing the uniform socialist education system:

1 the close link between education and socialist life;
2 the unity of theory and practice, link of school and university study with productive work and physical training;
3 the unity of personal upbringing and development and education at all levels;
4 the development of all of a learner's natural gifts and talents preventing anyone from being left behind;
5 close cooperation of all agents of society concerned with the provision of education, in particular establishments of the state, social organizations and the family;
6 the opportunity for each citizen to transfer to a higher including the highest level of education according to his or her talents and achievements.

The unity of aims and structure of the uniform socialist education system did allow for differentiation in the form of routes taken in education, in response to social requirements and individual preparation.

The time allocations for subjects and subject groups taught in the compulsory general polytechnical high school were as follows:[10]

	per cent
social sciences, mother tongue	41.1
mathematics/sciences	29.8
introduction into socialist production/productive work	10.6
foreign languages	10.6
physical exercise and sport	7.9

Even in the 1960s the key problems in the development of the ten-form general polytechnical high school were the exact definition of the polytechnical character of education, the polytechnical syllabus in the classroom, and the link between classroom and productive work. New demands caused by scientific and technical progress, new insights into the role of work in personality development, and activity methods in the acquisition of knowledge, perfection of skills and the learning of attitudes led to further developments in polytechnical education. The general education foundations for this were made legal in the *1965 Law*.

Between 1964 and 1971 a new curriculum for the ten-form school was introduced which gave a clearer Marxist interpretation to the whole concept of general education, affirming the status of socialist ideology as an exact science (unity of science and socialist ideology). This particular concept failed in practice leading to the formation of a double morality among young people. More successful were the new approaches in personality development.

The holistic view of the development of personality laid greater emphasis on active, independent, creative learning by stressing the unity of learning and working, insight and action, word and deed. The education content was designed so as to develop an interest in and the ability for perfecting one's own knowledge.

The introduction of the new curriculum was accompanied by attempts to make the process of teaching and learning more effective. Consideration was given to programming the teaching and learning processes. During the early 1970s it was recognized that although programming made certain elements in this process easier to master than other methods, exaggerated expectations of achieving a rationalization of the teaching process through programming had to be abandoned.

In all areas of education further curriculum developments were achieved on the basis of the *1965 Law*. Pedagogical work in *Kindergärten* was supported by the partial introduction of an education plan, and while the specific function and character of the *Kindergärten* was kept, more attention was paid to the preparation of children for mainstream schooling.

During the first half of the 1960s the function of the lower school (forms 1 to 3) was redefined. Systematic education in all subjects, based on their specific academic discipline profile, was available from form 1. The acquisition of solid knowledge and abilities was achieved by introducing pupils to the interrelations of nature and society, and by stimulating their capacity to think for themselves. Form 4 became the transition year from the lower to the middle school.

An important new development which affected the contents and structure of education during the 1960s were changes in teacher qualifications, which resulted in raising standards in teacher preparation. They were not unconnected with developments in the school sector, caused *inter alia* also by the greater attention given to the mathematical profile in the natural sciences, technology and economics syllabuses. The required changes in teacher training were announced in the *Draft for re-educating upper forms school teachers* of April 1963. This provided for a four-year teacher training course in two teaching subjects, one main and one subsidiary. All future teachers were required to obtain the minimum of a modern academic level science qualification. Compulsory study plans and detailed teaching programmes which allowed for some options were intended to provide a uniform, self-contained training course for each individual student teacher. Such courses were located in all teacher training institutions, universities, colleges of pedagogy and colleges of advanced technology. The training programme took into account the improved study opportunities resulting from the higher qualifications which future students would have acquired in their socialist schools.

In teaching methods and psychology courses closer links with practical work at school were established. Results obtained during the training course were evaluated during extensive practical teaching placement periods which again emphasized the dominant educational principle of the link between theory and practice. The systematic involvement of students in research projects, classroom teaching as well as psychology, provided by the option choices within core courses for the trainees, raised the quality and effectiveness of personality formation offered in the training course. The courses had gradually become oriented more towards the study of pedagogical science and professional skills, encouraging independent research activity. Teacher training institutions increased their research potential and their links with industry and agriculture both of which yielded remarkable research results.

Professional training was gradually changed, in step with the developments in production, towards training in so-called basic professions which allowed for specialization. The well-established form of vocational training which also provided a university entrance qualification (*Abitur*) was kept. This made it possible to bring education more into line with future requirements in science, production and technology.

The necessary tasks and measures to be taken were expressed in the *Principles for the further development of vocational training as part of the uniform socialist education system*, passed in June 1968 and in the *Principles for initial training and further education of the workforce*, passed in 1970. These radical changes in vocational training led to change in the decision-making process involving choice as to which profession to train for. In 1968 the first Vocational Advice Bureau was founded in Leipzig.

During the late 1970s tendencies could be detected in all areas of education to take preliminary steps for further developments based on insights and experiences gained so far, and in consideration of the new requirements demanded by the changing social conditions in the GDR. In all areas of education quantitative and qualitative changes were introduced in agreement with the laws of 1965 which increased the efficiency of all educational institutions and attuned them to social demands.

Encouraged by the sociopolitical measures, the birth rate in the GDR rose considerably during the 1970s. The great number of working mothers and greater numbers of children led to an increase in the demand for places in preschool institutions. This required considerable expenditure on staff and equipment, at the same time it posed the social task of further improvements in kindergarten education.

The conference on preschool education in the GDR, held in November 1977, decided that equal rights to education included the right to a place in *Kindergärten* for all children. This was a unique acknowledgement with far reaching consequences. Between 1970 and 1985 places in day nurseries were doubled, so that 73 per cent of children of preschool age could be provided for. By 1985 places in *Kindergärten* were increased by a further one-third, compared to 1970. Since the early 1980s all children whose parents wanted them to attend a *Kindergärten* could do so. Thus preschool education became a fully integrated part of the education system. Based on a new education plan full use was made of the opportunities for personal development during preschool attendance and to guarantee a good preparation for future steps in education and life.

Of equal importance from an educational, political, and social angle was the development of the day-home (*Hort*) for school children. By the late 1970s all children of forms 1 to 4, whose parents wished them to do so, could attend a day-home.

During the second half of the 1970s attention also centred on the development of special schools for mentally or physically handicapped children. The establishment, between 1974 and 1985, of 74 special schools, particularly for physically handicapped children, social and medical institutions, and the drafting of new education programmes made it possible to guarantee the right to education and vocational training of 75,000 physically or psychologically handicapped children.

The number of graduates from universities and institutions with university status working in the economy doubled between 1970 and 1985. By the end of the 1980s about 65 per cent of people working in the economy had received vocational training as specialist workers or master craftsmen. A census of one age-group cohort revealed that 90 per cent had completed the ten-form polytechnic high school, a *mittlere Reife* equivalent to the English General Certificate of Secondary Education.

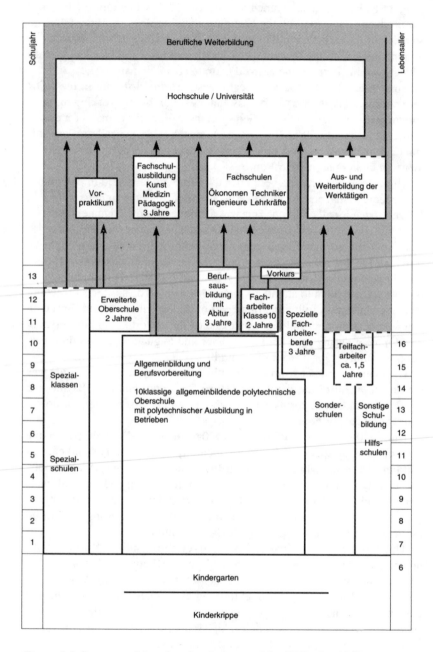

Figure 8.1 Structure of the educational system of the GDR after 1965.

CONCLUSION

It is necessary, when making an assessment based on facts of the achievements and failures of the education system of the GDR to bear in mind that this may lead to different conclusions. This is so because the education system is an integral part of the state in which it functions and its driving force. A flat rejection of its achievements takes no account of the humanist ideals which inspired the education laws of the GDR and the dedication of most of its teachers. The particularly close link between politics and education was responsible for much that was good in the system, at the same time it perpetrated ideological damage on those growing up in it. Predictably, the chance to transfer some of the constructive elements from the education system of the GDR into a unified Germany after 1989/90, and to encourage an urgently needed education reform in a country where education is a federal responsibility, have so far failed. The problem, however, may be back on the agenda when the necessary historical distance has been gained. [11]

ACKNOWLEDGEMENT

Translated from the original German by Dr Catherine W. Proescholdt.

NOTES

1 'Gesetz zur Demokratisierung der deutschen Schule' in *Dokumente zur Geschichte des Schulwesens in der Deutschen Demokratischen Republik*, Teil 1: 1945–1955, introduction by Karl-Heinz Guenther and Gottfried Uhlig. Monumenta Paedagogica, vol. VI. Volk und Wissen Volkseigener Verlag, Berlin 1970.

2 Kreuziger, Winzer and Wildangel were members of the *Reformpaedagogik* movement (see below) who with their interpretation of the ideas and reforms proposed were placed towards the political left. They became prominent in the future GDR. See also: Gerd Hohendorf, Helmut Koenig and Eberhard Meumann (eds), *Wegbereiter der neuen Schule*, Volk und Wissen Volkseigener Verlag, Berlin 1989.

3 See: *Dokumente zur Geschichte*, op.cit.

4 *Reformpaedagogik* is the term used for the German branch of a worldwide pedagogical movement (1890–1930), which despite a variety of directions taken was united in placing the child and adolescent at the centre of educational efforts, cf. Ellen Key, 'The Century of the Child', developing a child centred, anti-authoritarian pedagogy. See also: Stanley, W.B. *Curriculum for Utopia*, State University of New York Press, 1992. In Germany all such reforms were halted by the Nazis.

5 The main pedagogical principle of the *Arbeitsschule*, one of the directions advocated by the *Reformpaedagogik*, was pupils' manual work. Before 1933 there were three trends in Germany: help with vocational career choice

(Kerschensteiner), the harmonious development of all sides – intellectual and physical – of the pupil's personality (Gaudig, Scheibner) and the link of schooling with productive work in industry (Lunacharski, Krupskaya, Blonski). In one way or another they all were intended to be represented in the education system of the GDR.

6 Herbart and Ziller, influential nineteenth century German educationists, whose authoritarian, teacher-centred pedagogy was rooted in the principle of disciplining (ruling over – *regieren)* the child.

7 The structure and system of government of the GDR, illustrated by working examples, are discussed by Tulasiewicz, W., Cultural Identity and Educational Policy: the case of the German Democratic Republic, in *Cultural Identity and Educational Policy*, ed. C. Brock and W. Tulasiewicz, London, Croom Helm, 1985.

8 For details of the origins and theoretical assumptions of the 1965 Law, see: Meumann, Eberhard, *Entstehung und theoretische Grundkonzeption des Gesetzes ueber das einheitliche sozialistische Bildungssystem.* Akademie der Paedagogischen Wissenschaften der DDR, Berlin, 1973. Cf. also the diagram of the structure of the uniform socialist system of education, after the Law of 25 February 1965.

9 *Law introducing a uniform socialist education system* (25 February 1965): Gesetz ueber das einheitliche sozialistische Bildungssystem vom 25.2.1965 in: *Auf dem Weg zur gebildeten Nation*, Staatsverlag der DDR, Berlin, 1965.

10 *Das Bildungswesen der Deutschen Demokratischen Republik*, Gemeinschaftsarbeit der Akademie der Paedagogischen Wissenschaften, 2nd edn. Volk und Wissen Volkseigener Verlag, Berlin 1983.

11 For a West German assessment of the situation, see: Vergleich von Bildung und Erziehung in der Bundesrepublik Deutschland und in der Deutschen Demokratischen Republik. Herausgegeben vom Bundesministerium fuer innerdeutsche Beziehungen. Wissenschaftliche Kommission: Oskar Anweiler (Leitung), Wolfgang Mitter, Hansgert Peisert, Hans-Peter Schaefer, Wolfgang Stratenwerth. Verlag Wissenschaft und Politik, Koeln, 1990.

Part B

The law and education: institutions and the curriculum

9 The judicial control of the curriculum and court intervention in aspects of education: cases from the international scene

Jack Sislian

EDUCATIONAL LAW AND THE COURTS

It is a trite piece of wisdom to say that education is a controversial subject. Such controversy in education anywhere continually reflects social unrest caused by social change and problems of economic development. Every kind of educational administration faces conflicts and the law and courts are looked upon as problem-solving mechanisms. Many state constitutions give the aims of education and make provisions for the organization and administration of education with a view to attaining these aims. A variety of state constitutions exist: the centralized, the decentralized, the theocratic, the secular, and those that suit a ruling family or a single ruler or there might even be a mixture of these. For instance, Germany has a highly centralized system within a pronounced decentralized national educational framework. Some countries provide judicial protection to their citizens' individual rights while others forbid their courts from intervening in educational matters by law, for example, by depending on their constitution or by tradition. Teachers everywhere, especially secondary school teachers, wish to exercise academic freedom as this is understood in universities in matters dealing with freedom to lecture and do research. Students and their parents fight to retain their rights or, if lost or curtailed, desire these rights to be restored. Some school laws protect or prescribe the rights of students, of their parents and those of teachers and as a result restrict or proscribe administrative educational action. The legalization of education, which has now come to mean courts' sanctioning of educational laws, in contrast to legalizing, which means made lawful by the legislature, or the law of education in gestation or in the making, appears to be going on currently in various countries. Legalization simply means judicial review of statutory education law, for which provision obtains based on the law of any modern state. Not all sovereign states allow or even tolerate judicial review of educational litigation between the legislature and the public, let alone individual citizens. This is mainly because the genuine separation of powers does not obtain in them – the legislature, the executive and the judiciary. Dictatorships in history have invariably used the curriculum to further the dictator's ideology. The first thing any occupying power does is to close the schools and universities of the defeated country and then reintroduce their brand of curriculum, based on their own laws, through the administration of the occupied country.

Without administrative law in education no educational system can exist. Educational administration may be seen as a decision-making process which itself must be organized in an extremely hierarchical order to make sure who decides on what, and how such a decision is to be made legally binding in a given society. The law prescribes areas of procedure and competence and can block appeals if it is empowered by law to do so. Decision-making in matters dealing with education, including the curriculum, becomes a highly complex and sensitive affair since class, group, individual or national interests are involved. The aims of an administrative organization must be ascertained and how those aims are to be attained will have to be clearly delineated in order to forestall recourse to law by the citizens of a country.

Over and above every administrative law in education is the constitution which states the political aims of a nation and its people, such as social unity, social stability, a guarantee of due process and equal protection under the law, basic freedoms, and relations dealing with property acquisition and its retention. Whether a constitution is a political agenda or in fact law must be ascertained. It might be neither, but simply mean an indicator for or a guide to optimum social development towards an 'ideal society' based on a pious hope! The school and its curriculum are required not to contradict or run counter to the constitution of the land. Article 7 of the Constitution of the Federal Republic of Germany is clear on this point. 'The entire educational system shall be under the supervision of the state.' In sum, three things emerge: first, that any educational system is a decision-making process and includes educational administration; secondly, that courts of law play a conflict- or problem-solving role in educational disputes; and thirdly, that there is implicit in every school system the principle that the curriculum shall not be used against the state. Article 7 mentioned above is taken verbatim from the Prussian Constitution of 1794 whose aim was to create a unitary sovereign state. Schools and universities became state institutions, the curriculum was centrally prescribed and enforced by teachers in higher schools, all of whom had the character of 'state functionaries' or civil servants, as they are called today.

Certainly 1794 is a significant landmark when attempting to understand the development of modern Germany, but what currents were already at work before that must be borne in mind, which gradually culminated in that year. Compulsory education was introduced in 1619 in the duchy of Weimar with far-reaching implications for the spreading of the traditions and belief in education as being the birthright of every German child, boy or girl. In 1794 a unifying force was ushered into Prussia in law (already attained to a great measure in England), land reform, military matters and education. (The first state to introduce compulsory education, followed by compulsory military service was Germany.) Stein looked after the law and land reform, Scharnhorst after the military, W. von Humboldt after education and Fichte's ideas after the curriculum, through his 'Speeches to the German Nation'. Thus the social reform in Germany was massive and thorough, based primarily on a modern, new and purposeful curriculum, albeit tainted with 'nationalism'. Many countries in the world today, desiring to effect a speedy transition from the agricultural stage to industrial, can draw useful lessons from the German model.

THE VARIETIES OF COURTS EMPOWERED TO DEAL WITH EDUCATIONAL LITIGATION

A variety of social systems has given rise to a variety of systems of judicial control of educational litigation including curricular problems. Educational litigation takes place because of strongly opposing convictions between those in authority and those who feel they are being wronged by their decisions, which are made ultimately on behalf of the state. These decisions the state expects its citizens to accept and obey, even if a litigant disagrees with a court's decision. This is the coercive side of a constitution which extends to the educational provision of a state. Compulsory schooling means that boys and girls are *compelled by law* to attend school. About 150 years ago German parents refusing to send their children to school had to confront the policeman who would enforce the law or pay 20 gold '*thalers*' as fine to the local authorities, but they still had to send their children to school.

In the Federal Republic of Germany there are State Administrative Courts which are empowered to deal with educational litigation, whatever their nature, including questions of the curriculum. An example in this connection would be the litigation between parents and the school authorities concerning whether or not to include sex education in the curriculum in the 1970s. (A number of Lutheran parents in Denmark had a similar problem some years previously. In England the legal and moral framework of sex education is laid out in Sections 18 and 46 of the Education (No. 2) Act 1986.) In both cases the parents lost because the courts said sex education was part of general education, which was their children's right and that it would be a serious 'crime' to deprive them of that right. The teaching of Turkish and the tenets of Islam for migrant workers' children in Germany was another problem for the curriculum decision-makers (see below).

In England, Parliament is sovereign and the supreme decision-making body. Judicial review on the part of the House of Lords, as the highest Court of Appeal, restricts itself to principles of the political exercise of authority in educational or school administration rather than to individual subjects in the curriculum. An example in this connection is when in 1976 a Cabinet Minister's decision was challenged in the House of Lords. The decision of the then Secretary of State for Education and Science to compel the Tameside Metropolitan Borough Council to go comprehensive was not upheld in the House of Lords. Perhaps it is worthy of comment that that ruling by the House of Lords was not lost on the present British Government's policy of inviting rather than compelling schools to 'opt out' (i.e. seek Grant Maintained status directly under the Department For Education) of the Local Education Authorities' control.

In the USA, the Supreme Court may decide what is constitutional and what is not. It may not initiate educational policy or laws on its own. Locally raised tax-money may not support private schools for the teaching of religion or their curriculum since such financial help contradicts Article 1 of the American Constitution. This guarantees the separation of the state from the church. It therefore applies to any church which wishes to have its own schools and curricula but wants to teach its beliefs supported by public tax money. Congressional legislation in the USA may not be applied by the US Supreme Court if it is found by the US Courts to be inconsistent with the Court's interpretation of the constitution.

In France special constitutional courts decide on the constitutionality of an educational law including any changes in the curriculum. The French *Conseil Constitutionnel* decides on the constitutionality of the law of education automatically *before* the law is finally promulgated. In Japan, Austria, the Federal Republic of Germany, Belgium and Switzerland, for example, the courts may control the constitutionality of any educational measure *after* promulgation of the law. In Germany all Administrative Courts of Law are empowered to control both the federal and the individual state laws regarding their compliance with the federal constitution. Ultimately, it is the Federal Constitutional Court that decides on any educational matter including the curriculum, an example of this is the curriculum litigation dealing with sex education already mentioned.

In Belgium in the 1950s the *Conseil d'État'* decided on the question of priority of languages in the curriculum. It ruled that the medium of instruction, French or Flemish, had to reflect the language of the majority of citizens in a geographical region of the country, although Brussels was excepted where by law both languages became the vehicle of instruction. All multilingual societies will always face such problems, because of fear of possible dominance of one language over all the others. For example, Singapore, where the Malay language was superseded by Chinese. Brunei, today, is very conscious of such a situation repeating itself there. The decision concerning the medium of instruction is a highly political one.

In Switzerland, each of the 23 full Cantons and each of three half Cantons has its own sovereign constitutional arrangement in education and the curriculum. The Swiss Federal Court may control the compliance of Cantons' educational laws with the Swiss Federal Constitutional laws but the Swiss Federal Constitution itself forbids any judicial control of the Swiss Federal laws, thus the legislature, from the outset, does not allow its own constitution to be subjected to judicial review. The referendum is supposed to somewhat mitigate this state of affairs in Swiss Cantons. By law and tradition the highly federal nature of Swiss educational provision has always strictly set its sights on attaining two main objectives: to prepare boys and girls for the world of work and to develop their personalities fully. Both these objectives the Swiss sovereign state believes will enable individual citizens to lead useful and fulfilling lives. These two objectives are the *raison d'être* of each individual Cantonal curriculum. Parents or guardians of pupils may contest the Cantonal educational authorities if they think these objectives are not being met fully. But because of an extremely closely knit pattern of educational practice with educational theory, rarely does litigation come to light since very close monitoring of the curriculum and school inspections concerning standards take place frequently.

Despite the precise working of the Swiss educational system, reminiscent of high quality watches 'Made in Switzerland', there are, nevertheless, educational problems Switzerland cannot ignore, for example the under-representation of women in vocational and technical education, equality of educational opportunity to children of migrant workers or the role of the Swiss state in matters of lifelong educational provision. Such problems could usher in litigation in their trail between the public and educational administration.

In England and France, the theory of parliamentary supremacy prohibits court refusal to apply Acts of Parliament even when courts establish their unconstitutionality, since there can be no higher law-making body.

In Germany the Federal Constitutional Court may be resorted to even after the Bill has been passed as law by the *Bundestag*, its highest political law-giving body. It is the right and privilege of the German Parliamentary Opposition to make use of this possibility if it wants to delay the passage of a law from being promulgated. It can then, if it wishes, give further airing to the Bill in line with its own political programme, in the hope of mustering support for its views. Not only major social or economic laws in any modern state can suffer delays based on the laws of the constitution, but also major educational reforms such as that of Secondary Education or University reform, as in France or Germany in the past two or three decades.

In the German Federal Republic it is the Administrative Courts of Law that are empowered to look into litigation of an educational nature including the curriculum. There is a tier of three courts: the first and the lowest Administrative Court, the second and Higher Court and the third and ultimate one, the Federal Administrative Court. Each German *Land* has the first two kinds of Administrative Courts. The Higher Courts and the Federal Administrative Court are courts of appeal. Litigation of any kind takes place because the wording of a constitution is not clear or precise, which could cause citizens and the courts a lot of unnecessary trouble. Stuart Maclure, a close observer of the English educational scene for some four decades and a former editor of *The Times Educational Supplement*, is convinced that in matters of law and education the answer that comes back again and again is that the law is not clear and that there are areas that have been 'deliberately' left grey. It is also the writer's belief that such deliberate acts are common in many areas in many states behind which lawgivers can hide. (See below the case of the German civil servant seeking redress in German courts of law.) Basing itself on the principle of the sanctity of sovereignty any state will do its best to steer clear of social minefields at any cost, probably not always inspired by legal considerations only. Certain organs of state administration have access to sources of information denied to courts of law. It cannot be ruled out that subtle influencing of state official top administrative bodies or even courts could take place by decision-making committees, legally and constitutionally, placed between the legislature and the official state administration or executive. Educational law is anywhere an arm of the executive, which is protected by a highly trained bureaucracy, whose top echelons have had legal training especially in public administrative law.

Two examples can be cited in this connection, one having to do with understanding the meaning of control of education and the other with the meaning of control in employment in matters dealing with civil servants and their promotion to higher grades in their career. It must be remembered that in Germany almost all teachers and university lecturers are civil servants and Federal civil service laws are equally binding on civil servants in all the individual *Länder* – each *Land* may have its own constitution but Federal law overrides *Land* law (German Constitution: Art. 31).

The first example hinges on understanding the meaning of the word 'state'. Article 7 of the German Constitution states: 'The entire educational system shall be under the supervision of the State.' But we are left in the dark as to the meaning of 'State'. Is the State the *Bundestag*, is it the Legislature, i.e. *Bundestag* and *Bundesrat*, is it the Executive branch of Government, or is it the Judiciary? No definition is offered in the German Constitution for the 'state'. Only where there is a genuine separation of powers of these three branches of government can such a questioning make sense. Because of the principle of sovereignty of the state, it can use legally set up decision-making bodies called 'appropriate authorities', i.e. including complicated bureaucracies, to enforce its will despite the constitution. In higher education it can give full guarantee to an academic body called 'The Faculty and its Appointments Board', yet refuse to accept that body's decision, even if refusal is in breach of the constitution. (See the statutes of any European university on the appointment of university teachers.) The agenda and decision-making of such authorities is understandably highly secret, even in a *par excellence* decentralized country like England hardly anything is known about the 'Secret Committees' in the English polity. The present Prime Minister of the United Kingdom, John Major, has admitted to the existence of some 47 of such committees. In his efforts to make English society more open, the names, hitherto kept secret, of members of these committees are being made public. Agenda, policy, decision-making and minutes of these 'Secret Committees' will, however, remain inaccessible to the English public. 'Secret Committees' of pivotal significance for politicians, it has been reported, do not even record their deliberations in minutes of their meetings.

The second example has also to do with lack of clarity in the choice of words in the German Constitution which caused profound disappointment to a litigant who took such concepts on trust and good faith but who found that the courts from whom he had expected succour and comfort failed him. Article 19 (4) of the German Constitution says, 'Should any person's right be violated by public authority, recourse to the court shall be open to him. If jurisdiction is not specified, recourse shall be to the ordinary courts'.

Article 33 (2) of the same constitution says, 'Every German shall be equally eligible for public office according to his aptitude, qualifications, and professional achievements'.

A civil servant in Hamburg felt he was being discriminated against in not being promoted as a colleague of his doing the same work had been, and had recourse to the courts. The Administrative Court of Appeal in Hamburg dismissed the litigant's complaint because it was unable to find legal definitions for Aptitude, Qualifications and Professional Achievements. It ruled that, 'Regarding concepts of aptitude, qualifications and professional achievements, these concepts are juridically indefinite.' This example is an answer to the question whether or not all court rulings always become binding in every case. The reply must be unfortunately in the negative, despite the precise wording of the law.

In deciding whether sex education should be taught or not in German schools the litigation mentioned above between parents and school authorities in which the parents said they did not want sex education to be taught to their children, the courts took some seven long years to decide this point of including this subject in the curriculum. The children of these parents had by then left school. (One example of litigation known to the writer regarding a university appointment lasted some seventeen years, which the litigant lost, not because of the demerits of the case, but because of the procrastination by the bureaucracy in handling it. If the state so wishes, it can play its trump card, i.e. causing very long delays simply through bureaucratic obstinacy, which in turn allow the 'appropriate authorities' to score points because of changed circumstances that occur during those delays and which the state can use to its own advantage, all based on law. The Courts are then presented with these advantages and have no possibility other than to decide in favour of the position of the state's presentation of the litigation.)

A legally binding *modus vivendi* can also be reached on the sensitive issue of a national language or the teaching of a minority religion within a country. For instance, in certain German cities with Turkish workers the educational authorities cooperate with Turkish Ministries to appoint Turkish teachers of Islam and the Turkish language who are paid by the German authorities.

EDUCATIONAL SYSTEMS, THE EXECUTIVE AND THE COURTS

Educational systems form part of the executive branch of government whether they are the responsibility of the state, or local or private bodies. Any decisions, therefore, touching on the enormous and complex area of public life called education, including the curriculum, are subject to judicial review or control. Nowhere are educational problems with their numerous aspects beyond the reach of judicial control. In so far as decisions are made on curricular matters judicial review is allowed for the constitutionality of such decisions. The litigations in Denmark and Hamburg regarding sex education come readily to mind. Yet courts do not control curricular decisions, because constitutionally they are not empowered to do so. Jurisdiction regarding curricula is in the hands of education authorities, first and foremost.

For instance, courts in the USA and the Federal Republic of Germany might be prepared to control curricular decisions in so far as their constitutionality is concerned; courts in Austria, Switzerland and Japan resist such control and French and British courts abstain on principle from reviewing cases dealing with the curriculum. The various lines of action taken by these countries have to do with the various interpretations of their respective constitutions. Courts in Western Europe fight shy of dealing with problems arising from learning and teaching or from similar school situations. In Germany, as in most Western countries, curricular questions are the sole monopoly of the highest educational decision-making bodies. The rights of parents (except in the USA where parents can introduce a subject of their choice into the curriculum) are limited to expressing their views or criticism regarding the curriculum, with no right to participate in the decision-making legal process, which is a highly political, at times even a highly party-political, matter, for example 'comprehensive schools' as against the 'tripartite system'. It must be said that the 1944 Education Act did mention 'comprehensive education' but not 'comprehensive schools' – a nice distinction in law – which caused protracted and heated debate in England, soon after the end of the Second World War.

Judicial control restricts itself to 'discoverable' violations of competence and procedure in school situations such as assessment or the marking of exams. 'Discoverable', '*erfindbar*' in German, could be translated into English as 'inventible' (from Latin '*invenire*' and 'invent') or capable of being invented or contrived, with all its subtle undertones of possible fudging. The courts are prepared to look into disputes dealing with the consequences of teachers' wide-ranging discretionary powers over questions of discipline or the assessment of pupils' achievements, the assumption on the part of the law being that only this kind of judicial review will enable the courts to decide on the 'fairness' of such consequences. Courts basing themselves on Administrative Law stop short of decision-making in favour of those bodies or persons who were empowered to decide on a given case initially by law. This forbidden area for courts to enter and examine is known as *ultra vires* in English, *excès de pouvoir* in French and *Ermessensmißbrauch* in German. In its constitution a state might guarantee to respect a decision resulting from a pure exercise of academic judgement but it will always retain the final word, especially in matters of chair appointments based on the prerogative of sovereignty in decision making, and on the 'unprovable' assumption that the state knows best what is or is not in its citizens' interests.

It is said that when politicians do not do their homework properly when law-making, the work of the courts increases and citizens suffer unnecessarily. The latter sometimes have to wait for decades to obtain redress, or possibly they do not feel litigation with the State Administrative Office is worth pursuing in their particular case. In Germany, for example, only litigations having 'general significance' for the whole country are allowed by its Courts of Appeal to come before the Federal Administrative Court. As the overwhelming majority of disputes are of a highly individual nature and of a strictly private significance, precious few cases are reviewed by this Highest Court of Appeal.

CASES FROM THE INTERNATIONAL SCENE

Problems of law and education in Germany

Looking first at Germany, a country with which the writer is more familiar than others, its *'Bildungs- und Erziehungsziele'* have to do with the laying-down of educational aims which are legally binding on schools and their curriculum and which must conform to the German Constitution. Many *Länder* have now specified such aims in education, with perhaps Bavaria having the clearest ones. They are:

1 *Aims:*
  'To enable the child to identify conflicts and attempt to solve them; to understand the pupil as a subject and not as an object from the very beginning of his education; to impart knowledge and skills; to shape mind, body and character in the spirit of Democracy; to cultivate and nourish love for the *'Heimat'* and for the German people or *'Volk'* and to educate in the spirit of reconciliation among peoples.' Sex education, social studies or ethics also include aims laid down by the Law of Education, e.g. 'to impart knowledge on sex to children and youths commensurate with their age and maturity and to enable them to act responsibly towards themselves and others in the family and society'. (In this connection German law defines 'commensurate' as 'not in all details or aspects dealing with sex, as known to or practised by adults'.)

2 *Law and the curriculum:*
  Traditionally subjects taught at school, apart from Religion (in German simply 'Religion', which is Christianity taught separately to Protestants and Roman Catholics, not Scripture, Religious Knowledge, or Religious Education or Divinity as in England), were never regulated by law. No laws exist for including the traditional subjects in the school timetable, only new and controversial subjects have been voted on for inclusion in the curriculum by the Länder Parliaments, i.e. such as sex education, after both the German Federal Administrative Court and the German Federal Constitutional Court ruled that a parliamentary or legal basis for sex education was imperative. Other school subjects that were voted on for inclusion in the school timetable by the German Länder Parliaments

were Ethics and Philosophy as a substitute for Religious Instruction (if so intended by the education authorities of a *Land*, with voluntary attendance) and Social Studies and Sociology. With time the teaching of all school subjects old and new will be based on law. The different treatment of traditional and new subjects is based on the following consideration: the application of the constitutional principle of 'Statutory Reserve' ('Gesetzesvorbehalt' in German), or sovereignty of Parliament to the school system. It is a consequence of the so-called 'interpreted' constitution which amounts to changing the constitution to suit problems of the educational system including the curriculum.

3 *Law on pupils' progression from one form to a higher one:*
To date there are general but inadequate regulations on this aspect of school organization.

4 *Classroom management and discipline:*
German teachers are not allowed to inflict corporal punishment nor may they send a pupil out of class for this would be a 'criminal' offence, since denying a pupil his right to education would be tantamount to a breach of the Charter of Human Rights.

5 *Law on examinations:*
With regard to procedure in conducting examinations at schools there is no Federal uniform law available. The *Länder* educational authorities cooperate with the examining boards in the schools which are made up of senior staff members.

6 *Places at schools:*
German courts insist Parliament must decide on this question of demand and supply regarding places at school.

7 *Law on the organization of the school system:*
It is the function of the *Kultusministerkonferenz* (KMK) to deal with 'orientation years', 'comprehensive versus the tripartite system', 'additional tuition' or 'remedial teaching', and the 'reform of the Abitur' or 'Secondary Education for the 16–19 age group'. The KMK is a federal educational authority whose main aim is to unify the various federal educational policies of the 16 *Länder*. The 16 education Ministers make up the KMK. Decisions must be unanimous, a simple abstention would nullify the remaining 15 votes. The KMK is a progeny of the *Schulkommission* of 1868 having similar aims concerning German educational unification already at that time. Because of different weighting of schools subjects in various parts of Germany unifying efforts in curricular matters presents an especial difficulty to the KMK.

A survey of what courts around the world have determined on aspects of education

1 It is on record that some courts have decided on the structure of educational systems. In the USA in 1954 it was decided that segregation deprives children of a minority of their right to education. (Fourteenth Amendment: 'due process and equal protection under the law'.)

2 Since 1975 any of the 16 *Länder* (11 before reunification) of the FRG may organize a religious segregated school, but it must be open to all children and only if such a school protects the religious freedom of minorities, otherwise setting up purely denominational schools as a substitute for the general state-run public schools is not permitted by law.

3 On curricular matters the Japanese courts between 1974–9 ruled that the certification of school textbooks (especially History and Geography) was not unconstitutional but the Government was in breach of the constitution with regard to both academic freedom and freedom of expression if the Japanese state authorities censor or control the contents of such school textbooks. The Federal Republic of Germany between 1972/79 decided that the state authorities may impose sex education, yet not only did the German Supreme Courts decide in favour of sex education in German schools but so too did the European Commission on Human Rights. This means that all schools in the European Community may teach sex education against the wishes of dissenting parents.

4 Curricular litigation in England is conspicuous by its absence. Points contested in English courts of law deal mainly with matters of meaning arising from Education Acts, e.g. whether 'dyslexia' constituted a 'learning difficulty', or whether judges have jurisdiction to decide not only if the education a child was receiving privately was 'efficient' but also 'as efficient as he would have received at a public elementary school'. An English court's ruling that a 'dyslexic' child of school age had a 'special need' compels the LEAs to appoint a specially trained teacher and take on itself the financial burden of employing such a teacher under the 1944 Education Act .

Courts around the world have been involved in cases affecting the dismissal and reinstatement of teachers after strike action. Teachers in Switzerland and the Federal Republic of Germany have been dismissed for political reasons and a primary school teacher in England was dismissed because he propagated one-sidedly the views of the National Front (the famous Jordan case in the early 1950s).

5 It is also on record that some courts have decided on the governing and financing of education, on student participation in academic decision-

making bodies, on restricting the exercise of governmental powers in educational policy, and on decisions of the executive branch of government on whom to appoint as professors. The German state authorities of each *Land* have the power not only to refuse the appointment of a professor proposed by a university but also to appoint their own preference to an academic chair who has not even applied for the post. Under the Third Reich German professors as civil servants had to owe allegiance to the Nazi ideology. Only 'pure Germans' were required to express loyalty to the Nazi Party, non-Germans, especially Jews, were expelled from the university by Public Administrative Authorities.)

6 Teachers in Japan today are afraid that the Education Ministry might openly punish them by stifling their careers if they refuse to comply with the controversial government orders to fly the *Hinomaru,* the Rising Sun Flag, and sing the national anthem, the *Kimigayo,* at the beginning and end of each school year. *Nikkyoso,* Japan's powerful teachers' union, is ready for court action over this issue.

7 In the USA, the Supreme Court has ruled that public education authorities have broad powers to censor student newspapers, plays and other 'school-sponsored expressive activities'. This is seen by many US citizens to be a breach of the First Amendment to the US Constitution which guarantees freedom of speech and which they feel now stops at the classroom door (Hazelwood East High School, St Louis, Mo., USA, 1990).

8 In the summer of 1990 students in the UK were prepared to go to court if the examination-marking boycott by university lecturers, because of a pay claim, prevented them from sitting their finals, since this would delay their receiving academic degrees and getting work.

SUMMARY

In view of the fact that judicial orientation is influencing educational thinking and the work of schools more and more, it is the author's belief that both judges, since they are not educational experts, and teachers, since they are not trained as lawyers, ought to be introduced formally during their professional education, into each other's discipline. It would be in the interests of everyone if these two worlds – Education and Law – met and understood each other's idiom. Both law and education are problem-solving mechanisms in any society, and both guarantee some form of uninterrupted socialization of the rising generation in the interests of keeping a society's 'identity' for its ultimate survival. In this work of socialization both courts and schools have a common task, yet institutionally it is the courts that have to decide on legal problems of education as long as education continues to remain a controversial subject since, according to Michael Sadler (1861–1943), 'in the educational policy of a nation are focused its spiritual aspirations, its philosophical ideals, its economic ambitions, its military purpose, its social conflicts'. It might be said that the task of judicial control is becoming a widespread phenomenon in the educational world, and that the increasing orientation of the school system to parliamentary laws means nothing less than the growing control *of* the school *by* the centre *through* the courts.

Every state or society has an inner drive to survive. The instruments for survival are the constitution and its handmaiden, education. Both institutions are coercive forces and are based on the *raison d'être* of socializing a people. Socialization anywhere presupposes some form of overt or covert compulsion. Aristotle's reflections, some 2500 years ago, are as pertinent today as they were then:

> As things are . . . mankind are by no means agreed about the things to be taught, whether we look to virtue or the best life. Neither is it clear whether education is more concerned with intellectual or moral virtue. The existing practice is perplexing: no one knowing on what principle we should proceed – should the useful in life, or should virtue, or should the higher knowledge be the aim of our training; all three opinions have been entertained. Again about the means there is no agreement: for different persons, starting with different ideas about the nature of virtue, naturally disagree about the practice of it.
>
> (*Politics*, Book VIII, ch. 2)

> Of all things that I have mentioned, that which contributes most to the permanence of constitutions (i.e. states) is the adaptation of education to the form of government. We laid it down that the end of politics is the highest good, and there is nothing that this science takes so much pains with as producing a certain character in the citizens, that is, making them good and able to do fine actions.
>
> (Quoted by I.L. Kandel in his *Studies in Comparative Education*, New York, 1935, p. 46)

ACKNOWLEDGEMENT

The writer wishes to express his debt especially to H. Avenarius and H. Heckel, A. Laaser, and to K. Nevermann and I. Richter for their pioneering and authoritative publications on the subject. They are not, of course, in any way responsible for the chapter's overall presentation, interpretations or additional contents. (See some of their seminal works in the References section below.) For the understanding of the intricacies of English law and education, the following three publications are useful.

CANS – Citizens Advice Note Service (1991), Vol. I, The National Council for Voluntary Organizations, London. All aspects of the School Curriculum (e.g. Foundation Subjects, secular curriculum, Collective Worship, Religious Education, etc.) are looked into in great detail. CANS Trust is an independent charitable trust established for the advancement of education and the relief of poverty. Its editors and contributors are barristers or legal experts.

The Head's Legal Guide (1991), Cromer Publications, London.

The Law of Education, Issue 19 (1992), Butterworths, London. (Published in 'binder' form which is constantly updated as new changes are made in Education Law by the Looseleaf Textbooks Department of Butterworth.)

REFERENCES

Avenarius, H. and Heckel, H. (1986). *Schulrechtskunde* (German School Laws) 6th edition. Darmstadt: Luchterhand.

Feeley, M. (1979). *Schools and the Courts*. Eugene, Oregon: University of Oregon.

van de Graaf, J.H. (1978). *Academic Power. Patterns of Authority in Seven National Systems of Higher Education*. New York: Praeger.

Greenberg, J. (1979). *Schools and the Courts*. Eugene, Oregon: University of Oregon.

Harris, W.T. (1903). The Separation of the Church from the Tax-supported School. *Educational Review*, 26: 222–35.

Hudgins, V.C. and Vacca, R.S. (1979). *Law and Education. Contemporary Issues and Court Decisions*. Charlottesville, Virginia: Michie.

Kirp, D.L. and Yudof, M.G. (1974). *Educational Policy and the Law. Cases and Materials*. Berkeley, California: McCutchan.

Laaser, A. (1980). *Die Verrechtlichung des Schulwesens* (The Legalization of the German School Provision). Max Planck Institut für Bildungsforschung. Bildung in der Bundesrepublik Deutschland. Rowohlt, Reinbek.

Lischka, C.N. (1929). Limitations of the Legislative Power to Compel Education. Catholic Educational Review, 27: 22–3.

Max Planck Institute for Public International Law (1970). *Judicial Protection against the Executive* (National Reports). Cologne: Heymann.

Nevermann, K. and Richter, I. (eds) (1983). *The Legacy of the Prussian Enlightenment: the State as Trustee of Education*. In: Max Planck Institute for Human Development and Education. Between Mass and Elite Education: the Current State and Recent Trends of Education in the FRG. Albany, New York: State University of New York Press.

Parsons, T. (1967). Some Ingredients of a General Theory of Formal Organisation. In: Halpin, A.W. (ed.) *Theory and Research in Administration*. New York: Macmillan.

Paulsen, F.R. (1957). Jurisprudence and Education. In: *Educational Administration and Supervision*, 43: 65–82.

Sislian, J. (1988). *British and German Industrial Designers: Education and Training*. London: Anglo-German Foundation. Salient points, legal and social, between British and German approaches to aspects of educational understanding are compared as background information for the book's main research topic.

Schweizerische Konferenz der Kantonaler Erziehungsdirektoren (OECD – Länderexamen Bildungspolitik), n.d. This is the first report on Swiss educational policy to be published by the OECD whose main aim was to attempt to delineate a Swiss national educational typology based on six Cantons. This report is an excellent introduction to various kinds of educational and vocational training facilities that currently obtain in Switzerland.

10 The education of prisoners

Tessa West

The task of education departments in prisons is to provide a variety of learning opportunities for prisoners: academic, artistic, recreational and vocational. Currently huge variations exist in this provision nationally and internationally, depending on policies, resources and the type, function and regime of each establishment. Increasing discussion of conditions in prison, coupled with a greater awareness of the need for constructive activities are steadily moving education to a more central position. A more holistic approach is being sought, in which the cooperation of prison officers is a crucial ingredient.

The particular circumstances of working in a prison demand flexibility on the part of the teaching staff in terms of response to the client group, curriculum and methods of delivery as well as awareness of security implications. A recent report of the European Committee of Ministers rightly directs attention to prison education because the prevention of crime and the treatment of offenders is an international issue. Education can and should play a significant role in the lives of prison inmates during and after their sentences.

One-third of a million people in the member states of the Council of Europe are in prison. Many of them have access to educational facilities, but there is room for improvement in each country. Ideally, every prisoner should be able to participate in adult education programmes similar to those outside prison. The costs of prison education are low compared to the total costs of running a secure residential establishment, and there is a real need to take action which will reduce the harmful effects of imprisonment, enhance daily life in custody and attempt to reduce rates of recidivism. An account of the current situation in England is outlined below although it should be noted that significant variations exist in this provision.

A useful starting point is 'the right to learn' as defined in the declaration adopted by the Fourth International UNESCO Conference on Adult Education; the right to read and write, the right to question and analyse, the right to imagine and create, the right to read one's own world and to write history, the right to have access to educational resources, the right to develop individual and collective skills. How can these rights be established in prisons?

Every prison in England and Wales has an education department, whose staff are currently Local Education Authority (LEA) employees. From 1 April 1993 this will not necessarily be the case, for the Home Office Prison Department has sought competitive tenders to provide educational services from that date, and it may be that some of the three-year contracts it awards will be to non-LEA tenderers. At present, however, most prison education depart- ments are constituent departments of local Further Education Colleges, and where this is so the principal of the college is the LEA representative and usually the line manager of the prison education officer. Where this is not so a senior member of the LEA responsible for post-16 work, or for adult education, is the person actually liaising with the prison education depart- ment. The salaries of the lecturers are paid by the LEA which is reimbursed by the Home Office. After 1993 this will change and sub-contractors will have different arrangements according to their own organization which will have agreed a price schedule in its contract.

The staff of education departments currently consist of a number of full-time personnel including several vocational training instructors who, confusingly, are employed as civil servants under quite different conditions of service. In addition, there is usually a large contingent of part-time teachers each of whom may work between two and twelve hours a week.

It is important to note at this point that a special training for those who teach offenders hardly exists in England, so teachers appointed to prisons come from varying professional experience, such as secondary schools, adult or special education. In the USA, however, working 'in corrections' is a specific category of education with its own training and literature.

HM Prison Service has a Chief Education Officer's Branch with regional Principal Education Officers. The role of this Branch in the post-1993 structure has not yet become clear, but it is likely to include monitoring, evaluating and advising, and its relationship with sub-contractors will be an ingredient in the effective delivery of educational services.

Both the programmes offered and the mode of student attendance may be full or part time. At most, therefore, a prisoner could be a full-time student working a 50-week year. At least, he/she could attend classes for only an hour or two each week, excluding the summer months, and subject to the availability of prison staff to supervise or escort. Educational pro-vision is just one of the components of prison life, or, more specifically, the prison regime. This regime is determined by planning between the Regional Director of the Home Office Prison Department and the Governor of each establishment. A contract is agreed in which is stated, in quantifiable terms, the provision the Governor aims to make in a given year. This covers every aspect of prison life, for example from the number of clothes changes to the number of visits, to a certain number of hours of physical education and of general education, and so on, available to a certain number of prisoners.

The actual educational provision in any prison is therefore determined by Home Office policy, the ethos the Governor wishes to develop in line with his/her regime contract in accordance with the type of prison, the resources available in both physical, staffing and financial terms, the Education Officer's own policies, and the type of prisoner. The practical influence of the LEA varies in practice from minimal to substantial.

Recent trends in discussion of penal issues have led to the increasing promotion of education and training within prisons, and a distinct shift from the marginalized position they previously held. This is for two reasons.

Current thinking emphasizes the need for prisoners to have purposeful and active regimes in order to avoid, at best, growing apathy and, at worst, violent eruptions. Activity used to exist in the shape of industry: sewing mail bags, or their modern counterpart, T-shirts. The Prison Service Industry and Farms Department of the Home Office is slow to respond to the changing needs of prisons. It is a lengthy and expensive task to update machinery so inmates are sometimes working with out-of-date equipment. This puts them at a disadvantage when trying to re-enter the labour market on release. In Hungary industrial enterprises build factories inside prison walls, and every inmate works a 40-hour week, producing real goods and earning a wage. This, however, is difficult to sustain in a recession. In Estonia, for example, recent political and economic upheaval and instability have combined to make production an impossibility, leading to dissatisfied and idle prisoners. Here in Britain work is provided which is usually repetitive, unskilled and for which the maximum wage is about £4.50 a week.

Simultaneously, there is far more interest in promoting an ethos in prisons which might be more effective in bringing about changes in the behaviour of inmates, either on a temporary basis, or, better still, in the longer term, thus reducing the high incidence of recidivism. Education is one of the ways in which this hope might be realized. There are some prisons in Denmark which are designated as 'Education' prisons, and newly convicted prisoners are given information and advice under a scheme known as the *Skadhauge* plan, in which they can opt for a prison career plan which is training centred.

Education is therefore increasingly seen as an alternative which is not only more responsive, cheaper and more flexible than industrial work, but has the huge advantage of being considered attractive and useful by prisoners and, most importantly, to policy makers. It is the task of the Education Officer to ensure that this opportunity for education does not become diluted into mere occupation.

Where traditionally there has been reluctance or even resistance on the part of prison officers towards education and its providers there is now movement in at least some prisons towards a much better level of acceptance and indeed support. It is essential to engage the interest and skills of discipline officers in promoting education on a prison-wide basis. Thus a holistic model is sought – and is being achieved – rather than an insular one. The strategies for developing this include encouraging prison staff to use the facilities available to prisoners (e.g. computers, library, art facilities, advice on courses in local colleges), and to contribute to the programme as part-time teachers. Cooperation with staff everywhere: in the Physical Education department, on the farm, in the kitchen and on the landings must be promoted if mutual mistrust between officers and teachers is to be dispelled. Teachers sometimes tend to think that they have a monopoly on caring and humanitarian values; such beliefs do great damage to relationships, for there must be support from civilian staff for the everyday work of officers, too. It is interesting to note that prison officers in some American and Dutch prisons no longer wear distinctive uniforms with military overtones. This brings about a reduction of perceived or actual disciplinary ways of working and usually improves relationships. This practice has now been adopted by the first UK privatized prison.

The range of classes and courses offered includes academic subject-based work at levels varying from adult basic education through the General Certificate of Secondary Education (GCSE – the solid core of teaching) to Open University examinations. Provision has to be made for students with special needs, and for speakers of other languages; 40 per cent of prisoners in Dutch prisons are not Dutch, 20 per cent of those in Swedish prisons are not Swedish and Estonian prisons run half their classes in Estonian and half in Russian. Few prisoners in England are truly illiterate, but many find it hard, for example, to write their own letters home.

The curriculum (not exclusively aimed at GCSE, Royal Society of Arts or other examinations) in many prisons is likely to include mathematics, English, modern languages, business studies, art and design, cookery, sociology, information technology and social and life skills. Not every prison teaches everything, which may cause problems when prisoners are transferred, but liaison between some different Education Departments is well established and individual programmes can often be continued.

Distance learning is also being used increasingly, and it is well known that some prisons are Open University centres. The average class size in England is usually between 8 and 10. In Sweden and Canada it is likely to be half that, while in the USA it could be 25 (West, 1991).

Classes of a more recreational nature, such as could be found at an adult education institute, are also taught. They are often run as evening classes, and include activities like yoga, guitar playing and drama. In the USA and Canada there is more emphasis on the correctional side, such as trying to reduce alcoholism, or gambling, or to improve cognitive skills. This is increasingly the case in the United Kingdom with much direction and participation from the prison staff rather than just education staff. In China ideology is a third of the prisoner's activity; the other two-thirds are labour and straight education. The Chinese claim an extremely low rate of recidivism, about 5 per cent, whereas in Britain it is about 70 per cent.

Vocational courses are an important part of the provision. Brick laying, painting and decorating, and motor mechanics are typical courses offered. They lead to City and Guilds certificates, and it is possible for inmates to obtain a National Record of Achievement as industrial lead bodies decide on levels of achievement for the National Vocational Qualifications. In countries where there is minimal educational input, there is usually at least vocational training, as for example in Nigeria.

The library, provided by the local library service and staffed by a professional librarian, usually on a part-time basis in conjunction with prison officers and inmate helpers, is managed by the Education Officer. There should be regular access for all prisoners who should be able to enjoy the same facilities as in any branch library: a wide book stock, microfiche, newspapers, general information and a book request service. The library is an ideal place in the prison to address multi-culturalism.

In the UK participation in any part of the educational provision is voluntary although this is not necessarily the case for young offenders, that is those under 21. It is compulsory for children under the statutory school leaving age, who may find themselves serving their sentences in very secure establishments. In the USA some prisons insist that prisoners complete their school education. This also happens in Hungary. Depending on the mode of delivery students either lethargically agree to be taught, or they enjoy and profit from it.

Inmates being received into a prison should be provided with some kind of induction programme, in which the opportunities for education and training are pointed out to them, and information given as to how to apply for courses. 'Being on education' is usually seen as an attractive option, albeit not necessarily for educational reasons. There is often a waiting list, which is to the disadvantage for those with shorter sentences who are sometimes near to being discharged when their name reaches the top of the list.

Prisoners 'on education' can, in some British prisons, be full-time students and receive a wage. At present this is about £3.00 a week, which is less than could be earned by someone in a workshop getting good piece rates, but as much as many other workers and more than those who are unemployed. It seems unlikely that any keen inmate is unable to afford becoming a student, though sometimes one who has been on classes for some time will say that he has accepted another job because it pays better wages.

It seems to be the case that most prisoners choose to attend classes because they wish to make the most of their sentence, to achieve something for themselves, to make up for the schooling they missed, or to have better opportunities in the future. It is also the case that some choose to do so because they prefer to be with civilians, to be with women (many teachers in prison are women), to avoid the social control they believe the prison workshops epitomize, and to enjoy what they hope will be an easy option. But many are choosing to take advantage of educational opportunities not despite being in prison, but precisely because of it.

There are activities which the Education Department staff promotes in cooperation with other prison staff. Plays and concerts are performed both by inmates or by visiting groups. Lectures and information giving sessions from educational or community groups are organized, often as part of a pre-release course. Community work takes place outside (e.g. riding for the disabled) and inside (e.g. Christmas parties for old age pensioners) the prison. The Council of Europe and United Nations' recommendations emphasize the need to involve the community in working with prisoners. GENEPI is an organization in France which uses university student volunteers to visit prisoners for discussions and practical work.

Particular features of prison life make running the Education Department a different task to its equivalent in mainstream work. The status and offending history and potential of the students mean that staff must be cautious over security issues. Tool checks are essential, materials and resources must be watched for abuse, elaborate loan and tally systems must be operated, and relationships cannot be completely open. Every step must be taken to ensure that the prison is a safe place for prisoners to live in, and for staff to work in. This is something agreed on by all prisons, whatever country they are in.

Inmates do not arrive in neat batches at the start of every education term – and it is unhelpful to even think about terms – or even months. There are new arrivals (and leavers) at least once a week, indeed it can be every day, and in order to keep numbers up to strength, a roll-on roll-off system is necessary. This produces difficulties for all examination classes, for it is almost impossible to forecast in advance which of any existing class will still be there on the day of an examination.

Stereotypically an 'average' inmate is believed to have low self-esteem, low intelligence, a poor educational history and additional social problems. The growing areas of drug and sex related crimes have actually changed this, and there are now people in prison from right across the social spectrum. Many of them have trade or professional qualifications and a good employment record, and, of course, many of those with poor literacy and numeracy skills have at least average levels of intelligence. In Scandinavia it is rare to find any inmates who are functional illiterates. This fact is discouraging to those educationalists who believe that if people learn to read and write they will somehow also learn how to live in society without breaking the law.

However, although the social profile of prison inmates has changed it is still true that society's most disadvantaged groups are over-represented in prison. An obvious example of this is the Black and Asian inmates who form about 12 per cent of the British prison population, but only 3 per cent of the national population. Interestingly, this percentage doubles in many education departments, for example 25 per cent of those attending classes are likely to be ethnic minorities, although the percentage in the prison as a whole is 12 per cent. In the USA, about 80 per cent of prisoners are Black or Hispanic. In Hungary, about 80 per cent of prisoners are gypsies. In New Zealand and Australia, it is the Maoris and Aborigines who are over-represented (Government of New Zealand, 1989). These ethnic disparities can produce difficulties. Staff and prisoners may display racist attitudes. In Britain it is not easy to find Black teachers – or Black prison officers – in some of the places where prisons are situated, or indeed at all.

The type of prison has an effect on how much education can be achieved. A local prison, or anywhere where prisoners are on remand, means that sustained participation in anything beyond eating, sleeping, receiving visits and being produced at court is almost impossible to achieve. Such prisons offer classes, but find it difficult to make long-term progress. Sex offenders are another group for whom it is difficult to provide equal opportunities. Because the main part of the prison is usually a no-go area for them their options are restricted, with the exception of distance learning.

A so far small but significant indicator for the future may be the effect of privatized prisons. The 1991 Criminal Justice Act enabled the British Government to contract out the management of prisons. The company managing the UK's first privatized prison, Wolds Remand Prison, has decided to sub-contract the provision of educational services to the Adult Education Service of the LEA. The contract it has with the Home Office stipulates a minimum entitlement of six hours of education a week for each prisoner. This is a very different approach to that described above and means that any prisoner who wishes can have immediate access to education, thus demanding an immediate response from the prison: a very positive move towards implementing UNESCO's recommendations for 'a right to learn'.

The essential task is to pursue the aims of education, broadly defined as the promotion of opportunities through which people can acquire skills, knowledge and understanding of themselves and the world, in an environment where the mission (or purpose) statement is:

> Her Majesty's Prison Service serves the public by keeping in custody those committed by the courts.

> Our duty is to look after them with humanity and to help them lead law-abiding and useful lives in custody and after release.

This task is achievable, in the sense that help can be given in many ways, of which education is only one. At least, it is – or should be – achievable in our society, although while there are buildings with architecture which does not lend itself to a variety of activities there will be difficulties. In developing countries which are still struggling to enable each child to complete primary school education, it cannot be achieved yet. Nor will much progress be made in a country where penal attitudes and policies are essentially punitive.

Education should help blur the edges between prison life and the rest of society, as long as it can be achieved without risk. Integration should be possible at some stage of a person's sentence. This will mean developing strategies for dealing with offending behaviour, with victims, and with prisoners' families. It may mean rethinking sentencing policies so that those people who need sheltered accommodation rather than barbed wire are catered for more economically and with a more positive end result.

Few prisoners are anarchists. Many of them are extremely conservative and claim that there must be laws, and that people should be punished if they break them. They agree to be imprisoned, and when in custody they live without trouble for the most part. They do not want their children to commit offences. If education can contribute to their being able to thrive in the world without recourse to crime, it is worth time, energy and resources. Changes in the law should mean that education is established as a right rather than as a privilege. For some people, it may be a better opportunity than they have ever had before.

APPENDIX A

UNITED NATIONS ECONOMIC AND SOCIAL COUNCIL – COMMITTEE ON
CRIME PREVENTION AND CONTROL
Eleventh session, Vienna, 5–16 February 1990 Agenda item 4.

IMPLEMENTATION OF THE CONCLUSIONS AND RECOMMENDATIONS
OF THE SEVENTH UNITED NATIONS CONGRESS ON THE PREVENTION
OF CRIME AND THE TREATMENT OF OFFENDERS
Draft resolution submitted by Cheng Weiqui (China), Roger S. Clark (New
Zealand), Dusan Cotic (Yugoslavia), Ramon de la Cruz Ochoa (Cuba), David
Faulkner (United Kingdom of Great Britain and Northern Ireland), Vasily P.
Ignatov (Union of Soviet Socialist Republics), Simone Andrée Rozès (France),
Abdel A. A. Shiddo (Sudan).

The Committee on Crime Prevention and Control recommends to the Economic and
Social Council the adoption of the following draft resolution:

Prison Education

The Economic and Social Council

Affirming the right of everyone to education, as enshrined in article 26 of the
Universal Declaration of Human Rights, and in articles 13, 14 and 15 of the
International Covenant on Economic, Social and Cultural Rights,

Recalling rule 77 of the Standard Minimum Rules for the Treatment of Prisoners,
which emphasizes, *inter alia*, that provision shall be made for the further education
of all prisoners capable of profiting thereby, that the education of illiterates and
young prisoners shall be compulsory and that the education of prisoners shall be
integrated with the educational system of the country so far as practicable,

Recalling also rule 22.1 of the United Nations Standard Minimum Rules for the
Administration of Juvenile Justice, which stresses that professional education,
in-service training, refresher courses and other appropriate modes of instruction
shall be utilized to establish and maintain the necessary professional competence of
all personnel dealing with juvenile cases and rule 26, which underlines the role of
education and vocational training for all juveniles in custody,

Bearing in mind the long-standing concern of the United Nations for the humani-
sation of criminal justice and the protection of human rights and the importance of
education in the development of the individual and the community,

Bearing in mind also that human dignity is an inherent, inviolable quality of every
human being and a pre-condition for education, aiming at human development of
the whole personality,

Bearing in mind further that 1990, the year that the Eighth United Nations Congress
on the Prevention of Crime and the Treatment of Offenders meets, is also the
International Literacy Year, the objectives of which are directly relevant to the
individual needs of prisoners,

Noting with appreciation the significant efforts made by the United Nations, in
the preparation for the Eighth Congress, to give more recognition to prison
education,

1 Recommends that Member States, relevant institutions, educational counselling services and other organizations should promote prison education, *inter alia*, by:
   (a) Providing penal institutions with educators and accompanying services and raising the educational level of prison personnel;
   (b) Developing professional selection procedures and training of staff, and supplying the necessary resources and equipment;
   (c) Encouraging the provision and expansion of educational programmes for offenders in and outside prisons;
   (d) Developing education suitable to prisoners' needs and abilities, and in conformity with society's demands;

2 Also recommends that Member States:
   (a) Should provide various types of education that would contribute to crime prevention and the resocialization of prisoners, such as literacy education, vocational training, continuing education for updating knowledge, higher education and other programmes that promote the human development of prisoners;
   (b) Should consider the increased use of alternatives to imprisonment and measures for the social resettlement of prisoners with a view to facilitating their education and reintegration into society;

3 Further recommends that Member States in developing educational policies, should take into account the following principles:
   (a) Education in prison should aim at developing the whole personality, bearing in mind the prisoner's social, economic and cultural context;
   (b) All prisoners should have access to education, including literacy programmes, basic education, vocational training, creative and cultural activities, physical education and sports, social education, higher education and library facilities;
   (c) Every effort should be made to encourage the prisoner to participate actively in all aspects of education;
   (d) All those involved in prison administration and management should facilitate and support education as much as possible;
   (e) Education should have no less of a status than work within the prison regime, and prisoners should not lose financially or otherwise by taking part in educational programmes;
   (f) Vocational education should aim at the greater development of the individual, as well as being sensitive to trends in the labour market;
   (g) Creative and cultural activities should be given a significant role since they have special potential in enabling prisoners to develop and express themselves;
   (h) Wherever possible, prisoners should be allowed to participate in education outside the prison;
   (i) Where education has to take place within the prison, the outside community should be involved as fully as possible;
   (j) The necessary funds, equipment and teaching staff should be made available to enable prisoners to receive appropriate education;

4 *Urges* the United Nations Educational, Scientific and Cultural Organization and its International Bureau of Education, in co-operation with the regional commissions, the interregional and regional institutes in crime prevention and

criminal justice, the specialized agencies and other entities within the United Nations system, other intergovernmental organizations concerned and non-governmental organizations in consultative status with the Economic and Social Council, to become actively involved in this process;

5 *Requests* the Secretary-General, subject to the availability of extra-budgetary funds:
   (a) To develop a set of guidelines and a manual on prison education that would provide the necessary basis for the further development of prison education and would facilitate the exchange of expertise and experience on this aspect of penitentiary practice among Member States;
   (b) To convene an international expert meeting on prison education, with a view to formulating action-oriented strategies in this area, with the co-operation of the interregional and regional institutes for crime prevention and criminal justice and the specialized agencies of the United Nations and other concerned intergovernmental organizations and non-governmental organizations in consultative status with the Economic and Social Council;

6 Also requests the Secretary-General to inform the Committee on Crime Prevention and Control, at its twelfth session, on the results of his endeavours in this area;

7 Invites the Eighth United Nations Congress on the Prevention of Crime and the Treatment of Offenders and the Committee on Crime Prevention and Control, at its twelfth session, to consider the question of prison education.'

APPENDIX B

COUNCIL OF EUROPE COMMITTEE OF MINISTERS

RECOMMENDATION No. R (89) 12 OF THE COMMITTEE OF MINISTERS TO MEMBER STATES ON EDUCATION IN PRISON
(Adopted by the Committee of Ministers on 13 October 1989 at the 429th meeting of the Ministers' Deputies)

The Committee of Ministers, under the terms of Article 15b of the Statute of the Council of Europe,

Considering that the right to education is fundamental;

Considering the importance of education in the development of the individual and the community;

Realising in particular that a high proportion of prisoners have had very little successful educational experience, and therefore now have many educational needs;

Considering that education in prison helps to humanise prisons and to improve the conditions of detention;

Considering that education in prison is an important way of facilitating the return of the prisoner to the community;

Recognising that in the practical application of certain rights or measures, in accordance with the following recommendations, distinctions may be justified between convicted prisoners and prisoners remanded in custody;

Having regard to Recommendation No. R (87) 3 on the European Prison Rules and Recommendation No. R (81) 17 on adult education policy,

Recommends the governments of Member States to implement policies which recognise the following:

1 All prisoners shall have access to education, which is envisaged as consisting of classroom subjects, vocational education, creative and cultural activities, physical education and sports, social education and library facilities;
2 Education for prisoners should be like the education provided for similar age-groups in the outside world, and the range of learning opportunities for prisoners should be as wide as possible;
3 Education in prison shall aim to develop the whole person bearing in mind his or her social, economic and cultural context;
4 All those involved in the administration of the prison system and the management of prisons should facilitate and support education as much as possible;
5 Education should have no less a status than work within the prison regime and prisoners should not lose out financially or otherwise by taking part in education;
6 Every effort should be made to encourage the prisoner to participate actively in all aspects of education;
7 Development programmes should be provided to ensure that prison educators adopt appropriate adult education methods;
8 Special attention should be given to those prisoners with particular difficulties and especially those with reading or writing problems;
9 Vocational education should aim at the wider development of the individual, as well as being sensitive to trends in the labour-market;
10 Prisoners should have direct access to a well-stocked library at least once a week;
11 Physical education and sports for prisoners should be emphasised and encouraged;
12 Creative and cultural activities should be given a significant role because these activities have particular potential to enable prisoners to develop and express themselves;
13 Social education should include practical elements that enable the prisoner to manage daily life within the prison, with a view to facilitating his return to society;
14 Wherever possible, prisoners should be allowed to participate in education outside prison;
15 Where education has to take place within the prison, the outside community should be involved as fully as possible;
16 Measures should be taken to enable prisoners to continue their education after release;
17 The funds, equipment and teaching staff needed to enable prisoners to receive appropriate education should be made available.

REFERENCES

Biles, D. (ed.) (1988). *Current International Trends in Corrections*. The Federation Press, Sydney.
Council of Europe (1989). *Committee of Ministers: Recommendation No. R (89) 12 – Education in Prisons*. Strasbourg.

Council of Europe (1990). *Legal Affairs Report – Education in Prison*. Strasbourg.

Dunbar, I. (1985). *'Sense of Direction'*. Home Office, London.

Further Education Staff College (1990). 'Developments in Prison Service Education and Training'. *Coombe Lodge Report*. Coombe Lodge, Bristol.

Government of New Zealand (1989). 'Te Ara Hou: the New Way', *Prison Review*, Wellington.

Little, McAllister (1989). 'A Right Liberty'. *Butler Trust*, London.

UN Committee on Crime Prevention and Control (1990). *Draft Resolution: Prison Education*. UN Economic and Social Council.

West, T. (1989). 'A New Education Department in a New English Prison', *Journal of Correctional Education*, Vol. 40, Issue 2.

West, T. (1991). 'Curriculum Development in a Prison Education Department', *Correctional Education Yearbook 1991*, S. Duguid (ed.), Simon Fraser University, Vancouver.

West, T. (1992). 'Out of Prison – into Society', *Social Work Monograph*, Norwich.

11 Education for citizenship: school life and society - British-European comparisons

Witold Tulasiewicz

INTRODUCTION

The impact of legislation upon education is usually perceived to operate on the macro-level of state intervention in matters such as compulsory school attendance or the legal age for juvenile employment. This is perhaps particularly so in the United Kingdom, where the teacher had traditionally been seen as in possession of the 'freedom of the classroom', and where the interplay of legislation and politics and the other interests affecting the school curriculum in the twentieth century have been slow to become uncovered (Lawton, 1984; see also Lawton, 1992; Aselmeier *et al.*, 1985; Kron, 1989).

Citizenship and citizenship education have been a component of the school curriculum in most nation states whenever there was a need to remind citizens of their allegiance to their country, and as such subject to control on security grounds, and a variety of interpretations ranging from the inculcation of ideology and specific civic duties – as in the former communist states, where in the German Democratic Republic *Staatsbuergerkunde* was a compulsory part of the school curriculum in years 7 and above – to the simple mention of citizenship among the aims of education in the United Kingdom coupled with a warning against making it the supreme end of education by 'erecting the State into an august symbol of worship' (Findlay, 1928). While in Britain there has always been a measure of distrust of the macro-state and its influence, in countries such as France or the United States with a more clearly defined concept of republican citizen- ship, both formal and informal teaching of contemporary history and institutions can be linked with reminders of a patriotic education often equated with a civic education. Although this is not entirely unknown in Britain in times of crisis, with civic groups and committees exhorting the subject to do his duty to his sovereign and country, the Report of the Speaker's Commission on Citizenship (*Encouraging Citizenship*, RCC 1990) with its recommendations was an innovation.

SOME DEFINITIONS

Because of the varieties of emphases given and the different status and scope of legislation in curriculum terms it is not easy to identify *education for citizenship* in narrow terms. In the Federal Republic of Germany the recommendations for schooling of the standing committee of Ministers of Education (1969 *Kultusministerkonferenz*) recognize 'the demands made on young people as citizens *(Buerger)* to be capable to accept . . . certain responsibilities', but the texts continue with explicit mention of 'rights and duties . . . in *society*' *(Wahrnehmung von Rechten und Pflichten in der Gesellschaft).* In the declaration *(Erklaerung)* made by the aforementioned committee of Ministers of Education in 1973, no exact civic reference to the Federal Republic appears in the section: *Aufgabe der Schule.* This is in contrast to the right to a socialist education in the German Democratic Republic where according to Article 25 of the *Zweite Verfassung der Deutschen Demokratischen Republik* (1968) pupils were expected to dedicate themselves fully to service to the community *(Dienst der Gemeinschaft des Volkes)* of the 'democratic' Germany. The duties of citizens of the German Democratic Republic (and the term *Buerger* is very explicit) were frequently referred to, society being that of the new republic after the earlier era of exploitation and oppression. This can be seen for example in the *Gesetz ueber das einheitliche sozialistische Bildungssystem* of 1965 and especially explicitly in the communication about military education *(Mitteilung zur Wehrerziehung)* of 1963 issued jointly by the Ministry of People's Education and the Central Committee of the Association for Sport and Technology in the German Democratic Republic (GDR). French educational legislation also provides for citizenship as an integral part of the school curriculum, the *annexe (Bulletin Officiel,* no. 44 of 12 xii 1985) to the decree *(arrêté)* of 14 November 1985 lists 'love of the (French) Republic', *(l'amour de la République)* as part of education for democracy, law and order. In the United Kingdom the 1990 Speaker's Commission on Citizenship submitted 'Outline Conclusions . . . to the National Curriculum Council' on 'Learning to be a Citizen' and 'The Place of Citizenship Within the Curriculum'.

To the national legislation must now be added the Resolution on the European Dimension in Education (Resolution of 24 May 1988 (88/c 177/02) of the Council of the European Communities, with 'European citizenship' a part of the dimension. This resolution, with some reservations according to article 126 of the Maastricht Treaty, is binding on member states of the European Community. An earlier initiative had been taken by the Committee of Ministers of the Council of Europe in 1983 (R (8) 4 and R (85)7) (Tulasiewicz, 1993; see also Department of Education and Science, 1992).

The syllabus details will inevitably vary not only between different countries but also in the same country at different times, emphasizing a more or less national education, whether it is in Europe or outside Europe. In the United States we note Dewey's acquisition of 'dispositions' through 'education which holds the key to orderly social reconstruction', in his *Quest for Certainty.*

It is possible briefly to sum up education for citizenship as social and political education through knowledge of the law, where the state *may have little or no jurisdiction* over the actual teaching materials and styles used. In France there is specific reference to the limits of ministerial powers in this respect, so that the programmes themselves in most cases provide an outline syllabus only. It is necessary therefore to distinguish between the general formulations and the actual teaching practice within a particular school structure to obtain a more complete picture of what citizenship education really entails. Brief working definitions of the terms *civics, education for citizenship, political education* and *(personal and) social education* applied to the teaching of 'citizenship studies' may be useful.

Civics may be taken to refer to concise factual instruction about a country's constitution and its system of government, as in the English Advanced Level subject 'British Constitution', either as a discrete element or referred to in teaching other parts of the school curriculum, such as history. Such instruction may on occasion also be available elsewhere, for example outside polling stations during elections, or indeed during mock elections organized in schools. *Education for citizenship* is taken to mean a more ambitious programme which may be taught as part of school pupils' *moral* or *personal and social education* (PSE) and which attempts to instil values as well as skills which enable them to *function* as educated members of civic society. An account of society itself is usually provided in such courses, which may also be part of other subjects of the curriculum, like history or geography. A Department of Education and Science (now the Department For Education) definition of PSE refers to 'the ability to make choices sensibly in the light of available evidence' (DES, *Curriculum Matters No.14*) which implies an *educational* stance. *Political education* informs about the political nature of society. This includes the family, and the school, and by concentrating on controversial issues sets out to enable pupils to make use of their critical faculties and negotiating skills. It attempts to tackle questions such as how people align themselves on issues and why. *Political education* as *political literacy* teaches the use of political procedures and the skills to understand the meaning of messages received and to prepare and communicate one's own. In some English schools the term *communication* is used for lessons about contemporary society and the skill of reading texts. This was the content of *political competence* defined in a 1977 Her Majesty's Inspectorate document (Curriculum 11–16, DES/HMI, 1977). *Social Studies* refers to a study of society which may include discussions about 'what it is like to be a citizen', often without the literacy or communication skills required elsewhere.

The definitions overlap, since as taught at school all of the above themes are concerned with preparing the young for life in their own society. However, it is important to distinguish between education and instruction according to *how* the curriculum is delivered.

A short course which informs is often reduced to instruction. On the other hand, the transmission of values though intended as education may degenerate into *indoctrination*. Since schools have traditionally served the interests of the ruler, who may also have been the school's founder, and his state, their main task was turning out obedient or at least loyal citizens ready to work in his service. Church schools served a similar purpose.

Like other parts of schooling, civics/citizenship or political education *socializes* the young into the society in which the school is located. The term is used openly in France, but has less currency in Britain. World or global education which transcends the nation state is a relatively new development and not taught in all countries. Socialization does not appear as one of its aims. The situation is compounded by the fact that societies as states are not identical, the detailed workings of democracies like France or the United Kingdom are very different, and civic education will differ considerably as a consequence. Literature on topics like society, democracy, citizenship and the study of the school curriculum confirm the difficulty of distinguishing among *instruction, education, socialization* and *indoctrination*. Only a course which will teach about society and present different viewpoints will *educate* the pupil rather than *instruct* him. A simple transmission of values is akin to catechetical instruction, an approach which may only be appropriate in the initial stages of a course intended for the younger age groups.

SOME ASSUMPTIONS

The first assumption of citizenship education, whether it is taught as a discrete subject, as in France, or as a theme across the curriculum, as practised in England and Wales, is that it aims to prepare the learner to live in society, in community with others. This poses the question as to the nature of society or community into which socialization is undertaken. The lack of an exact, agreed definition of terms like 'community' or 'society', let alone the extent of 'world' or 'rights', and the width of the concept of 'citizen' complicates the fixing of boundaries. Applied to membership of political units which do not have a government in the sense that sovereign states do in the West, 'citizen' may be the wrong term altogether. If a different allegiance attaches to the recently coined 'European Citizen' (as in Citizens' Europe), how do the civic duties and rights of a 'world citizen' differ from those of a citizen of a European or American nation state? The nature of the imperative behind the concept of 'community', for example in a 'community of writers' or the 'community of first nations' (in Canada), has to be grasped to see what membership of one entails.

Socialization presupposes the recognition of the potential for conflict, whether between individuals or between authority and individuals, which requires a peaceful resolution. This assumes agreement on the curtailment of certain liberties, entailing submission to laws, in return for which society offers the individual enjoyment of a variety of rights. There is a problem of scale between a small community and a nation state, but in either case socialization is not expected to be imposed by force. The necessary legislation should be negotiated and contracts freely entered into. Since one usually becomes a citizen by being born into a society one is presented with a definition of citizenship, in other words the citizenship course prescribes what one does *do* to function as a citizen.

Citizenship education will distinguish between rights which can be bestowed directly, for example civil or political rights of a state, and human rights, some of which may not automatically be enforceable outside the juridical competence of a state unless acknowledged and the conventions adopted by the government. Given the growing convergence and collaboration of states, whether through supranational organizations like the United Nations or the Council of Europe or through economic/political units like the European Community or the North American Free Trade Association, relations between individuals in society and whole societies are increasingly being played out in the context of more than one country. Concern with the environment seeks to extend the application of rights and duties worldwide. This would assume that citizenship education courses in different countries are taking these developments on board, and that this is reflected in the wider contents of courses to include universal and human rights and comparisons made with the legal situation in different societies.

No citizenship course should exclude a discussion of the distinction between freedom and anarchy, aptly presented by one of the first English school inspectors Matthew Arnold in a cultural context, and by the German poet Goethe in his dramatic hero Egmont in a wider political sense. Teaching about society must therefore present the outcomes of actions undertaken.

The learning process itself is facilitated and the citizen at the end of the course is improved by the inclusion of *procedural attitudes*, like tolerance or reasonableness (Stradling, 1978; Crick and Porter, 1981) which make for a rational dimension to living with others without compromising one's convictions. Moral interpretation of values and the discussion of moral and sociopolitical codes in citizenship education are both found in courses like Moral Education (in continental Europe) or Personal and Social Education (in the United Kingdom) to fulfil some of the aspects at least of an education for citizenship.

However desirable a particular society or model of society may appear to the educator (or indeed pupil), no dogmatic comments by the educator can be allowed (Council of Europe R (85)7). The objective of the course is to educate the pupil to keep an open mind, to 'believe with a doubt' (Russell), and the educator must encourage the search for truth, rather than claim to be presenting the truth at every opportunity. Only an honest statement of teaching aims by the teacher will produce honest learners. This presupposes a classroom ethos where discussions of intent are possible. In the 1960s the model of the *'neutral teacher'* whose teaching accepts the principle of 'balance' was advocated for the teaching of controversial issues (Stenhouse, 1970). Some features of this model may be applicable for the teaching of citizenship, using principles like impartiality. The procedural skills, too, will help in the increasingly multicultural context of schooling. In view of the cross-disciplinary nature of citizenship education, drawing on history and geography, including topics like health and safety, or service to the consumer, there is much resource material that can be used in teaching. It is important therefore to make an unbiased selection. This is not a realistic option in many citizenship studies courses worldwide.

Certain types of school community encourage an acceptable mode of presentation. Laws are not presented in long lists, in isolation from their societal, national or international contexts, which makes their presentation dry and boring. With human rights accepted as the ethical base for civic education, pupils are made to face the wider human context at the same time as being taught to be citizens of their own country. Republican citizenship may have made the concept of citizenship more transparent in a qualified way, but attempts to confine courses to one society are irrational, although imposing limits may make teaching and learning easier. With civic instruction advocated as necessary to achieve desirable citizenship ends, the complexity of the course will take account of the age of the pupils and the time allocated to the teacher.

Since the school is accepted as the mouthpiece of its commissioning society, demonstrated particularly clearly in the school curricula of countries with a non-Western style of government, genuine curriculum reform can only be effected if the reformer has the power to do so. This is a point often forgotten by enthusiastic curriculum planners. A reminder about 'the art of the possible' (Heater, 1990) must therefore precede any curriculum development proposals which may be implied in this chapter.

THE NEED FOR CITIZENSHIP EDUCATION – NEW DEVELOPMENTS IN THE CONTENTS OF COURSES

After the Second World War, with the immediate threat of Fascist or Communist domination removed, the urgency for education for democracy and freedom had disappeared. In Britain, where civics was identified with these more general aims, there were to begin with mixed responses affecting the fortunes of politics or citizenship studies or pupils' school councils (Porter, 1983). In a number of European countries citizenship courses had become subsumed under social studies courses, the discrete citizenship element less to the fore. The arrival of a variety of new factors has complicated the simple socialization process. The responses in nation states have been different. In the long run, simple instruction may not necessarily be the most appropriate solution.

1   The decline of the welfare state and the emergence of a multitude of private initiatives has brought to the fore the strong nationalism of its proponents. The greater involvement of many individuals, especially in matters affecting the welfare of the community, requires the preparation of differently qualified and motivated people to replace the state, with the preparation undertaken by different agents altogether. Many of the young must be reminded more of their civic duties and obligations than of their social rights.

2   The fast growing immigration particularly into the countries of the 'Western' world and the general mobility of populations requires the education of an increasingly more multicultural school population against racism and for tolerance, in mixed groups of members previously unknown or little known to each other.

3   The rise of supranational political units, like the European Community with its free movement of people including students, as well as the changing demography of established, more homogeneous nation states in receipt of waves of immigrants, require an education which accounts for interdependence rather than dependence.

4   International structures require the training of a multicultural work-force and the education for international understanding of people who would see themselves as world citizens, while the changing economic structures and the poor economic performance of many countries require the training of a more diversely qualified citizenry.

5   The growing concern posed by the abrogation of human rights in many societies, the worldwide destruction of the ecology, the multiple conflicts which lead to escalating poverty, health and education problems, require an education which has been variously described as human rights, global, ecological, developmental or peace education. The accelerating

crime rate especially among the young requires the education of responsible and committed citizens. This has been finding an echo in civic education also.

6 The growing dissatisfaction with the performance of educational services is another factor calling for curriculum reform and *inter alia* for the introduction of a more widely conceived citizenship education component.

There are variables across the sets (1) to (6).

The sociopolitical realities sketched above can be perceived as either:

1 A threat to the established order in societies due to the loss of at least some of their values, or
2 An impulse towards the creation of a new order, for example in the context of the European Community, requiring the reaffirmation of additional values.

Either scenario requires a civic education of a new, stimulating kind, still largely absent in schools including those of the European Community, and shows the need for socialization to help to meet the challenges.

The contents of citizenship education courses in the school curriculum have varied according to the acceptance of the priorities of the criteria discussed above. Often education which assumed the form of imparting basic facts about the duties of its citizens and their political rights, especially as far as using the right to vote is concerned, was deemed sufficient. In the United States the use of ritual which emphasizes the element of patriotic socialization implicit or explicit in citizenship courses has been deliberately excluded from post-war social science syllabuses in the German Federal Republic. But the patriotic stance is practised by explicit order of the government in countries like Taiwan or Singapore, reinforced in school subjects like history, geography or teaching the mother tongue, a process encouraged in countries where the state government or church are involved in prescribing teaching guidelines. In the case of the National Curriculum (1988) in England and Wales, central government and its many new agencies like the Schools Examinations and Assessment Council, its members appointed rather than elected, have become heavily involved in revising syllabuses. In the case of 'a predominantly Christian' Religious Education the decisions have actually gone against established Church policy. In the case of the English syllabus they went against the professionals. The acknowledgement of pluralism, especially when values become involved, makes citizenship education a more difficult and tricky task than simple induction.

Even so, in most democracies the contents and mode of presentation usually leave the road open for some pupils at least to be *educated* in citizenship, that is to learn about alternatives, as suggested in the PSE document referred to at the beginning of this chapter. This practice has probably increased with the 'shrinking world'. The mass migration of peoples requires courses at least partly to reflect the multicultural nature of society (Cambridge University, Department of Education 1992), and the introduction of courses on human rights in an international context. Legislation and advice to this effect is available in member states of the European Community. For a British example, see the National Curriculum Council *Guidance*, 1991; in France there is the Hannoun Report of November 1987 to the French Government, '*L'homme est l'espérance de l'homme*' which made 53 recommendations. The difficulty is that awareness of world problems or tolerance of others may not be associated with the same intensity of commitment as socialization into a clearly defined civil unit.

The 'global' courses springing up in the wake of current world developments are not normally available in the form of simple 'patriotic kits'. Often the organizations which inspired them had no legal power to enforce them, even though they may be acceptable in the general climate of public opinion, with or without specific government encouragement. For reasons of expediency and simplicity as well as political ideology, the swing still tends towards the model of preparing the dutiful citizen in receipt of transmitted information on which he or she can act promptly, rather than encouraged to examine it in detail, so as the better to question it and to demand change (Slater, 1991). This is often the fate of popular programmes like global education. Increasingly, some become a part of citizenship education in a nation state. It is the right thing then to help the hungry or to show concern at the widening hole in the ozone layer, but this may be accompanied by less prominence accorded to those aspects of civic society likely to be regarded as potential threats to the preservation of the *status quo* at home (developed from Durkheim, 1925). Citizenship education courses themselves may be regarded as such a threat in societies on both the right and left wings of the political spectrum. There may be particular reluctance to the provision of full citizenship *education* for those likely to demand more radical change (Brownhill and Smart, 1989). Three different civic systems into which pupils can be socialized in Western democracies will be referred to in a later section.

Teachers' individual or professional rights in the delivery of the curriculum are also affected by legislation. In England and Wales only those teaching in maintained schools have to teach the National Curriculum as published. It is possible for teachers to concentrate more or less on the issues outlined. That they are subject to assessment, as is the legal position in England and Wales, rather limits this freedom. In France and in Germany as well as in most other European countries the curriculum prescribes a fixed number of hours to be given to all subjects, including citizenship studies. Assessment may take a different form.

Crick and Porter (1978) address the three political attitudes: acknowledgement *of*, participation *in* and desire *for change* in the status quo which arise in political education courses. This impacts the work done by teachers with pupils in citizenship studies and their nature, which are about society as it is. Sideglances at what it was like or what it could or should be can also be present.

Socialization achieved through the simple transmission of values is characterized by a predominantly static (approval of the status quo) and local (confined to one society) approach. It is possible to see a good citizen as one who operates within his community making use of his rights while going about his duties without giving it another thought. The nature of a global and human rights education approach on the other hand determines that the best practice is dynamic, it is freer to draw attention to the *need* for change when using a broader canvas. The 'art of the possible' in citizenship education would attempt to combine the best of the two in an act of *controlled* change. 'Human Rights' recognizes the preservation of existing rights where already available while calling for change in societies where they are not. Global and human education approaches may be seen as providing education presenting alternatives rather than instruction and simple socialization, the latter explicitly discouraged in French programmes. This is facilitated by the use of complex programmes, the inclusion of moral, personal and social, philosophical, religious, civic and other school subject elements, presented in the form of themes for discussion and debate. It is worth continuing to examine the potential of cross-curricular themes in this light, as was attempted for PSE in *Curriculum Matters*.

The European Dimension in Education contains ingredients which demonstrate both the static and dynamic qualities. The citizen of Europe, still to emerge, will be expected to identify with Europe, take part in the economic and social development of Europe, as well as becoming involved in more global concerns. It is a measure of the changing priorities and definitions of education that citizenship studies are beginning to include human rights, peace and environmental education. A discussion of the implications of the European contents appears in Tulasiewicz (1993). European citizenship seems to be developing differently from existing citizenships: social and civic rights (cf. the Social Chapter in the Maastricht Treaty) appear before European political rights. The usual civic pattern has been for citizens' social rights to arrive last, and to disappear first! (Roche, 1992).

This development indicates a significant change and extension of the term 'citizen', with implications for citizenship education in schools. It is also an area which has been largely untested, legislation being too diffuse for interpretation in nation states, although a number of human rights are currently being tested before the European Court.

TEACHING CITIZENSHIP (CONTENTS AND METHODS) IN SCHOOL

A survey of citizenship education conducted by the author in seven schools in the European Community (Tulasiewicz, 1990) revealed that work had been mainly of the *cognitive* type, imparting knowledge of facts and emphasizing values in formal lessons, encouraged by the practice of isolating the discrete 'citizenship' component in more general social science or current affairs courses, with prescribed syllabuses as in most German *Länder*. Not very dissimilar findings have come from two schools in East Anglia and several schools in the Paris region (the latter researched by Eliane Monconduit (1991), with pupils responding in stereotypes and with little constructive citizenship thought, also in response to unduly cognitive approaches. This one-dimensional approach, found boring by a large majority of pupils, may have gone a little way to train the unthinking but law-abiding citizen; it did not do much to encourage the reflecting, articulate participant capable of considering controlled reform.

Although knowledge of details of political party programmes or achievements may constitute a component in the French courses, political education does not feature, since details are not usually presented as the result of a conflict of interests. In England and Wales the Education (No. 2) Act of 1986 forbids the presentation of political party programmes to younger age groups altogether. There is the danger that problems are presented as awaiting a charitable solution rather than being made the object of reflection. Pupils get involved in enthusiastic acts of fund raising without much of an idea as to the exact reason for the need for their generosity. It is clear that a different moral game of duties is being played out here from one which involves the use of civic social rights. Citizenship education and political education cannot be kept separate without damage to both.

Cognitive teaching may be relieved by simulated civic and political practical activity, such as mock elections or the encouragement of directed student activity, such as fund raising or visiting the sick. In these school-sponsored activities, which often they do not find themselves, young people of school age often exercise minimal decision-making functions. Meaningful involvement in functions and responsibilities outside the school community decided exclusively by pupils is rare. The disbursement of the paltry sum of £200 to be decided by the school council quoted by

Edwards and Fogelman (*Citizenship in School*, 1991), is typical. In the former Yugoslavia, under the Self-Management constitution, school pupils over the age of 16 were deemed capable of being responsible for their own progress at school (Tulasiewicz, 1979), so that no parents' evenings were necessary for this age group. They were not *politically* active since the system in the country precluded the *choice* of political views. However, in a limited respect young people could learn by practice to judge on some of their priorities for themselves.

Practical involvement, the skills side of pupils' learning is said to be widely accepted and encouraged, especially in Britain, but this is revealed to consist mainly (90 per cent!, cf. *Encouraging Citizenship*, Appendix E, RCC, 1990) of the fund raising activities already mentioned. The recommendation of the Taylor Committee (Taylor, 1977) that pupils over 16 should be eligible to serve as school governors was not implemented under the 1980 Education Act or any subsequent legislation. Though the various participatory schemes in running the school may occasionally (ca. 8–9 per cent, Appendix E, RCC, 1990) allow pupils the political right of consultation, this still leaves them politically disenfranchised when it comes to decision making. Not being involved in making school rules which directly affect them for example cuts pupils off from involvement in school organization as opposed to school activities. British pupils are less in evidence in non-school sponsored, out of school community activities of their own choosing, than their French or German contemporaries (Tulasiewicz, 1990). Implications of this for citizenship will be developed later.

EXCURSUS ON CITIZENSHIP

Dewey's recognition, without recourse to the Marxist view of the link between education and politics, that 'education will vary with the quality of life which prevails in a group' (Dewey, 1961) may be taken to argue that the status of representative democracy in a country will impact the nature of its citizenship courses.

In the Western world pupils are broadly socialized into one of the three civic systems, viz. *republican*, of the kind associated with being established after a revolution, *liberal*, where citizenship is an entitlement to enjoy rights while law making and administration are someone else's business, the citizen's business being private, and *discursive*, which acknowledges equally the rights *and* duties and a knowledge of the activities performed by an informed, educated electorate enabling it to participate politically through a process of practical argumentation in associations (Habermas, 1990; see also Kreide, 1992).

The French and North American models can be seen clearly to fulfil the criteria of the liberal system; the British probably only partly. The third is often canvassed, but remains an ideal.

The status of British citizens who are *subjects* of the monarch, and whose rights and duties are residual in that they are not explicitly stated in a constitution or a bill of rights but are those which Parliament had not determined that they should be curtailed, differs from that of their fellow Europeans. Individual freedom in Britain being vulnerable to any subsequent enactment of Parliament the individual is often concerned not with the areas which Parliament has 'left alone', but with challenging the extent to which the authorities encroach on rights which the individual thought he had. The validity of legislation, moreover, unlike in other democracies, cannot be challenged in the UK courts (Gardner, 1990). Though non-adherent to the European Convention on protecting citizens' rights, the United Kingdom has granted the right to *individuals* directly to petition the European Commission of Human Rights which has led to legislation in the case of corporal punishment in schools.

Prominent in the current British debate on citizenship is the emphasis on participation in voluntary activity (RCC, 1990), which has no parallel in other countries. This does not take sufficient account of the fact that the control of the purse is voluntary only to a limited extent, creating a distinctive stratification of citizens. The spate of Citizen's Charters which came in the wake of the Report outline the rights to financial compensation for the failure of services provided. This accords rather uncomfortably with all the voluntary activity advocated.

In Germany not all those living there are in possession of full citizenship rights, a situation which the European Commission seeks partly to change by allowing all inhabitants to vote in local elections. Because immigrants enjoy the protection of human rights, however, they can participate in civil rights indirectly by joining full citizens in assemblies (Articles 19 and 20 of the Universal Declaration of Human Rights) which may ultimately aim at political rights.

The fact that in many democracies which have become multicultural people live in a much greater cultural, economic and political proximity to each other widens their socioeconomic and cultural outlook. Developments in 'European Citizenship' encourage this happening. In Britain the position occupied by the personal monarch tends to concentrate the focus on the national aspects of citizenship.

THE SURRENDER VALUE OF CITIZENSHIP EDUCATION COURSES

Two questions may now be asked:

1 Does the socialization/education they receive enable and encourage young people actually to participate in their democracies?
2 Do they become citizens at the end of their citizenship studies course?

Most teachers, including those with civil servant status in the European Community, can be expected to transmit the information, values and practices which accord with those of their society's establishment. The *contents* alone, however, may fail to deliver if the methods used by teachers are unsuitable.

The traditional type of cognitive and affective methods of citizenship studies have not always succeeded in instilling the basic fundamental civic values of fairness and reciprocity. There is evidence that many young people do not act as citizens. This is not only so at the macro level, that is involvement in government, but also in active commitment at the micro level of community life. There is not only reluctance on the part of adolescents (especially those aged 14–19) to become involved, their distrust of and inability to work with the agents representing the various sociopolitical structures of their society, but widespread total rejection of society and authority, paradoxically often to establish strongly authoritarian structures of their own. Young people, and not only the young, opt out in order to join in anti-democratic and anti-civic causes and crime.

Courses which in their choice of contents and method do not take sufficient account of the stages, posited by Kohlberg and Piaget, of young people's moral development and readiness are felt to be peripheral to real life. School may reinforce young persons' sentiments towards their community likely to foster emotion rather than reason, dependence rather than responsible initiative. Imposed 'do gooding' activity finds release in 'independent', anti-social group activity. Only activity clearly understood and supported by the young themselves gives them the opportunity of a say (Haines, 1967) and enables them to act objectively in matters concerning it within their groups. Narrow national or other group identification is partly to blame for chauvinistic tendencies which find expression in xenophobic acts. The educator's task is to teach so as to allow the young to 'find' worthy alternative pursuits. Both partners must be open on this.

Meanwhile French citizenship education programmes give prominence to the study of multiculturalism and relevant legislation, and stress the 'neutrality of the secular school' as a factor in good intercultural relations. The study of topics such as 'identity' entails learning the appropriate legislation concerning foreigners in France. Helene Nico's study concerned with the '*comprehension du droit et son application dans les manuels*' (1991) confirms the heavily cognitive approach which contrasts with the more experiential British way of becoming aware of multiculturalism by studying 'similarities and differences' or 'the diversity of cultures in other societies', as suggested in the National Curriculum Council's *Guidance* (1991) mentioned above. Unlike the French *annexes* the abstract noun 'identity' does not appear in the English *Guidance* document. That pupils' behaviour in the urban *colleges* and the British comprehensives can be equally bad is an incentive to investigate the connection further.

Participation in voluntary activities as suggested earlier has been widely advocated, particularly in Britain, but non-school matters, like the environment, unemployment or social concern, are not sufficiently in evidence, especially so among the urban school population. Teachers' failure to engage pupils' enthusiasm increases the already existing imbalance between theory and practice, both in terms of ratio of school and out of school time allocated and the kind of opportunity for practical activity, and stunts pupils' experiential, autonomous development. The autonomous citizen is an active citizen, but the converse is not necessarily true. Social life involves a greater part of the total human person than any other pursuit, academic or recreationary.

THE SITUATION IN THE UNITED KINGDOM

The above findings can be confirmed in a closer look at the British situation, where current developments in citizenship education are topical on two counts at least:

1 The Parliamentary Commission on Citizenship report *Encouraging Citizenship* (RCC, 1990) provides evidence for a commitment to citizenship education and practice.
2 The use of activity methods in school teaching and the institution of pupils' school councils coincides with current Council of Europe initiatives to investigate the link between citizenship education and school life. *Éducation Civique et la Vie Scolaire* was the topic of a 1992 Council of Europe conference chaired by François Audigier of the French Institut National de Réchèrche Pédagogique (INRP).

In the United Kingdom the intermittent interest in citizenship education in the 1930s coincided with the rise of Nazism. The 1960s period was marked by the introduction of new citizenship and politics teaching methods and in particular of the original concept of procedural values in political education (Stradling, 1978). It also saw a growth of pupils' school councils and a revival of teaching with participation in the life of the school community. Traditionally much of that takes the form of debate. A promising, less exclusively school community based pupil parliament and debating chamber, a state maintained school equivalent to the Oxford Union, disappeared with the abolition of Inner London Education Authority under the third Thatcher administration. The revival of citizenship studies at the end of the 1980s and the early 1990s coincided with an era of intense privatization, a cult of consumerism, cultural pluralism and the loss of identity, all affected by the strategically placed reform of the school curriculum legislation in 1988.

The thrust of the report of the Citizenship Commission *Encouraging Citizenship* was twofold: teaching the young civic knowledge and skills through the *cross-curricular theme* of citizenship in the National Curriculum and fostering democratic behaviour by encouraging participation in the work of predominantly voluntary associations and services. The slogan 'Active Citizenship', a different concept from the earlier political literacy and personal and social education, illustrates the emphasis of this new aspect of community membership. However, 'duties', 'information' and 'factual knowledge' give little real guidance on how to put across 'living and working for the community' and a sense of identification and involvement with it, especially in view of the 'Citizen's Charters' which emphasize the consumer citizen's rights to an appropriate standard of service. Several hundred of these, national (like the railway user's) and local (services in the city of Cambridge), are now in place.

The already mentioned National Curriculum Council *Guidance* expects pupils to 'understand the duties, responsibilities and rights of every citizen'. Participative citizenship can be taught by 'helping pupils to acquire and understand essential information' and giving them 'opportunities and incentives to participate in all aspects of school life'. Knowledge extends to what constitutes a community, roles and relationships in a democratic society, the nature and basis of duties, rights and responsibilities, learnt in themes listed on pages 5–9 which include: the nature of community, the pluralist society, the family, democracy in action, the citizen and the law, work, employment and leisure and public services, all of which together cover the aim of 'Being a Citizen'.

The task of how these can be adequately taught through subjects, the specific subject knowledge of which does not include the overall object of citizenship in the community, is not easy. Among the skills emphasized are the communication skills, such as detecting bias. Highlighting the responsible use made of facilities available without identifying the reasons for decisions taken and those responsible for making the decisions about priorities in provision in the first place leaves no room for the all important community principle of reciprocity, particularly absent in the Citizen's Charters.

The *Guidance* makes scant reference to communities other than British, nor does it highlight the historical and comparative perspective or an involvement in global education worldwide. Some of this may of course be available among other syllabuses or cross-curricular themes, nevertheless the absence of the exposure of controversy and competing priorities in political programmes, including an analysis of government plans, is striking. The school ethos, listing its authority clusters, pupil/staff, staff/local authority, intra- and inter-society relations, is not mentioned. In contrast to the Attainment Targets for the discrete curriculum subjects there are no time allocations or detailed schemes of work.

The activities seem suitable for a child centred teaching approach, but this is no longer favoured by the ministers of state, who have created a vast number of regulations, affecting curricula, school government, parental choice, to refer to but the most recent legislation 1988–93, to push through their rather different ideas of programmes. An evaluation will not be possible until the effect of the guidelines has worked itself through teaching all the stages, including Key Stage 4 (pupils aged 16).

A brief survey of school textbooks and other teaching materials confirms a rather summary treatment, on the whole, of choice, and the lack of a thorough historical and sociopolitical content analysis of texts. (In the case of the Department For Education prescribed English literature anthology for schools there is evidence of direct ministerial interest in teaching materials.) In citizenship and politics lessons, the series of school texts widely used in the former Inner London Education Authority schools, entitled *A Social Life* (Whitburn, 1980), with specific reference to the political nature of problems, has been replaced by texts which obtain a wider perspective by the different expedient of presenting developmental, racist or family issues largely as facts, as in the series *Humanities Insights* (Daly, 1989), or *Society in Action* (Moss, 1988).

The second area, activity teaching, which impacts the development of a sense of citizenship in a *community*, is the experience of living in a democratic community which provides a preparation for life in one. The school can encourage democratic management, relations between staff and pupils being based on mutual respect, and allow pupils, within reason, the opportunity of running parts of it themselves, especially giving them a share in decision making. The arguments both in favour and against this are many, the educational one that 'democracy in education is that of a common interest in pursuing knowledge' (Wringe, 1984) is very pervasive and persuasive, though the claim rings somewhat hollow with the present level of administrative interference from above. The possibilities and limitations of pupils' work in school councils are critically examined from practitioners' experience by Ungoed Thomas (1972). How independent and meaningful are decisions made in a school council for which the funding does not come from the pupils? How can pupils become involved in independent and responsible activity in wider society? How important are the procedural skills in such activities? These are problems for a school already suggested within the general context of pupil involvement.

The status of the distinctive mode of simultaneous learning (= reflection) and practising citizenship (= governing), with the duties of social life present in school life itself, including involvement in a school council, which has traditionally been a feature of British schools, may be seen as to some extent affected by the nature and status of British citizenship which has no written rights. Marshall (1963) and Barbalet (1988) give an authoritative account of citizenship (cf. also the points listed in the previous section on Excursus on Citizenship).

Like the school councils, so the status of school as a community is an imperfect model for teaching democracy. In her critical account Slee (1991) describes the English school as 'a clan, a micro-state of which the pupil is the citizen', and where s/he can learn the importance of an ordered democratic society. But Slee goes on to comment on both the excessive official involvement in prescribing activities and the 'pride of belonging'. The author's own researches into British pupils' political involvement saw the school 'rather like a club, with little concern for the wider community, and often the only or major focus of pupils' and old boys' attention and affection' (Tulasiewicz, 1990). The practice of substituting school for *'real adult life'*, identifying the one with the other, may encourage an emotional sense of permanent juvenile loyalty which can lead to exclusiveness, fostering partisanship, creating 'a curious mixture of a *passively active submission* to authority' (Tulasiewicz, 1990). The comment in *Citizenship in Schools* (1991): 'if active citizenship only means helping one's own group then selfishness is not removed' is rather damning. The author's research goes on to note the attitudes senior school pupils and young adults adopted to political activity; particularly in Britain there is less inclination by voters to intervene or to 'check what their representatives and government agencies are up to'. School councils in Britain are not alone with little *active* pupil involvement. Flitner Merle (1991) finds a wide gap between the poor reality of school pupils' actual freedom of their own representation and activity, and the rhetoric of the political rights granted to them in France and Germany.

The point made by Helen Marks (1990) that many schools which do concern themselves with school-sponsored community service activities manage to turn out 'autonomous individuals' and at the same time instil 'accountability to members of the community' shows that the school community can be organized on rather more open and independent lines. As argued by Bryk (1988) this has to do with the organization of the school, since 'the structure of the school sends a moral message'.

Whether the latest education for citizenship initiative, against the background of the clannish school, will encourage young people in Britain as citizens to be more autonomous and active is too early to say. Earlier attempts to see schools as 'unique opportunities to participate' showed 'few examples of democracy in action' (Stradling, 1987). The figures quoted for involvement in the Young Volunteer Resource Unit and others (Edwards and Fogelman, 1991), while undoubtedly impressive, leave out hundreds of thousands of youngsters not involved. Listing Youth Training Schemes (YTSs) as citizenship education and participation confuses the issue since they are only a substitute for real employment. The statement by a British MP: 'refusal to give the young any serious responsibility for the society in which they live merely encourages the kind of anomie which undermines citizenship' (Rowe, 1991) sums up the situation.

If instead of 'active decision makers' the 'Active Citizenship' movement were to produce 'thinking *consumers*' only, the outcome would not be at all encouraging for democracy. There are far too many variables to take into account to answer it here, nevertheless the question whether problems are the effect of government legislation on an aspect of the curriculum or the result of a particular slant attached to it in practice, or both, should be asked. The recommendation (No. 4) in the Report of the Commission on Citizenship that 'evidence of activities undertaken as part of learning citizenship skills' should be recorded in a pupil's Record of Achievement could be reinforced by evidence of pupils' continuing meaningful involvement.

REINFORCING CONSIDERATIONS

Detailed syllabus legislation or guidance affecting the *contents* of all compulsory subjects of the school curriculum, like the National Curriculum in England and Wales, is common practice in Europe, but legislation does not go on to prescribe classroom approaches, for example the *extent and nature* of participation. Though aims may be clearly stated, they are discussed and negotiated with pupils only in the most 'progressive' schools. Only a full course, with comparative surveys and histories of society, is educationally valid. How many school pupils are aware of the gap between reality and rhetoric where it occurs, the socioeconomic background of the different types of rights – civil (e.g. freedom from unlawful imprisonment), political (participation in the democratic process) and social (entitlement to welfare, like health and education) – and how it may affect them? The understandable lack of reciprocity between rights and duties, for example that the opportunity for work and the responsibility for self and family has functioned differently in different types of society, can begin to be discussed at school; otherwise only the few pupils who go on to study sociology or politics in higher education will become aware of the complexities of social life and citizenship. The contents of courses for the majority of pupils still take too little account of the political priorities of policies of the national state and of post-national supranational communities, although this situation is beginning to change.

If citizenship is the possession of all, then citizenship studies must be available to all pupils. That is part of the legislation in England and Wales. Exempting pupils educated in independent schools from learning the National Curriculum syllabuses is part of the same legislation. Legislation rarely gives reasons for such decisions, although in this case independent schools may be said to have been offering an appropriate syllabus independently from the state. That courses slanted towards an elite group who after school may go directly into decision making in politics may alienate those whose courses did not offer the same advantages is not legislated for. Middle-class values in the school syllabus are difficult to recognize by pupils not used to them. It is possible to argue that some of the proposed syllabus changes in the National Curriculum, for example in the teaching of language, have been ignoring this fact. The procedural values by contributing to peaceful solutions by all have gained validity in this context.

Education for citizenship aims at teaching the pupil to *become a citizen* at both the macro and micro levels of participation. What citizenship involves must be known to both learners and their teachers. It is significant that unlike previous exhortations to learners' 'loyalty and patriotism', the report of the Speaker's Commission on Citizenship gives an account of British citizenship, which may bring the United Kingdom closer to practice in other European countries. Indeed one of its recommendations (No. 15) was 'the proposal for the review and codification of the law'. The recommendations concerning monitoring citizenship studies go a long way to making such studies an important part of the compulsory curriculum. This is especially necessary if with the pursuit of standards of excellence, which are legislated for in the discrete subjects of the curriculum including tests at regular intervals, the civic parts of education are not to become neglected.

In matters of actual presentation the teacher is much more, if not completely, independent. Presentation can slant pupils' education, if for example prejudice or abuse of rights are illustrated exclusively by racism, or inequality shown in the third world only. Material cannot be left out because of political fear, for example change in the status of citizens' rights, since otherwise some pupils would not see themselves represented. Learning the facts of the government system alone for examination purposes is unlikely to prepare for citizenship. Independent professionals will claim that political knowledge and participation in politics do not destabilize society. This is more likely to be the result of ignorance and marginalization. The right presentation here is crucial.

For pupils to act as citizens they must be provided with the necessary tools and skills, such as being able to distinguish between general and political skills, as advocated by Maitland Stobart in *The Challenge of Human Rights Education*. Recent legislation concerning language education in British schools has begun to see to that. Recognizing the cause and effect of actions is more difficult to teach than extending the range of one's vocabulary. It can be taught as a discrete unit drawing on examples from a variety of subjects tested for the validity of their message. Though profes- sional expertise rather than legislation may be the first to recognize a need such as this, in many societies legislation is necessary to sanction its introduction in the first instance. Legislation may take a long time to arrive. Advice on whom to approach for help when organizing an action, is made easy in the case of actions approved, such as under a Citizen's Charter. In other cases, one has to learn how to take the initiative and to know the consequences of actions taken. Pressure group activity is unlikely to be government-funded, and yet in a democracy it may be the law tomorrow, as in the case of physical punishment in schools in Britain after the work done by the organization STOPP (Society of Teachers Opposed to Physical Punishment).

Teacher education has paid too little attention to pupils' process of maturation from biological dependency to complex social relations in the teaching of citizenship. Teachers are poorly informed about the legal situation, which would help them in discussing the implications of laws and regulations, a dimension which has been taken up in the recently created Institutions Universitaires de Formation des Maîtres (IUFMs) in France. Professional opinion differs on many details, historians prefer the historical approach to a sociological survey; often legislation cuts short a long debate.

CONCLUSION

If there is a single principle that must not be omitted from citizenship education courses it is that of reciprocity, of cause and consequence. A simple *quid pro quo* cannot be expected, as recognized by the distinguished political educationist Ralph Dahrendorf. This too must be learnt. Nor must citizenship be equated exclusively with too narrow a unit. While such a skill is necessary to be able to function in such a unit, the larger unit, like that of European Citizenship championed by French legislation (*Journal Officiel* of 14.vii.1985 – '*l'élève doit devenir un citoyen européen*'), provides a dynamic visionary quality which can counteract the lack of appeal of traditional citizenship education, for which there is much evidence from most countries, where citizenship education is equated with the imposition of a particular ethnicity: cultures or values.

The last thought must be reserved for the British audience: there are some, like Colin Geary in *The Guardian* in February 1993, who actually welcome the relative lack of legislation, such as a written constitution, in the United Kingdom, arguing that it is easier to find new solutions by act of Parliament after a debate than to overturn legislation. One thing is certain: having to learn legislation will make citizenship education more like other subjects of the school curriculum.

REFERENCES

Aselmeier, U., Eigenbrodt, K-W., Kron, F.W. and Vogel, G. (eds) (1985) *Fachdidaktik am Scheideweg*, Muenchen/Basel: Reinhardt.

Barbalet, J.M. (1988) *Citizenship*, Milton Keynes: Open University Press.

Brownhill, R. and Smart, P. (1989) *Political Education*, London: Routledge.

Bryk, A. (1988) Musings on the Moral Life of Schools, *American Journal of Education*, 96.

Cambridge University Department of Education (1992) Adams, A., Convey, A., Taverner, D., Tulasiewicz, W. and Turner, K. (eds), *The Changing European Classroom: Multicultural Schooling and the New Europe*, Cambridge: Department of Education, University of Cambridge.

Crick, B. and Porter, A. (1981) Political Education, in White, J. *et al.*, *No Minister: A Critique of the DES Paper 'The School Curriculum'*, London: University of London Institute of Education.

Daly, B.J. (1989) *Humanities Insights*, London: Hodder & Stoughton.

Department of Education and Science (1977) *Curriculum 11–16: Working Papers by HM Inspectorate: A Contribution to the Current Debate*, London: HMSO.

Department of Education and Science (1989) *Personal and Social Education from 5 to 16, Curriculum Matters 14*, London: HMSO.

Department of Education and Science (1992) *Policy Models: A Guide to Developing and Implementing European Dimension Policies in LEAs, Schools and Colleges*, London: HMSO.

Dewey, J. (1961) *Democracy and Education*, New York: The Macmillan Company.

Durkheim, E. (1961) *Moral Education*, Glencoe: Free Press of Glencoe.

Edwards, J. and Fogelman, K. (1991) Active Citizenship and Young People, in Fogelman, K. (ed.), *Citizenship in Schools*, London: David Fulton.

Findlay, J.J. (1928) *The Foundations of Education*, Vol. 1, London: University of London Press.

Gardner, J.P. (1990) What Lawyers mean by Citizenship, in RCC, *Encouraging Citizenship* Appendix D, London: HMSO.

Habermas, J. (1971) Verfassungspatriotismus – im allgemeinen und im besonderen, in Habermas, J. *Die nachholende Revolution*, Frankfurt/M: Suhrkamp.

Haines, N. (1967) *Person to Person: A Workout in Principles and Values*, London, Melbourne, Toronto: Macmillan.

Heater, D. (1990) *Citizenship*, London and New York: Longman.

Kreide, R. (1992) Toward Citizenship Education, Unpublished paper, Cambridge University.

Kron, F.W. (1989) The Nature and Limitations of Teachers' Professional Autonomy, in Tulasiewicz, W. and Adams, A. (eds), *Teachers' Expectations and Teaching Reality*, London and New York: Routledge.

Lawton, D. (1984) *The Tightening Grip, Growth of Central Control of the School Curriculum*, London: Bedford Way Paper 21, Institute of Education.

Lawton, D. (1992) *Education and Politics in the 1990s*, London and Washington DC: Falmer Press.

Marks, H. (1990) The Effect of Participation in School Sponsored Community Service Programs on Students' Attitudes toward Social Responsibility, Unpublished dissertation, University of Michigan.

Marshall, T.H. (1963) *Sociology at the Cross Roads*, London: Heinemann.

Merle, F.M. (1991) L'éducation civique en Allemagne. Bases juridiques et debats in *La formation du futur citoyen par le droit dans le collèges*. Paris: Laboratoire de Sociologie Juridique Université Pantheon–Assas – CNRS.

Monconduit, E. (1991) Enquête sur l'éducation civique auprès d'établissements scolaires de la région parisienne, in *La formation du futur citoyen par le droit dans les collèges*, Paris: Laboratoire de Sociologie Juridique, Université Panthéon–Assas–CNRS.

Moss, P. and Moss, J. (1988) *Society in Action*, London: Oxford University Press.

National Curriculum Council (1991) *Curriculum Guidance 8, Education for Citizenship*, York: National Curriculum Council.

Nico, H. (1991) La formation du futur citoyen par le droit et les manuels français d'éducation civique des collèges, in *La formation du futur citoyen par le droit dans les collèges*, Paris: Laboratoire de Sociologie Juridique, Université Panthéon-Assas-CNRS.

Porter, A. (ed.) (1983) *Teaching Political Literary: Implications for Teacher Training and Curriculum Planning*. Bedford Way Paper 16, London: Tinga Tinga.

Report of the Commission on Citizenship (RCC) (1990) *Encouraging Citizenship*, London: HMSO.

Roche, M. (1992) *Rethinking Citizenship*, Cambridge: Polity Press.

Rowe, A. (1991) in Fogelman, K. (ed.) *Citizenship in Schools*, London: David Fulton.

Slater, J. (1991) Introduction, in Conley, F. (ed.), *Political Understanding Across the Curriculum*, London: The Politics Association.

Slee, B. (1991) L'education civique en Grande Bretagne. Citoyennété et éducation, in *La formation du futur citoyen par le droit dans les collèges*, Paris: Laboratoire de Sociologie Juridique, Université Panthéon-Assas-CNRS.

Stenhouse, L. (1970) *The Humanities Project: An Introduction*, London: Heinemann; revised by J. Rudduck (1983) Norwich: School of Education Publications, University of East Anglia.

Stradling, R. (1978) Notes for a Spiral Curriculum for Developing Political Literacy, in Crick, B. and Porter, A. (eds), *Political Education and Political Literacy*, London: Longman.

Stradling, R. (1987) *Education for Democratic Citizenship*, Strasbourg Conference on Parliamentary Democracy, Strasbourg: Council of Europe.

Taylor, T. (chair) (1977) *A New Partnership for Our Schools*. London: HMSO.

Tulasiewicz, W. (1979a) *Political Education in Yugoslavia: Education for Participation and Communication*, Paper presented at the 14th annual conference of the

Comparative Education Society in Europe, British Section, Bath: University of Bath, pp. 102–112, mimeo.

Tulasiewicz, W. (1979b) Political Education in Yugoslavia: Practice in Self-management, *Cambridge Journal of Education*, (9)1.

Tulasiewicz, W. (1990) Unpublished research into the political awareness and political activity of school pupils in seven schools in the European Community.

Tulasiewicz, W. (1993) The European Dimension and the National Curriculum, in King, A. and Reiss, M. (eds) *The Multicultural Dimension of the National Curriculum*, London and Washington DC: Falmer Press.

Ungoed Thomas, J.R. (1972) *Our School*, London: Longman.

Whitburn, R. *et al.* (1980) *A Social Life*, London: Macdonald Educational.

Wringe, C. (1984) *Democracy, Schooling and Political Education*, London: George Allen & Unwin.

12 Teacher mobility and conditions of service in the European Community

Andrew Convey

While there is nothing especially new about a small number of qualified teachers taking up teaching posts in a country other than the one in which they qualified and are ordinarily resident, such teachers have always constituted a very small minority of the total teaching force. They have tended, moreover, to make such moves for personal reasons of one sort or another. With the development of higher levels of unity, mobility and exchange of ideas in Europe, what is anticipated by some is that, in common with other professionals, teachers may begin to make career moves to posts in other European countries in much greater numbers than ever before. At this early stage, therefore, it is perhaps prudent to look into the kind of migration which may develop, and how these moves might relate to the status of teachers in legal, social and professional terms.

There seem to be three preliminary thoughts to bear in mind when considering this question, each of which will tend to affect the number of teachers who are likely to move:

1 The recent mutual recognition of diplomas by the member states of the European Community, coupled with the original Treaty of Rome stipulations on the free movement of labour, means that in career terms at least, teacher movement within the European Community is likely to be greater than that with other European countries at present outside the Community. However, one should in no way eliminate the rest of Europe, or indeed the rest of the world, from a consideration of this question. There is, for instance, already a significant movement of European teachers on short-term or semi-voluntary contracts with third world countries.

2 This chapter limits the study to the movement of already qualified and newly qualified teachers in the European context and not of movements via ERASMUS, LINGUA and other student-based European Community programmes, even though quite clearly in teacher education

terms these are closely related and experience of schools in another European country, while undergoing training, might well encourage a young teacher to move to work in that country after qualifying.

3 It must be noted that modern foreign language skills remain of special if not crucial importance when teaching in another country. Such skills may at present be more of a problem for teachers originating from some European countries than from others. What is certain is that little progress will be made in the field of teacher mobility without enhanced levels of modern foreign language abilities across all countries and an awareness of language with its cognitive and social implications.

WHAT ARE THE CONDITIONS THAT LEAD TO MOBILITY?

Several features related to teacher mobility in Europe seem to have come together in recent years. These include the recognition of Initial Teacher Education qualifications across the European Community member states; the 'opening-up' of Central and Eastern European countries; the attempts by the government of the United Kingdom to recruit teachers from other European Community member states; the new European Community Teacher Exchange Scheme for Secondary Teachers, and other similar schemes which allow for a level of mobility. In addition to this, for new teachers in training in the United Kingdom, the existing Teacher Education Regulations (DES, 1989), also known as 'CATE II' call for all courses of Initial Teacher Education to take account of the European Dimension in their design a point absent in the latest (November 1992) proposed version. At the same time, the National Curriculum Council in England and Wales has produced its own definition of what constitutes the European Dimension in Education so far as the schools are concerned and has also formulated aims and objectives for its delivery in all school courses for the 5 to 16 age groups (NCC, 1990).

In respect of the stipulations in 'CATE II', it is perhaps worth noting that Her Majesty's Inspectors have stated that the clauses in question, which urge all institutions to take account of the European Dimension in the design of courses, will mean that courses in institutions of initial teacher education will be looked at quite closely as far as provision for the European Dimension is concerned, as those courses come up for review from time to time. Even now there are some institutions which are perhaps not fully aware of this situation. In parallel to this, the National Curriculum Council's identification of the place of the European Dimension in Education in schools is being published in many of its subject documents. It is possible to see a progression from, for example, an early English syllabus document which stated hopefully that, 'English should be regarded as part of the family of European Languages'; to the later Geography syllabus documents which had 'The Study of the UK within the European Community' as a major Attainment Target! Encouragement to work with other European countries is also found in many of these documents, as for example in the cross-curricular theme of Environmental Education. It is evident that British teachers operating within this framework are going to be progressively much more aware of Europe as a whole, and are therefore more likely to look for career opportunities within Europe.

While respecting national autonomy, it should be borne in mind that much of the impetus towards a European Dimension in Education had started with European Community initiatives. The well-known Resolution of May 1988 from the Education Ministers of the European Community on 'The European Dimension in Education' (Commission of the European Communities, 1988a) had much to say about the training and re-training of teachers, on the development of contacts between teachers in different parts of the Community, in addition to setting out certain guidelines for the delivery of the European Dimension in schools. This resolution led to the 1991 State- ment from the Department of Education and Science (DES) on the delivery of the European Dimension in English and Welsh schools (DES, 1991). In November 1989, the European Community Ministers produced further Conclusions on the main criteria for education and training 'in the run-up to 1993' (Official Journal of the European Communities, 1989). More recently, in January 1992, there was the new 'Memorandum on Higher Education in the European Community' (Commission of the European Communities, 1992) which once again stresses the important role to be played by teachers. It makes the point that 'it is essential that a European experience should form part of the professional education of all teachers', and that 'means of providing European experience for teachers who cannot avail themselves of a study period abroad should be developed'. At the same time, the Department For Education (DFE) (formerly the Department of Education and Science) has produced its own 'policy models' (DES, 1992), intended as guidance for schools and higher education in their implementation of the European Dimension.

There is also some suggestion that teachers in the United Kingdom are now more aware of the conditions of service and the opportunities which exist in other European education systems. Whether this will ever lead to a 'brain drain' of teachers to these countries, as is suggested by some, is still a matter of conjecture. Much of the evidence is still anecdotal, but it is not unreasonable to suppose that if individuals from professions other than teaching are increasingly involved in jobs in other European countries, then why should this not also apply to teachers in due course? This would have implications for their training, as it may well be true to say that teachers, more than any other professionals, are trained to serve the needs of their own nation state. Certainly, an increasing number of student teachers are looking at possibilities and in reverse, it is not unusual these days when visiting teacher training institutions in other parts of Europe to be asked about teaching opportunities in the United Kingdom! As more trainee teachers take part in ERASMUS and other structured exchanges during their courses of preparation, we can perhaps expect more such questions and subsequent movements. An interesting survey in the United Kingdom (*The Independent*, 1990) of what 18 year olds wanted from their working lives suggested that, while a majority wanted to continue working in their own home area, 36–40 per cent said they would like to work abroad, at least temporarily, and this figure was well in advance of those who wanted to work in another part of the United Kingdom. London was particularly unpopular. If this is true of young people at the start of the higher education age group and it is a view which is maintained, then it is likely to be reflected to some extent a few years later in the career decisions which new teachers take. Meanwhile, Nigel Forman MP, formerly a Junior Minister of Education, has supported the increased European mobility for teacher trainers and lecturers in higher education, 'the time has therefore come to think about alternative means of bringing Europe into higher education for the majority of students who are not internationally mobile . . . encouraging lecturers to move from country to country could be one way of bringing a European element into higher education' (DFE, 1992).

IF TEACHERS MOVE, WHAT MAKES THEM GO AND WHAT WILL THEY FIND?

In the light of such developments in the United Kingdom and with their equivalents elsewhere, it becomes increasingly necessary to understand how conditions of service for teachers vary across the European Community and to know more about the differing legal status of teachers (Shaw, 1991, pp. 35–8). In most European countries teachers are civil servants, while in some others, notably Britain, they are not. Research has been done in this field by Joanna Le Métais (NFER, 1990) and there is also the Commission of the European Communities document, 'The Conditions of Service of Teachers in the European Community' (1988b), which covers all countries except Spain and Portugal. The study of In Service Training of Teachers in the European Community (Blackburn and Moisan, 1987) and the *70 Millions d'Élèves* of Francine Vaniscotte (Vaniscotte, 1989) give attention, respectively, to teacher training and to the position of teachers within the education system as a whole.

Table 12.1 outlines some of the salient features of appointment procedures and contracts of employment in ten European Community member states. This differentiates between how applications are to be made; probationary periods; the nature of the appointment; the teacher's legal status, and the employer's status. It can be seen that much variation exists and that the 'national' characteristics of the individual systems would tend to prevent, as yet, a large scale 'European' recruitment of teachers. Many of these features could be amended to allow for a broader European recruitment, but the most intractable is likely to be civil servant status of teachers at certain levels of seniority. There is quite clearly room for tension here, between the interests of a nation's own teachers and the desire of a national or federal education system to expand its European base. Perhaps a future test of a nation's European credentials will be the extent to which it is willing to provide 'civil servant equivalent' status to incoming teachers from other European countries! In general terms, there have been suggestions that recently 'job barriers' in the European Community area may be becoming more significant, rather than easier. At the beginning of 1992, the International Bar Association reported that 'we have got the ability to shift data, finances and the products of intellectual work without ever going near a border, an airport or a dock, but we are in our infancy in moving staff around' (*The Independent on Sunday*, 1992). In terms of teachers in Europe, Matthew Hancock has stated that, 'in reality, however, most European Community countries already have a surplus of teachers and they are doing all they can to ensure that their native teachers do not lose out to rivals from other member states!' (*The European*, 1992).

There is further the question of the social security situation, entitlements and emoluments, and regulations governing such things as workloads. There are variations in pensionable age (up to age 67 in Denmark); there are different interpretations of what can be included as pensionable service, for example compulsory military service counts in some countries and not in others. In the United Kingdom this affects former national servicemen. The approved normal workload varies quite considerably; in the Netherlands it adds up to about 24 hours per week and in Luxembourg to only 15 hours (the United Kingdom is at a mid-point of 21 hours). This is just normal teaching time; in certain countries, for example Germany, 'extra' time is paid for as a matter of course.

While most of these variations are of a technical nature and could presumably be resolved by the adoption of European norms, or by the agreed automatic inter-European transfer of rights and contributions, others are more fundamental, especially that of status. A number of very difficult questions remain to be worked out in the area of civil servant status or its equivalent, and the security of tenure this entails.

Table 12.1 Employment characteristics of teachers in selected European countries

	Appointing agency	*Probation*	*Nature of contract*	*Teacher status*	*Employer status*
B	school	1 yr (can be 2)	permanent; may extend temps with no limit	civil servant (in state schools)	Ministry; local authority or school board
DK	school	2 yrs	as in B	majority are civil servants	Ministry
D (west)	school	< 5 yrs	as in B	civil servants	*Land*
F	national exam	Sec: 1 yr Prim: none	as in B	civil servants	Ministry
GB (England and Wales)	school	1 yr (2 for foreign teachers)	conditions same for permanent and temps	not civil servants	local authority or school board
GR	national exam and selection	2 yrs	as in B	civil servants	Ministry
IRL	school	1 yr (can be < 5)	as in B	not civil servants	school board or school manager
I	national exam and vocational training	1 yr	as in B	civil servants	Ministry
L	national selection	can be < 2 yrs	permanent: temps only in secondary schools	civil servants	Ministry (secondary); municipal (primary)
NL	school	1 yr (can be 2)	permanent; temps only for 2 yrs	civil servants (in state and municipal schools)	Ministry; municipal or school board, according to sector

Source: Adapted from table 5.1, 'Appointment procedures and contract of Employment', in 'The Conditions of Service of Teachers in the European Community' (Commission of the European Communities, 1988).

Table 12.2 Teachers' salaries in the primary sector in selected European countries (in ecu and pps)

	Minimum (ecu)	Maximum (ecu)	Minimum (pps)	Maximum (pps)	Average (ecu)	Average (pps)
B	12596	21144	15274	25640	17555	21287
DK	17645	23404	17112	22697	20525*	19905*
England	9859	19988	11187	22679	16690	18937
F	11890	18347	12896	19900	14528	15758
D (west)	17092	25338	17979	26653	21215*	22316*
NL	12006	24181	13045	26275	17706	19239
IRL	11493	21728	13600	25712	16611*	19656*
I	10227	14599	13285	18966	12413*	16126*
L	15098	35284	17725	41423	25191*	29574*

* denotes estimate.

Source: Compiled from salary tables (Commission of the European Communities, 1988b).

Table 12.3 Salaries in the secondary sector, in selected European countries (in ecu and pps)

	Minimum (ecu)	Maximum (ecu)	Minimum (pps)	Maximum (pps)	Average (ecu)	Average (pps)
B	12905	29478	15649	35746	21192*	25698*
DK	17645	28558	17112	27694	23102*	22403*
England	9859	24269	11187	27537	17308	19638
F	12087	25552	13110	27715	18820*	20413*
D (west)	19320	31309	20323	32933	25315*	26628*
NL	13584	35226	14760	38276	24405*	26518*
IRL	11493	21728	13600	25712	16611*	19656*
I	10814	16016	14048	20806	13415*	17427*
L	20618	41805	24206	49078	31212*	36642*

* denotes estimate.

Source: As in Table 12.2.

1 If a teacher is not a civil servant in his/her own country, can that status be expected in another country?
2 If civil servant status is not conferred on incoming teachers in a member state whose own teachers have it, do the visitors then become 'second-class' teachers, as well as presenting a form of foreign competition; (lower pay for example)?
3 Can one envisage the development of an 'international civil servant' status for teachers in the European Community or would eventual European citizenship be sufficient?
4 Is the question sufficiently important for those more mobile teachers who will normally only reside and work in another European country for a limited time?

In terms of salaries it is possible to see considerable variations. Tables 12.2 (primary) and 12.3 (secondary) demonstrate some of the characteristics of the salaries' structures. In an attempt to achieve a degree of standardization, they rank the salaries received in terms of 'purchasing power standard' (pps).

There are considerable differences shown in these tables, and they exclude Greece, Spain and Portugal, countries which would only serve to accentuate the differences. The main variations are shown in Table 12.4.

There are of course the so-called 'perks' to consider. Housing and other residence allowances are not uncommon, and in Belgium and Germany, for example, end-of-year and holiday bonuses can add very considerable amounts to the annual total salary of the teacher. With such variations in remuneration, and with the range of benefits of various kinds in the different countries (and with the lack of them in others), the relative attractiveness of teaching in the different member states of the European Community from the point of view of salary and associated benefits is going to vary substantially.

It is possible to make a start considering which countries might be more attractive to potentially mobile European teachers, and which might be less

Table 12.4 Main salary variations for European teachers

	Highest	*Lowest*
Primary teachers	in ecu: Denmark	in ecu: England and Wales
	in pps: Germany (west)	in pps: England and Wales
Secondary teachers	in ecu: Luxembourg	in ecu: England
	in pps: Luxembourg	in pps: England

Source: Derived from Tables 12.2 and 12.3 above.

so. With apologies to Colin Clark and his principle of 'economic potential' (Clark, 1966) which represented the relative potential for economic development of a particular area, we might consider the notion of the 'pedagogical potential' of a country, this being the degree to which that country might be attractive to teachers from other countries. To arrive at a satisfactory analysis, it is necessary to use certain key variables for the countries concerned, and those which seem appropriate at this stage might be the following:

a the number of teachers per total population;
b the average size of classes;
c the percentage of gross national product devoted to Education and Training;
d the number of teachers in training;
e the legal status of teachers (e.g. civil servant);
f the size of salary (primary/secondary mean);
g other 'perks'.

The value of these key variables for different countries may then be ranked in a matrix diagram as in Table 12.5, with ranking points being awarded according to the listing position of the country concerned, with the highest ratings (i.e. 12 points) being awarded to the most favourable situations.

In the language of a well-known consumers' magazine, this would mean that in terms of a teacher's perception of the attractiveness of various European countries, the 'best buy' might be Luxembourg; that 'also worth considering' would be Denmark and the Netherlands; and that 'not worth considering' would be Portugal, Spain and Greece. However, this analysis does not take full account of the fact that the preferences of individual teachers will vary a great deal, and that the variables shown above can change quite rapidly from year to year. It should be stressed again that this is an initial analysis and that it needs further expansion and refinement in order to become more reliable. It remains a certainty, however, that potentially mobile teachers within the European Community will make mobility decisions based upon this kind of information, evidence and perception. The data could be expanded further by rating such variables as the teacher's professional status and standing in the community (there is considerable variety in the respect enjoyed by primary school teachers and independent school teachers in different countries (Walford, 1989). It would be difficult to rate such variables as teacher's independence in the use of syllabus guidelines, classroom discipline and the state of buildings, a situation brought to public attention by curriculum developments and other changes in the United Kingdom, or the job market situation and prospects for teachers in France compared with Germany (Brock and Tulasiewicz, 1993).

Table 12.5 Ranking of key variables (selected European countries)

	B	DK	F	D*	GR	IRL	L	I	NL	P	E	GB
a	12	9	8	2	1	7	6	11	10	5	3	4
b	7	6	3	10	6	4	11	12	8	1	2	10
c	8	10	7	4	1	11	9	6	12	3	2	5
d	11	12	2	4	7	4	9	1	10	2	7	4
e	6	12	12	12	12	1	12	12	6	12	12	1
f	7	9	5	11	4	8	12	4	10	4	4	6
g	9	8	7	10	4	5	12	4	11	4	4	6
a–g	60	66	44	53	35	40	71	50	67	31	34	36

* D is the former Federal Republic of Germany.

Source: Various; compiled from sources in the bibliography.

If mobility among teachers is set to increase in the European Community in the future, it is important to try to anticipate its likely main features. What, for example, might be the effect of a 'brain drain' on a particular country or on a particular subject (or on both); what part will language competence continue to play in the scale of mobility; what part might be played by the teachers of 'shortage subjects'; is there a need for a pan-European 'job description' for teachers, something which teachers' unions are working on at present (Jones, 1990, p. 15); is there room for the 'internationalization' of civil servant status for teachers in order to get over the variations which exist at present, and what will be the effects of the recent changes in Central and Eastern Europe? The role of the European Community itself in creating programmes and removing constraints becomes ever more important in these fields, as do the roles of individual national governments. Useful evidence which might provide pointers to the future may be gained from those teachers who have already made such moves, and also from the local education authorities such as Havering (in the UK) which have already been involved. And a final thought might be that if the mobility of teachers in Europe does not increase along with that in other professions, then there must be significant reasons for that situation which will also require investigation in due course.

REFERENCES

Blackburn, V. and Moisan, C. (1987). *'The In-service Training of Teachers in the Twelve Member States of the European Community'*. Education Policy Series, Presses Interuniversitaires Européennes, Maastricht/EURYDICE.

Brock, C. and Tulasiewicz, W. (eds) (1993). *Education in a Single Europe*, Routledge, London.

Clark, C. (1966). *Lloyds Bank Review*. London, June 1966.

Commission of the European Communities (1988a). *'The European Dimension in Education'*. Resolution no. 6171/88 of the Ministers of Education meeting within the Council, Brussels.

Commission of the European Communities (1988b). *'The Conditions of Service of Teachers in the European Community'*. Report on a Study carried out for the Commission of the European Communities and the Netherlands Ministry of Education and Science, by the Stichting Research voor Beleid, Luxembourg.

Commission of the European Communities (1992). *'Memorandum on Higher Education in the European Community'*. Brussels.

DES (1989). *'Initial Teacher Training; Approval of Courses'*. Circular 24/89, London.

DES (1991). *'The European Dimension in Education; a statement of the UK Government's policy and Report of activities undertaken to implement the EC Resolution of 24 May 1988 on the European Dimension in Education'*. London.

DES (1992). *'Policy Models: A Guide to Developing and Implementing European Dimension Policies in LEAs, Schools and Colleges'*. London.

DFE (1992). *UK Presidency Press Release No. 234/92*. London.

The European (1992). 'Class wars hold teacher back; opportunities to work abroad are still limited despite the Single Market', in *International Education Special Report*. London.

The Independent (1990). 'Thatcher's children want job satisfaction', (4 September 1990) London; see also, 'Thatcher's children; what 16–18 year olds want from their working lives', The Stapleford Partnership, Wilton, Wilts. 1990.

The Independent on Sunday (1992). as reported in 'Job barriers go up in EC market'. 2 February 1992.

Jones, R. (1990). *'A pan-European Teaching Profession?'* Report in AMMA, Vol. 12, No. 6, June 1990.

NCC (1990). *'Education for Citizenship'*. Report from Special NCC sub-committee on the European Dimension in the National Curriculum; see also Curriculum Guidance Series No. 8, York.

NFER (1986). (as reported in) *'Employment and Status of Teachers in State Schools in the European Community'*. EURYDICE European Unit, Slough.

Official Journal of the European Communities (1989). *'Conclusions of the Council and the Ministers of Education on Co-operation and Community Policy in the field of Education in the run-up to 1993'*. No. 89/C277/5, Brussels.

Shaw, J. (1991). 'Equality of Treatment for Teachers under EC Law', *Education and Law*, Vol. 3, No. 1, 1991.

Vaniscotte, F. (1989). *'70 Millions d'Élèves; l'Europe d'Éducation'*. Hatier, Paris.

Walford, G. (1989). *Private Schools in Ten Countries*. Routledge, London.

Walford, G. (1990). *Privatization and Priviledge in Education*. Routledge, London.

13 The changing roles and responsibilities of school governors

Dan Taverner

BACKGROUND

The Royal Commission of 1888 in describing the qualities of a School Governor stated the need for:

> A general zeal for education . . . , breadth of view, business habits, administrative ability and the power of working harmoniously with others . . . , some amount of education, tact, interest in school work, a sympathy with the teachers and the scholars . . . , residence in reasonable proximity to the school, together with leisure time during school hours.

It can be argued that for many schools these criteria were not strictly followed, certainly after the Robert Morant Education Act of 1902 when School Boards and Attendance Committees were taken over by newly appointed Local Education Authorities (LEAs). It can also be argued, however, that as a result of measures since 1944 these requirements now match much more closely the demands made upon governors by schools and their communities.

In reviewing the responsibilities now being faced by governors it is worth examining the stages by which these have been achieved from 1944.

The Education Act of that year helped to clarify the role of governors and stressed the importance of their functions in linking schools with the LEAs and the intermediary role which they should play. Instruments and Articles of Government covering the constitutions and the responsibilities of governing bodies were established. The 1944 Act, however, did not envisage the appointment of parents or teachers to governing bodies.

The Plowden Report of 1967, however, stressed the importance of parental involvement in the education of their children's schooling and advocated to LEAs that they should encourage parental representation on governing and managing bodies. At this time many schools, particularly in city areas, were grouped for the purposes of governors' and managers' meetings and a single body could be responsible for as many as 10 schools. In some LEAs, the Education Committee itself was responsible for these functions. This often meant that many members were unaware of the individual requirements of schools and were unable to exercise their responsibilities as envisaged in the 1944 Act.

In these circumstances it was not possible to monitor school developments and one of the most important functions of governors and managers – that of appointing headteachers and staff – was not always carried out successfully. Appointment procedures were often unsatisfactory and often took the form of presenting candidates for headships with a series of written questions upon which they were asked to comment. Decisions, which depended upon knowledge of the school organization, of the experience and ability of its staff and of its individual problems were often not able to be made by interviewing panels. This meant that LEA officers and inspectors (where they existed) had considerable responsibilities in advising interviewing committees on the strengths and weaknesses of candidates. It also meant that very few governors or managers found time to visit schools and many were unknown to teaching and non-teaching staff who tended to view them as remote people, only seen at a distance on functions such as speech days or at social gatherings. Under this system certainly few governors or managers were able to be aware of the individual needs of pupils or of the aspirations of their parents.

During the late 1960s and early 1970s pressure groups such as the National Association of Governors and Managers, the Campaign for the Advancement of State Education (CASE) and the Advisory Centre for Education were formed. These groups campaigned for governing bodies to be more representative of the communities which served the schools and which they, in their turn, were encouraged to reflect in the educational and social policies they adopted.

In 1977 the Taylor Committee was set up with the aim of reviewing the existing arrangements for school government. The report of this committee recommended that governing bodies should fully exercise their responsibilities as outlined in the 1944 Act. It also recommended, in order to reflect the needs and wishes of the local community, that all schools should have their own governing bodies. It was anticipated that the implementation of this recommendation would go some way to overcome the problems mentioned above. In order to further this aim the Taylor Report recommended that no single group on a governing body should have a dominating presence and that each body should be seen as a forum for all those representatives of the community who have legitimate interests in the affairs of the school.

Three years later the 1980 Act was passed and this went some way in meeting the Taylor recommendations. The grouping of schools under one governing body (except in the case of two closely linked primary schools) was abolished and no individual was allowed to hold more than five governorships. In addition there was a widening of representation on all governing bodies to include parent and teacher governors. The Act also stated that the term 'managers', which had been applied to primary schools only, should disappear and from that time all bodies would be called governors.

The recommendations of the Taylor report were further implemented in the Education (No. 2) Act of 1986. This considerably increased the powers of governors and, with them, their responsibilities.

The Act made new provision for the composition of governing bodies with four basic categories – parents, LEA representatives, teachers (and the headteacher if he or she so wished) and others co-opted by the rest of the governors to develop links with local business communities. Elections were to be by secret ballot and no one under the age of 18 would be eligible. In many schools this precluded the election of students as governors and a number of LEAs appealed unsuccessfully to the Secretary of State to have this clause changed.

There were clear moves in this Act to make schools and their governors more accountable to their communities. Minutes of meetings were to be made available to members of the public and governors were required to prepare a report to parents on the running of the school, the actions of the headteachers, the governors and LEAs. This would be presented at an annual parents' meeting and 'could be published in other languages in addition to English'. It was compared by some to a shareholders' meeting in which the members of boards reported on the success or otherwise of the company for which they were responsible.

The 1986 Act also gave governors powers to make decisions relating to the curriculum and they were given the responsibilities of playing a major role in pupil disciplinary cases. Clause 42 of the Act required governors to make reports and returns direct to the Secretary of State and 'to provide any other information he may need for the exercise of his functions'. This meant that links between the Department of Education and Science (DES – now the Department For Education or DFE) and governors were considerably strengthened and the intermediary functions of LEAs correspondingly weakened.

One of the most important responsibilities – that of appointing headteachers – was largely moved from the LEA to governing bodies who would have a majority on selection panels. The LEA was not able to appoint anyone as a headteacher unless recommended by these panels.

THE PRESENT POSITION

As a result of these measures school governors now have hugely increased responsibilities and the 1988 Education Reform Act whose purpose according to the Secretary of State was 'to put power into the hands of parents and governors' refined this process. Many of the powers which had previously been in the hands of LEAs are now held centrally or are in the hands of governors.

It is significant that the 1888 Royal Commission should refer in its criteria for governors to 'business habits', for governors now have a major say in matters of funding.

Finance

One of the major concerns of governors in the early 1990s has been that of managing school budgets. By 1993 all secondary schools and primary schools with 200 or more registered pupils have delegated powers and many smaller primary schools are also taking on these responsibilities. The allocation of funds is determined by formulae devised by LEAs and agreed by the DFE which, among other elements, depend upon the number of pupils (age-weighted pupil units) and above average numbers of pupils with special needs. From these funds governors, with the headteacher, decide upon their priorities. These include decisions on staffing (about two-thirds of the budget), the costs of day-to-day premises maintenance (about 10 per cent including services such as heating, water, and telephone charges), purchase of books, equipment, stationery and other goods and services.

Some spending remains under the LEAs direct control. They keep, for example, responsibilities for school transport and, as the landlords, for major building items relating to structure. A number of Authorities are delegating an increasing proportion of their funds which they receive from national and local sources to schools, in some cases with the aim of pre-empting 'opting out' (see below under 'Grant Maintained Schools').

This has meant that many governors for the first time are faced with important decisions on their financial priorities which may vitally affect the future of their schools. How does one decide for example whether the school needs another teacher, or indeed whether it should lose one? Does the school need more books or computers to meet the statutory require-ments of the National Curriculum and what additional insurances should be taken out? These are just a few of the decisions which governors and their headteachers need to make and most governing bodies have found it necessary to establish finance committees in order that they may resolve them. Many of the larger schools are also appointing bursars to advise them on this, and a number of smaller schools are clustering together in order to share expertise.

As a major proportion of the funding is dependent upon the size of the school roll a number of schools are actively recruiting pupils and popularizing what they have to offer. This follows the 'open door' policy which allows parents (with certain limitations) to chose for themselves the school they wish their children to attend. Here again a number of governing bodies have established committees dealing with school admissions and the development of public relations. In addition, many are actively seeking funds through a whole range of activities and, through their links with industry and commerce, are arranging funding schemes which range from raising money from sponsorship agreements to the hiring-out of school display boarding to local firms.

Many governors then are undertaking entrepreneurial work in the spirit of the 1988 Act and are raising considerable sums of money, but it is felt that such funding can only supplement and not replace statutory provisions. One of the problems, however, is that the amount raised is very much dependent upon the nature of the community which the school serves and as communities vary widely so does the amount of money raised in this way. This means that there can be great differences between schools in their available resources with a number losing out. The spirit of competition between schools is a natural result of the thinking of the 1988 Act and is receiving further impetus as schools publish the results of assessment measures at the Key Stages (see below in 'Assessment').

Curriculum

In introducing the 1988 Act the Secretary of State considered the National Curriculum as the bedrock of his policy. Whilst the headteacher is responsible for day-to-day decisions about the management and curriculum of the school, the governors are given powers to modify the LEA's curriculum policy to match the aims of their school 'so far as this is compatible with the National Curriculum'. They are charged with establishing a policy on sex education, including decisions on whether or how this should be provided and are required to produce a written statement about this, and they must also hear complaints about the curriculum according to agreed procedures. In the terms of the 1988 Act the curriculum is seen as all the activities which are designed to promote 'the spiritual, moral, cultural, and physical development of pupils'. Within this broad area the governing body is responsible with the headteacher and the LEA for ensuring that the National Curriculum is followed.

It is in this area that some confusion has arisen. It has been argued that whilst governors have the overall responsibility for the curriculum, the teachers are responsible for its delivery. This, however, is a simplistic view for content cannot always be separated from presentation and there is a grey area between the governors' curriculum responsibilities and those of teachers. Many governors feel that they do not have the expertise to pronounce on these matters and given the many other demands they face tend to leave this to the 'professionals'.

At the same time education is now in the centre of the political arena and is receiving a great deal of attention from all political parties and the media, particularly over the question of 'standards'. The debate on the teaching of reading, for example, has raised concerns about levels of achievement, and governors are being faced with an increasing number of questions from parents and the community about the quality of children's reading, their spelling and handwriting.

Assessment

As part of the 1988 Act, Statutory Orders were made indicating Attainment Targets in Foundation Subjects and determining ten levels of achievement for pupils between the ages of 5 and 16. Subsequently Orders were made for the assessment of pupils at the Key Stages for children aged 7, 11, 14 and 16. With the exception of 7 year old children the results of assessment at these ages are to be published and there are increasing pressures for schools to publish the results also at Key Stage 1.

The publication of these results (which may not always reflect the quality of education within a school) could lead to the establishment of 'league tables' of schools. In this way the 'market place' philosophy inherent in the 1988 Act could result in further competition for pupils. Certainly questions are being raised at annual parents' meetings about assessment results, and as the size of school budgets will be largely dependent upon school rolls, these present an added challenge to governors in representing the achievements of their schools.

Grant maintained schools

The 1988 Act contains provision for schools to 'opt out' of LEA control, gain grant maintained status and become funded centrally by the DFE. If the majority of parents voting in a secret ballot are in favour, then it is for the Secretary of State to decide whether to approve the application. This is a move which is being encouraged by the present Government whose expressed wish is for all schools eventually to become grant maintained.

A minority of governors faced with these increasing powers and responsibilities have moved to consider grant maintained status. One argument is that opting out of the system is only taking it a further stage down the road of independence from LEAs. Another, based upon evidence so far, is that grants from central government for such schools have been generous and result in larger funds at their disposal for the provision of increased resources and staffing. In certain areas this has raised problems for governors of those secondary schools remaining in the system which may have been in the process of reorganization, particularly if rolls are falling in their LEA areas.

A strong impetus to the opting out process was given in the White Paper of 28 July 1992. This proposes to ease procedures with the scrapping of a second parental ballot and to allow voluntary bodies to start up new grant maintained schools. It also proposes to abolish the requirements of local councils to have education committees. The White Paper recommends the establishment of a funding agency with a network of local offices for planning and administering grant maintained schools for which there is a target number of 1,500 by April 1994 and of 4,000 by the following April.

These recommendations end 'more than 100 years of local authority participation in education – and the local political action which has made the schools and colleges both the victim and the beneficiaries of civic and county pride and ambition. No more will local politics reflect arguments about the funding of education or the quality of local schooling' (Stuart Maclure, former editor of *The Times Educational Supplement*, in *The Times* of 3 August 1992). These recommendations were published in an Education Bill in the Autumn of 1992 and given the Royal Assent in July 1993.

This 'Revolution in our schools', 'the biggest shake up in state education since the Second World War' (*Evening Standard*, 28 July 1992) will result in fundamental reappraisals by governors of all schools of their responsibilities and commitments.

Staffing

Despite the many problems associated with managing their delegated budgets there is increasing evidence that headteachers and governors are coming to terms with them. One major area of concern which still remains involves personnel. The quality of the head and school staff is crucial to the quality of education which the school provides and although the LEA is still the employer of teaching staff, it is the governors who are responsible for appointments to the school. For schools with financial delegation this involves initial decisions on establishment levels. These include agreement on how many teachers are required, the number and allocation of incentive allowances and placement upon the incremental scale. As these are dependent on finance and as staffing involves a considerable portion of the school budget (see above) these may not be easy questions to resolve. There is some evidence that, where budgets are tight (perhaps with a falling school roll), teachers who have not had a great deal of experience, and are therefore lower on the incremental scale and thus 'cheaper', have taken precedence over more experienced teachers who may require higher salaries.

Once they have agreed that a vacancy exists governors then need to go through the process of appointment from advertising, through to long-, then short-listing to interviewing and appointing. These latter stages can be a matter of concern for governors for although LEA representatives may be present during interview they can only advise upon suitable candidates for senior posts and have no vote at interviews. For other posts up to deputy headteacher level the headteacher's guidance will generally be sought, but for the most important appointment – that of the headteacher – this of course does not apply. Other problems may arise if it is decided that the school needs to 'lose' a member of staff. Here the governors can require the LEA to dismiss a teacher but must be prepared to defend their actions if there is a complaint to an industrial tribunal.

All these decisions call for informed judgements based upon a knowledge of the school and its pupils which must involve time spent in visiting the school and making contacts with pupil and with teaching and non-teaching staff.

Children with special educational needs

The Warnock Committee of 1978 suggested that up to 20 per cent of children might need special educational help at some stage in their school career. In some schools this is much higher. It is estimated that about 2 per cent of all children are likely to need attention beyond that which an 'ordinary school' can provide. There are therefore many pupils who require additional attention and under the 1981 Act governors have a duty towards these children. They must try, for example, to ensure that the right provision is made for them, that teachers know of those needs and of ways of identifying them, and that the LEA knows of any pupils in this category.

To meet these requirements of the 1981 Act considerable specialist knowledge on the part of governors is needed. They are also faced with the financial implications of providing additional resources for these children.

Organization and discipline

Governing bodies decide the dates of school terms and holidays with schools meeting for not less than 380 half-day sessions in any academic year and they decide on when sessions should begin and end provided certain minimum weekly lesson times are followed.

They are also responsible for making sure that attendance registers and admission registers are kept. This process is a reminder of pre-Second World War days when registers were examined regularly and entries such as 'registers examined and found correct' were made in school log books. It raises questions of relationships between governors and teachers as well as of the demands made upon governors' time in order to carry out these duties.

Governors also have powers to draw up a written statement on general principles of discipline which they may offer to the headteacher. The headteacher alone is responsible for deciding to exclude a pupil but, where this is permanent, governors may direct the head to reinstate the pupil. This process has been the cause of some friction in a few schools where the head (and staff) have felt that the return of an excluded pupil is not in the best interests of the pupil or the school.

It is probable that these more recently defined responsibilities of governors could present some headteachers and their governing bodies with relationship difficulties if carried out to the letter. In many schools, however, it is likely that liberal interpretations of the rules will apply.

Problems facing school governors

The challenges facing a governing body are now more demanding and complex than ever. Decisions on the deployment of finances, on teaching appointments, on the curriculum and on disciplinary cases require a good working knowledge of the ways in which a school is organized and run. Governors of locally managed schools have, for example, the power (but not necessarily the money) to pay incentive allowances, incremental enhancement on the standard scale, and headteachers and deputies can be paid at any point on the pay range depending upon their responsibilities. The need to make these decisions which will be most beneficial to the school and its pupils, involves regular visits in order to further the development of sound relationships.

These decisions demand a breadth of expertise on the part of governors, who are attempting to resolve this through the establishment of committees (see above). These have proliferated and include responsibilities for staffing, finance, curriculum, discipline, buildings and lettings and many governing bodies in the larger schools have eight or nine such committees which can co-opt 'experts' to advise but who have no voting rights (except for control of premises used during out of school hours).

Many governors have been able to draw on teacher representatives in their decision making and these have made valuable contributions to debates on priorities. There have been suggestions, however, from the DFE that governing bodies are teacher dominated (31 per cent of school governors are teachers) and it is proposed that teachers will not in future be able to sit on governing bodies in the Authority which employs them, other than on those of their own schools. This has caused some concern as it is not considered to be democratic in the spirit of the 1988 Act.

All governors should receive on appointment a copy of a DFE publication which gives guidance on the legal aspects of their role and which is constantly updated. This publication, together with the Instruments and Articles of Government for the school provide the basis for their work.

These are not the only publications with which governors need to come to terms and many are concerned with the number of updating circulars and occasional papers which need to be read and which reflect the pace of changes in education. This can put a heavy load on the Clerk to the governors who may or may not be a member of the body, who may not be remunerated, and who with the headteacher, often has the task of sifting and of processing policies from central government.

Funding (a proportion of which is now being directly allocated to governing bodies) has been delegated from central government for governor training schemes in order to assist them in meeting these responsibilities and LEAs have appointed co-ordinators for training. Through these training officers many Authorities have provided valuable support for governors.

All these duties are, nevertheless, very time consuming and whilst, at one time, governors met on average once a term they need now to meet much more frequently which is of major concern to many governors. Whilst in 1988 it was possible to consider with some confidence the availability of 'leisure', this now very rarely applies. Under the employment laws employees must be given 'reasonable time off to perform their duties'. What constitutes this has to be agreed with the employer and there are wide variations of interpretation of what is 'reasonable'. An employer may give time off with pay but there is no legal requirement for this. The great majority of governors are volunteers and may claim from a few LEAs the costs of attending meetings. These are very much in the minority and with increases in the speed with which budgets are delegated the system is not likely to be continued.

THE FUTURE

Recruitment and tenure

In May 1991 the Association of Metropolitan Authorities undertook a survey of governing bodies which revealed that in a quarter of the 34 LEAs examined, the proportion of governors who had resigned rose by more than 50 per cent. In this survey three of the LEAs mentioned a drop in attendance, with LEA representatives being the group most likely to resign, just ahead of co-opted governors. It mentioned that teacher and parent governors were the most loyal in terms of attendance and membership. It needs to be asked if this is a continuing trend, particularly in view of the proposals to reduce the numbers of teacher governors.

Governors and LEAs

One of the major effects of the Acts of the 1980s is felt by LEAs. They no longer have the powers to undertake many of their previous responsibilities. This has profoundly affected governors who may, if they wish, negotiate contracts with LEAs to provide many of the services previously supplied by them. The functions of LEAs have changed from control to advisory and it is suggested that they may become little more than 'post boxes' for the passing on of information from the DFE to schools.

The changes following the Acts of the 1980s which affect governing bodies have still fully to be realized. It may be that Local Authorities will be re-organized into regions or will work as members of consortia. One of the results could be a gradual lessening of the powers of governors with a corresponding increase of those of headteachers.

Whatever the future may be, governors will need to face continuing challenges in the ways in which they are expected to run their schools. As Chris Patten the Secretary of State stated in the White Paper of July 1992, 'The objective has been both to put governing bodies and Headteachers under the greater pressure of accountability for better standards and to increase their freedom to respond to that pressure.' How governors will react to this and to its support of moves towards grant maintained status remains to be seen.

REFERENCES

DFE (1992) *Choice and Diversity: a New Framework for Schools*. HMSO, London.
DFE (1992) *School Governors: a Guide to the Law ('The Governors' Handbook')*. HMSO, London.
Education Act (1944) 'The Butler Act' (R.A. Butler, Minister of Education).

Education Act (1980) The first attempt to implement some of the Taylor Commission recommendations. HMSO, London.

Education (No. 2) Act (1986) Further implementation of the recommendations of the Taylor Commission. HMSO, London.

Education Act (1988) *The Education Reform Act*. HMSO, London.

Plowden, B.H. (1967) *Children and Their Primary Schools ('The Plowden Report')*. Advisory Council for Education, HMSO, London.

Royal Commission (1888) 'The Cross Commission', chaired by Lord Cross.

Taylor, T. (1977) *A New Partnership for Our Schools ('The Taylor Report')*. HMSO, London.

Warnock, M. (1978) *Special Educational Needs: Report of the Committee of Inquiry into the Education of Handicapped Children and Young People ('The Warnock Report')*. Cmnd 7212, HMSO, London.

14 Local management of schools: an English case study

Peter Downes

INTRODUCTORY BACKGROUND

As a new headteacher starting in September 1982 but appointed at the end of April, I had the advantage of being aware of what I was undertaking, but the disadvantage of not having taken a personal part in the negotiations preceding the implementation of local financial management (LFM). It was in fact the chance to be involved in this scheme which was one of the major attractions of the post. While head of a comprehensive school in Oxfordshire, I had been becoming increasingly concerned about the need for greater financial autonomy and had been advocating that experiments should be tried out. To arrive in a Local Education Authority (LEA) which was actually putting into practice what I had been thinking about as a theoretical and rather remote hope was an exciting prospect and brought me to Cambridgeshire full of great expectations.

In my previous post, I had become increasingly frustrated with the inflexibility of the system and more and more convinced that a measure of marginal flexibility to increase and decrease spendings under different headings would improve the management and efficiency of the school. I also felt that headteachers should be encouraged to use their buildings and lands as much as possible for public use and to keep for school purposes any profits they could make by their own initiatives and enterprise. My third main belief was that there is much greater incentive to save energy and to function cost-effectively if the savings you make are available to the school itself.

Hinchingbrooke School in Cambridgeshire is the largest school in the pilot scheme and one of the largest in the county. It also has its own Foundation which makes other small but useful sums of money available for the use of the school. Although this naturally increases the flexibility and resources at my disposal, it should be understood at the outset that the finances referred to in this chapter are only those of the Local Education Authority, which has the responsibility for the maintenance of the school.

THE HEADTEACHER'S SCOPE FOR MANAGEMENT

The first benefit of the local management of schools (LMS) scheme has been to give me the opportunity to find out a great deal more about the management of the financing of schools. It has been an extended on-the-job in-service experience and I have found it fascinating. If one believes that it is better for people in senior management positions to have a greater understanding of the pressures affecting the running of their establishment, local financial management is certainly a way of increasing that under-standing. The day-to-day management of the scheme has been carried out by me personally since the end of the first year of the pilot scheme. During the first year, one of the deputy heads was responsible for finance. When he moved to a headship in another county, I decided to take on the running of the scheme myself so that I could experience in detail the difficulties and opportunities first-hand. After further staff changes, a deputy head appointed in 1985 is now sharing the responsibility and could step in if I were indisposed or away from school for a period of time for any reason.

What, in fact, have I managed? Although the annual budget for a school as large as Hinchingbrooke is well over £1.5 million, the amount of money actually moved from heading to heading is no more than 2 per cent and usually nearer 1 per cent. Why such a fuss for such a small amount? The major costs of running a school – salaries and wages, council tax (of which more later), fuel – are fixed to a large extent. However, a flexible margin of £15,000 can make a great deal of difference if effectively applied to meet local needs in an individual way. The purchase of a piece of equipment for as little as £500 can enable a teaching programme to go ahead, or make the working conditions for teachers and learning conditions for pupils much better. £2,800 can provide an ancillary colleague for 20 hours per week term-time only and this person, employed, say, as a reprographics assistant, can greatly reduce the pressure on teachers and therefore make them more effective in the classroom.

Another great benefit of the management aspect of the scheme has been the speed with which decisions can be made. When an emergency arises and if you have set aside a contingency sum, you can call in help im-mediately without having to get permission from an official of the County in Shire Hall or in the Area Education Office.

Our experience has shown that the main underspendings have occurred in the following areas:

1 *Fuel costs* have been reduced by a mixture of great attention to careful use of premises and by mildish winters.
2 *Teacher salaries* by not re-appointing full-time staff when vacancies occur late in the year, thus saving on the time released from examination

classes after Whitsun.

3 Teacher salaries by *fortuitous appointment of slightly younger teachers.*
This has never been done as a matter of policy – all appointments are made by committee and our only consideration is the quality of the applicant chosen.

4 *Cleaners' wages* because we have been unable to recruit our allocation of cleaners at the normal wage-rate offered (as agreed with Shire Hall).

5 *Water charges* by identifying a leaking fish-pond and swimming-pool. Our water is metered.

6 Teacher salaries by the retention of *money not paid to teachers taking industrial action.*

At the same time the main overspendings have been incurred in the following areas:

1 *Teacher salaries* by appointing above the number of staff allowed by the Area Education Office formula and by using, temporarily, more scale points than our official allocation.

2 *Supply cover* by calling in supply staff whenever the situation demanded it, rather than by one-day, three-day rules.

3 *Ancillary staffing salaries* by appointing at least two extra part-timers to look after reprographics and libraries and by operating our own ancillary supply cover arrangements.

4 *Caretaker's wages* by the need to do overtime to cover for the shortage of cleaners.

5 *Rates, now council tax*! The only serious area of disagreement between myself and the LEA team has been on this question. I have maintained from the beginning that rates ought not to be included in the scheme as they cannot be managed by the head. My point was made when, in 1984–5, we incurred a £12,000 overspend because the Rating Officer re-rated the school on the basis of new buildings which had been open several years but the LEA refused to alter the sum allocated to us for rates. This decision was justified on the principle of taking the rough with the smooth! I have been allowed to repay this overspend over the next four years.

The amount of money nationally moved from one heading to another in the course of a year has always been under 2 per cent and the general direction of the moves has been to increase ancillary staffing, increase teacher staffing, increase supply cover, buy more equipment and books, and to set up our own in-service training account to allow us to support staff going on in-service training, who had been refused assistance by the LEA. The pecking-order of priorities was established by consultation with the whole staff at the end of the first year of the scheme, when we found ourselves with an underspend of £42,000 to allocate.

The oversight of the management decisions is vested in a Financial Management Committee on which are four governors (including a head of department and the chairman of the common room), the head teacher and accountant. They meet four or five times a year to receive a report on the balances and to consider priorities for the future. The accountant does the bulk of the routine checking and it is important to note that neither she nor her predecessor had any training before taking up this responsibility. Training was introduced for those in schools joining the scheme later. Neither should one be misled by the title accountant; the salary scale is the same as that of ancillary clerical staff and below what would normally be associated with trained accountants.

The main area of frustration for the accountant and myself has been our lack of confidence in the figures appearing on the monthly budgetary control print-out. The main areas of concern have been:

1   changes occurring in our budget allocation without explanation;
2   straightforward errors occurring through mis-coding of invoices (another school paid for all our toilet-rolls for two years before it was discovered!) and through what was recently described by the education officers as an unfortunate quirk in the computer;
3   the 'expected to date' column is based on county averages and does not necessarily match the pattern of spending for my particular school, thus producing strange apparent underspends or overspends at different times of the year;
4   the alterations to the budget through inflation happen at different times of the year according to the heading, oil prices, salary settlements, etc. This has caused particular difficulty in the last two years with back-dating of pay awards and assumed settlements;
5   the detailed tabulations accompanying the summary print-out do not give enough detail to allow a proper check to be made. This has caused a lot of frustration and innumerable telephone calls to Shire Hall, thus increasing our telephone bill and the workload of the staff at Shire Hall. Steps are now being taken, as the scheme goes county-wide, to improve this aspect of the computerized information;
6   the teacher staffing budget heading has great difficulty in coping with secondments: sometimes the seconded teacher is removed altogether from the payroll, sometimes he/she remains but a sum is added to the budget. This makes the fine-tuning of the staffing budget very difficult. To help me in this critical area of my work, my computer colleagues in school have devised a programme which forecasts the teacher salary

budget for the coming year, taking into account the incremental element due each September for many of the staff. This has proved helpful but I am slightly uneasy that this major component of expenditure is still not water-tight.

There has not always been the best liaison between ourselves, Shire Hall and the Area Education Office. Quite often we have received clarifications and instructions direct from Shire Hall about which the Area Office knew nothing. Some areas of the allocations and the administration remain with the Area Office but they do not always seem to be aware of the procedures we adopt. This is an area of muddle; matters usually get sorted out but it takes time.

We have come to the conclusion that certain aspects of the routine management of the finances could be improved, as follows:

1 If we could computerize all our accounts, a step we have been requesting for three years, time would be released from other matters (School Fund, for example) to allow for greater checking of the print-outs.
2 If we could have our own cheque-book and pay suppliers direct, one stage in the handling of invoices would be removed and with it the possibility of greater error. We would also know with greater accuracy the state of our accounts at month and year end.
3 If we could have a direct link to the Shire Hall main frame computer we may be able to question it direct and reduce the pressure on staff in Shire Hall.
4 If we could have a copy of the monthly salary bill, broken down by payments to individuals, we could keep a much tighter check on the accuracy of payments.
5 If we could be told much sooner the salary of new appointees, i.e. at exactly what incremental point they will be placed, the salary account could be fine-tuned. At the moment, I have to guess and then wait for confirmation when the September printout arrives.
6 The time-lag between 1 March and 5 March print-outs needs to be reduced. At the end of year, adjustments are made and a large number of internal transfers take place. By the time we know exactly the final under/overspend for the preceding year, we are well into June or even early July, by which time most of the critical decisions for the following academic year have been taken.

There are some important areas which lie outside the scope of the scheme, including debt charges and central management services. In addition, I have become concerned about other aspects which could come usefully under individual school control, for example, maintenance and re-decoration, grounds maintenance, school meals and school transport.

Some steps have been taken, however, to bring these areas within LFM; notably the fact that Hinchingbrooke School has become one of the pilot schools, with Comberton Village College, for the property bursar scheme. An experienced person, usually a former Area Surveyor, is placed in the school and takes over all day-to-day maintenance and re-decoration, reporting regularly to the Head and other members of staff as appropriate. This has been in operation for a few months at the time of writing and has had a very positive effect on the school, partly through the merit of the scheme and partly through the quality of the person appointed. It should be noted that at the present stage of the property bursar pilot scheme, the bursar is following the traditional funding arrangements and is not working to a school-specific budget. Nor are his salary costs debited to the school in the LFM printout.

The property bursar has an office in the school with a direct terminal link to Shire Hall, and has computerized control of all the heating equipment in the school. His responsibilities also cover a further 15 County Council establishments in the near vicinity and we shall wait to see how this works out in practice. At the time of writing, his salary and the costs of work done are being borne centrally in the traditional way. Discussions will shortly be taking place to see to what extent these costs can be brought within the schools' LFM budget. We shall also need to consider how energy conservation costs and savings can be apportioned between the County and the school. A further report on this development will have to be produced in due course. Grounds maintenance is still organized on an area basis, however, and there is no connection with the LFM budget. It is soon to be taken under the wing of the property bursar.

After many months of negotiation, we have been allowed to take over responsibility for our own catering service for a trial three-year period. We have appointed our own catering manager who reports to the headteacher and governors and not to the County school meals service. The aim of this scheme is above all to improve the quality of the catering and to increase the take-up by pupils. It is not primarily a money-making enterprise. The County has agreed to let us have, if we need it, the deficit that would have been incurred if the school meals service had been running the catering, on the basis of a 100 per cent of the deficit for the first year, 66 per cent for year 2 and 33 per cent for year 3. The governors have agreed to underwrite any extra deficit (from Foundation funds). It is too soon to draw any conclusions from this experiment and a further report will no doubt emerge in due course.

The absence of plans to give the school responsibility for its own transport is a source of much irritation to my colleagues responsible for bussing, in that they receive the criticisms from parents but are powerless to do anything about it except pass on the complaints.

THE WORKLOAD ON THE HEADTEACHER, SENIOR STAFF AND ANCILLARY STAFF

I am often asked how much time I spend on LFM and regret not having kept a more accurate record of this over the last four years. The pattern of work seems to be that I have a short burst of concentrated work and then never give it another thought for several weeks. The busy time is when the budget for the following year has to be worked out and when the staffing allocation for the following year is known. Other than that, the regular monthly printouts need to be checked and matters followed up. I have to attend meetings of my own Financial Management Committee and the LFM interferes with my work as a headteacher. My firm answer is that I still feel like a headteacher (!), that is my major concerns are the well-being of the school, the conduct and work of the pupils, the appointment and deployment of staff, relations with parents and governors and I still feel that I am in touch with pupils. I teach four periods per week in a 20-period timetable and participate in school music and sport as well as some of the school exchanges. I am active in a very thriving parents association and rarely miss a school social or cultural event. I think I can honestly say that I do not feel that LFM is a barrier between me and the school; on the contrary, it is an enabling factor which allows me to make good things happen much more rapidly and effectively than they might otherwise have done. The satisfaction given in this way more than outweighs the notional increased workload.

It is very difficult to quantify the extra workload on senior staff. The before-and-after LFM analysis is complicated by the changes in personnel: a new headteacher, followed by two new deputy heads and by three new heads of house, together with several new heads of department. There would have been changes in any event so it is impossible to disentangle the LFM element. I rely on my three deputy heads, each of whom has day-to-day responsibility for a section of the school, to deal with the majority of the immediate crises of school life, perhaps to a greater extent than I would otherwise. There is an increased workload on the ancillary staff responsible for accounts. I have explained above the reasons for the extra work and I hope that many of these will soon be solved. My personal view is that the senior member of the ancillary staff in charge of accounts, whatever title he or she is given, deserves remuneration on a scale towards the top end of those available.

THE HEADTEACHER'S RELATIONSHIP WITH THE LOCAL EDUCATION AUTHORITY

One of the great benefits of the pilot scheme has been to give officers and headteachers the opportunity to work closely together. The contact has gone beyond officers in the Education Department and has involved people in finance and administration, as well as property and other sections of Shire Hall. This working together has been fruitful for both sides, I believe. It has given people whose work is somewhat removed from the daily realities of school life the direct contact with the issues and problems we face in school. At the same time, those of us who work in school and are used to seeing everything in terms of our own patch have been given the chance to see the wider problems of educational financing. It is all too easy for those in school to see those in Shire Hall as 'them' who are out to make things difficult for 'us', who, we naturally think, are doing the real job. This pilot scheme has helped to reduce that divergence. In discussion with officers in other authorities thinking of taking up LFM I have more than once detected an anxiety that LFM might threaten the job security and challenge the mystique of those who work in central admini- stration. I do not think that there is any real danger of this. LFM in Cambridgeshire has increased the pressure on central staff and it has been necessary to take on five extra staff, for two years, in order to implement the scheme across all the secondary schools in the county.

THE EFFECT ON THE HEADTEACHER'S RELATIONSHIP WITH . . .

School governors

The responsibility for the successful working of LFM lies jointly with headteacher and governors. It is therefore clear that such a scheme brings governors more closely into contact with the life of the school. As it happens, Hinchingbrooke has always had a governing body which has prided itself on its detailed interest, meeting twice a term in full session, with a number of sub-committees as well as informal meetings with the staff. A number of governors have experience in the world of business and of management and this gives them the opportunity to put their talents at the disposal of the school.

School staff

The teaching staff have rightly not shown any great interest in the detailed workings of the LFM scheme, although they have been pleased to receive the benefits and to be asked for their advice on the best use of available resources. I say rightly, because the last few years, and the present time in particular, have seen a vast range of innovations within the curriculum and the examining system and it is to those tasks that the teaching staff should be putting their major energies and not worrying about the minutiae of the LFM scheme. It is, however, important that the staff should be fully informed and their support canvassed if there is to be a successful concerted effort to reduce waste, e.g. in fuel costs. Unless the whole staff is united in this approach, no amount of energy conservation will have any effect.

As with any scheme which is innovative, it is all too easy for staff to see the headteacher as being obsessed with his or her particular hobby-horse. Whether or not LFM has seriously harmed my relations with staff is scarcely for me to say but I am aware of the danger of appearing to be only interested in money! I hope that the majority of my colleagues appreciate that I have been able to use the flexibility of the LFM scheme to improve teaching conditions and resources.

By its very nature, the LFM scheme brings me more directly into contact with the school ancillary staff at all levels. This has enabled me to appreciate more personally the invaluable work they do for the life of the school, usually at relatively low rates of pay. I hope that they have begun to feel more part of the team of the school by dint of having a more direct working contact with the person who inevitably is the focal point for the financial management and all that flows from it.

Parents

The official contact for parents with the scheme is through the parent governors, one of whom is on the Financial Management Committee and is currently chairing it. On a wider level, mention of the scheme has been made at the annual meetings held in all parts of the catchment area and will need to be repeated at regular intervals as the school parental population changes.

What has emerged most clearly from the special meeting with parents has been their amazement at the pitifully small amount of money available to spend on books and equipment. Starting with a global sum of over £1.6 million to run a school of 1,700 pupils, by the time all the other expenses had been accounted for the school was left with approximately £25 to spend on books and equipment for each pupil. This had the merit of making them realize how valuable their fund-raising activities are and even if they raise only £1,000 per year, it adds proportionately quite a lot to the disposable income for books and equipment.

It has been said to me that parents are pleased that the school is in the LFM scheme because of the flexibility it gives to the headteacher to meet some of the crises of school life and also because it gives the head greater credibility with those parents who spend their professional lives working in industry and commerce. At least I am now able to give them well-informed replies when they want to know why certain aspects of the conditions or equipment in school are unsatisfactory.

Pupils

There is no formal structure for allowing pupils to participate in the decision-making process related to LFM. However, I do from time to time take the opportunity to explain to them aspects of the school's finance and have attempted to get them to understand that whatever we can collectively save by not wasting light or heat comes back to them in better facilities. In a more practical way I have involved them in the spirit of LFM by allowing each School Council (one for the Lower School, one for the Middle School and one for the Sixth Form) to retain the entire income from the typical School Fund collection at the beginning of the school year and to have responsibility for allocating its use. Their deliberations have been characterized by great seriousness and by a reluctance to grant funds to those unlikely to make good use of them. In practical terms, they have bought extra outside benches for seating in the school grounds, equipment for lunch-time entertainment, improved display facilities and smartened up and re-furnished their common-room areas.

THE BENEFITS FOR THE SCHOOL AND THE PUPILS

People who are unconvinced by the philosophical arguments behind LFM often ask me to prove that it has made education better for the pupils in my school. I am unable to do so in any clear and statistical way. Instead, I would point to what has been achieved and I would argue that these actions have brought significant advantages to the education of the pupils, mainly through making teaching conditions better for their teachers. For example, the fact that we now have a part-time librarian means that the libraries are open more often and the books better organized than before. The fact that we have a reprographics assistant means that teaching staff may spend less time duplicating their own teaching materials. We can point to specific items of equipment, particularly in the sphere of technology and computing, and say that we would not have been able to buy those when we did, had it not been for LFM. I can indicate that we have been able to reduce the occasional over-sized class by buying in an extra couple of teaching periods to enable a class to be split in two. Perhaps the most important, yet intangible, advantage to the school as a whole is that, compared with the previous system of financing, we are aware of much greater job satisfaction.

PERSONAL CONCLUSION

It should no doubt be apparent from the preceding paragraphs that, in spite of some specific points of criticism in relation to the mechanics of the system, I am wholeheartedly in favour of local financial management. I am acutely conscious that anybody involved in a new idea is predisposed to be in favour of it and that is why it has been valuable to have external evaluation. Although the evaluation was carried out at other schools in the pilot scheme, it broadly coincides with my own perception of its strengths.

In response to enquiries received from people in other countries which are considering adopting some version of LFM, I would respectfully and tentatively offer the following pieces of advice:

1 *To finance officers* – try to get their computer systems operating in a way which is comprehensible to the layman.
2 *To governors* – make sure that the system is fully explained to all concerned, staff, including non-teaching, and parents, and set up proper consultation procedures from the beginning.
3 *To headteachers* – not to expect too much of the scheme: it is not dramatic in its effects and it does not make overnight miracles possible. But it is certainly going to make the head's job more satisfying by enabling him/her to circumnavigate a number of the obstacles faced at the moment.
4 *To headteachers and deputies* – not to be overawed by the first impressions of complexity. It is not necessary to be a financial genius; what is needed is a firm commitment to doing the best possible for all the members of the school, a pocket calculator, a reliable accountant/secretary and lots of applied common sense.
5 *To accountants* – to keep asking the questions until the answers come in a form you can understand.
6 *To local authority elected members* – to commit themselves to not using LFM as a way of reducing expenditure on education. Make it clear time and again and keep repeating that the main intention is getting good value for money and avoiding waste by putting the point of decision as close as possible to the place of work, and if one does find oneself in the unfortunate position of having to cut education expenditure, do not use LFM to pass the blame for the cuts on to the headteachers. Make it clear in public pronouncements why cuts have had to be made, for example

because of 'rate-capping', but give the LFM headteacher discretion in deciding how the least harmful cuts can be made.

7 *To chief education officers and deputies* – LFM offers a spring-board for bringing the schools and the local education offices closer together. It is an in-service exercise with a real carrot.

8 *To all concerned* – to be prepared for the possibility that LFM may not work with smaller schools. When I say not work, what I mean is that the effort expended by the headteacher and his or her colleagues on understanding and checking the paperwork may be greater than the flexibility created by the scheme. The Cambridgeshire pilot scheme only had one primary school in it, a large one which reported positively on its experience.

LFM has clearly not yet reached its definitive form. Other refinements need to take place and there is much to be learned by exchanging experiences with other local education authorities who are trying similar schemes. There may well not be one perfect answer but I am convinced that we are at the beginning of a process of devolution which will gather momentum. My hope is that it will not be long before LFM is regarded as the normal way to run schools. Perhaps by the year 2000 people will look back on recent educational history and wonder how in Britain we allowed a system to last for so long which, however benevolent and wise, separated the decision- makers from those responsible for disbursing the available finance – those who had to make those decisions work out in practice.

My earnest hope is that LFM will not be hijacked by any political party, of whatever persuasion, and thereby get tangled up with other contentious issues, such as vouchers or direct-grant funding, which may prejudice teachers and parents against it.

NOTE: THE ORIGINS OF THE LOCAL FINANCIAL MANAGEMENT SCHEME IN CAMBRIDGESHIRE

All schools in Cambridgeshire have, for a number of years, had delegated to them a wide range of financial powers. The most important of these are: the freedom to decide on the type of ancillary staff employed (clerical, general and technical assistants but not the caretakers and cleaners) within a limit relating to school size, and to spend the capitation allowances made to them as they see fit, subject only to the use of county contracts and to compliance with financial regulations.

During Autumn 1977, a scheme for delegating certain other matters of financial administration to schools was made available to schools. Known as Increased Financial Responsibility it gave schools the responsibility for the control of orders, the certifying and coding of accounts and perhaps more importantly, for the budgetary control of capitation and other minor items of expenditure during the year. The Increased Financial Responsibility Scheme has now been wound up and is superseded by LFM.

A pilot scheme for local financial management was initiated by a county council resolution in November 1981. The Education Committee was asked to consider more flexibility in the control of their finances in 1982–3 by giving authority to the Governors of secondary schools to control their own budgets within a total cash limit. This limit was established by the council's budget and accountancy backup was made available from the Director of Finance and Administration. As a first stage the practice was to be introduced in establishments which agreed to accept this responsibility.

The county council then determined that with effect from 1 April 1986 the scheme of LFM was to be applied to all secondary schools in the authority, and a pilot scheme established for primary schools. The LFM scheme was subordinate to the Articles of Government of the participating schools and should be operated in the light of them. A number of costs were excluded from the LFM scheme and controlled centrally. These included cover for maternity and long-term sickness of teachers, property and playing fields' maintenance, home to school transport, school meals, insurances, debt charges, in-service training costs, as well as the costs of inspectors and advisers.

15 Opting out and legal challenge

Paul Meredith

INTRODUCTION[1]

One of the most deeply controversial reforms enshrined in the Education Reform Act 1988 was the establishment in England and Wales of a new category of maintained schools, known as grant maintained schools, inde- pendent of local education authority (LEA) control and funded directly by central government grants. Parallel legislation has been enacted for Scotland under the Self-Governing Schools, Etc. (Scotland) Act 1989, though the discussion in this chapter will focus on England and Wales. The Government's main justification for the creation of this new category of school, as spelled out in its 1987 consultation paper,[2] has been largely in terms of the promotion of the autonomy of schools from the strictures of LEA control and, in some cases, allegedly unwelcome curricular pressure (though the evidence for the latter was extremely slight); the opportunity for governors to run their schools as individual institutions with their own identifiable ethos and spirit; the responsiveness of schools to parental wishes and thus the enhancement of accountability on the part of the direct providers of educational services (teachers) through the school's governors to the consumers (parents), leading to greater efficiency, cost-effectiveness and higher standards; and the enhancement of parental choice of school through increasing the diversity of provision of schools within the maintained sector and hence expanding the scope for the operation of market forces in this context. It is, however, worthy of note that there is a major overlap between some of these justifications – notably autonomy, parental involvement and accountability – and those given for the provisions of the Education Reform Act concerning open enrolment and delegated financial management. This would appear to raise an implicit assumption that the new policies of open enrolment and delegated management would not go far enough to achieve these goals: hence the need for a new category of school free even from the residual powers of control and influence remaining to LEAs following implementation of the 1988 Act. There may well, however, have been a more fundamental underlying purpose behind the government's opting out proposals, namely the determination further to erode local authority functions in respect of education through the destruction of the LEA monopoly over the provision of maintained schools, this being consistent with the government's approach to central–local relations over a wide spectrum of governmental functions. The extent of this erosion will depend largely upon the scale of opting out: Baroness Margaret Thatcher spoke of her vision of opting out on a substantial scale. It remains to be seen whether Baroness Thatcher's vision was accurate, but in the early period before the general election of April 1992 the movement towards grant maintained status was undoubtedly slow, the majority of proposals having come predictably from schools threatened by unwelcome closure, amalgamation or other structural proposals. By May 1992, 217 schools were already operating as grant maintained schools in England, 33 had been approved but were not yet in operation, and five were close to ministerial approval.[3] But it is likely that there were many schools waiting in the wings, content to observe the initial fortunes of the early grant maintained schools or preferring to await the outcome of the general election, before themselves taking positive steps towards opting out. The return of the Conservative government to power in 1992 will undoubtedly add considerable impetus to the opting out movement, and this was perhaps the most important element in the government's White Paper of July 1992, 'Choice and Diversity: a New Framework for Schools'.[4] This projected that there could be over 1,500 grant maintained schools by April 1994, and that by 1996 most of the 3,900 maintained secondary schools, as well as a significant proportion of the 19,000 maintained primary schools, could be grant maintained.[5]

Legal challenges hitherto have come both from parents opposed to opting out on political, social or educational grounds, and from LEAs dismayed by the potential impact of one or more schools opting out on the provision of schools in their area as a whole, particularly if opting out comes at a time when wide-ranging, carefully co-ordinated, socially and educationally viable and cost-effective plans for reorganization of their schools in the area in the light of falling rolls are pending. As will be seen later in the context of the City of Bath dispute, even one school opting out is likely to throw wider LEA reorganization proposals into serious disarray.

LEGAL CHALLENGE TO THE ACQUISITION OF GRANT MAINTAINED STATUS

Two major legal challenges have been brought in the context of the acquisition of grant maintained status, one against the governors of the school concerned (the Birmingham Small Heath case), the other against the decision of the Secretary of State to approve opting out proposals (the City of Bath case): these cases are analysed below. As would be expected, other litigation elsewhere has since occurred, notably in the London Borough of Newham in relation to Stratford School, and this case is analysed briefly in the postscript at the end of this chapter.

The Birmingham Small Heath case

The first litigation arose out of the bitter struggle in Birmingham over the proposal by the governors of Small Heath School that a ballot of parents should be held, and involved parallel applications for judicial review by Birmingham City Council (the LEA) anxious to retain the school within its control, and by a group of parents opposed to opting out.[6]

Small Heath School was (before becoming grant maintained) a co-educational comprehensive county secondary school for pupils aged 11 to 16 years. Its catchment area was 'one of the poorest parts of Birmingham's inner ring',[7] and some 80 to 90 per cent of its pupils were Muslim, coming mainly from Pakistan or Bangladesh. There was evidence that no more than about 60 per cent of the parents understood English, and that at least 16 different languages were spoken among the parents, and with a variety of dialects among those 16 languages. The school faced many problems, but its social and ethnic mix undoubtedly served to give it a strong element of cohesion and identity, and it was generally perceived as successful both in educational terms and as a significant community resource. This perception gave focus to strong feelings among a group of parents that the school should remain as a community resource under LEA control rather than opt out. Other parents, strongly supported by the headteacher, however, argued that the school could be more responsive to community needs if its governors enjoyed full managerial control as a grant maintained school independent of the LEA.

The composition of the governing body of the school had been revised with effect from 1 September 1988 by virtue of section 3 of the Education (No. 2) Act 1986. There were 16 members, comprising four LEA nominees, the headteacher, four elected parents' representatives, two elected teachers' representatives, and five co-opted members. One of the elected parent governors happened to be a non-teaching staff employee at the school. The governing body met on 9 November 1988 to explore the merits of grant maintained status. The governors formally resolved at this meeting[8] by a majority of 13 votes to 2 that a ballot of parents on the issue should be held. Those present and voting in favour of this resolution included the headteacher, the two teacher representatives and the 'employee parent' governor.

Certain consultations and communications – which will be examined in more detail below – then took place between the governors and the LEA. Then, as required by the Act,[9] a second governors' meeting was held on 14 December 1988 for further consideration of the issues: the governors voted on this occasion by 10 votes to 3 in favour of holding a parental ballot. On this occasion too, the headteacher, the two teacher representatives and the 'employee parent' representative were present, although the two teacher representatives abstained from voting.

On 13 January 1989 the ballot papers were sent to parents under section 61, and the ballot closed on 3 February, the parents voting by 435 to 338 in favour of seeking grant maintained status. Formal proposals for the change were then published by the governors on 1 March,[10] and on 14 June the Secretary of State gave his approval to the proposals[11] which were scheduled to come into effect on 1 September 1989. The legal challenges were directed expressly at the governors' resolutions and at the activities of certain of the governors, and not at the Secretary of State's approval. The major grounds of challenge will now be considered.

The LEA's first challenge was based on their contention that they had been inadequately consulted[12] by the governors as to their decision to hold a ballot between the governors' two formal resolutions. 'Consultation' is not defined in the Act, but the LEA contended that it must at least involve clear identification of the governors' 'proposals' for the school in the event of its becoming grant maintained, and that proper consultation at this stage was of critical importance to the LEA given the short period of time available between the two resolutions.[13] The LEA contended that the consultation process had been defective in that the governors' plans had failed to make clear, in particular, the governors' proposals in respect of pupils with special educational needs and the proposed use of recreational and library facilities at the school which had hitherto been available for use by the general public. The governors, on the other hand, argued that they were not obliged at this early stage to produce fully formulated 'proposals' for consultation, and that on the facts they had in any event carried out sufficient consultations with the LEA. Various communications had in fact passed between the headteacher and the Acting Chief Education Officer, and meetings had taken place between LEA officials and governors at which officials had set out what they saw as the disadvantages of opting out 'in clear and forceful terms'.[14] The Acting Chief Education Officer and another officer had attended the governors' meeting of 14 December at which the second formal resolution was passed and at which there was an extensive discussion of the issues.

Lord Justice Woolf in the Divisional Court was clearly of the view that the LEA's submissions as to inadequate consultation were without substance: the governors could not be expected at this stage to have formulated their plans on all points in highly specific terms; adequate efforts had been made to communicate the substance of the proposals to the LEA, and sufficient opportunities had been afforded to the LEA to communicate their views to the governing body. The judge clearly regarded it as significant that no complaint about the process of consultation had been made by the LEA while the process was continuing. Birmingham City Council, as a large LEA with legal advisers and experienced education officers on its staff, could readily have been expected to have requested further information if they had felt it necessary, yet this had not been done. In a sense, they had by their silence waived any right to demand further information.

The second major ground of challenge by the LEA was that the headteacher, the two teacher governors and the 'parent employee' governor had improperly taken part in the governors' deliberations as they had had a direct pecuniary interest in the outcome, contrary to paragraph 2 of Schedule 2 of the Education (School Government) Regulations 1987.[15] The LEA relied principally on the earlier decision of the Court of Appeal in *Bostock* v. *Kay*[16] in which it had upheld the decision of Mr Justice Jowitt at first instance, declaring that teacher governors were disqualified from taking part in a governors' meeting on the issue of whether a school should become a City Technology College. In order for the regulations to have the effect of disqualifying the employee-governors, it would have to be shown that the change to grant maintained status was sufficiently probable and that the consequences which might flow from that change for the employee-governors were sufficiently radical. The courts have traditionally taken a stringent approach to provisions of this kind disqualifying parties from participating on account of financial interest, placing considerable emphasis on the need to prevent conflicts between private interests and public duties.

In *Bostock* v. *Kay*, the Court of Appeal, in holding that the employee-governors were disqualified, had been influenced by the possibility that teachers employed at a City Technology College might earn more money than their counterparts in LEA-maintained schools, and by the prospect that, if not offered a position by the governors of the newly created City Technology College, they might be made redundant. It had been argued by the governors that these possibilities were too remote to be operative as disqualifying factors, but the Court of Appeal disagreed, endorsing the opinion of Mr Justice Jowitt at first instance that, 'Any teacher invited to vote on these proposals would understandably be tempted at the very least to ask how it would affect him financially.'[17]

In the Small Heath case, Lord Justice Woolf, although aware that the change to grant maintained status was less radical than that to City Technology College status, nonetheless felt bound to follow the decision in *Bostock* v. *Kay* and thus upheld the LEA's contention that the employee-governors were disqualified. He went on, however, to express concern over this consequence of the 1987 Regulations, given that it is widely recognized that the headteacher and other teacher representatives on the governing body ought to have a particularly important contribution to make to these very important deliberations about a school's future.

When the governors challenged this finding on appeal, however, the Court of Appeal declined to follow its earlier decision in *Bostock* v. *Kay* on the basis that there were significant differences between City Technology Colleges and grant maintained schools. Lord Justice Glidewell (who, co-incidentally, had also delivered the leading Court of Appeal judgment in *Bostock* v. *Kay*) emphasized that:

> The only necessary changes when a county school becomes a grant maintained school are that the cost of the school's financial support is transferred from the local education authority to the Secretary of State, and that the governors gain a greater measure of autonomy. The school itself need not alter at all. If a voluntary, or county, school becomes a CTC the change is much more fundamental. The old school ceases to exist, and a completely new institution takes its place, albeit in the same building. The staff of the old school may well be, but need not be, engaged by the governors of the CTC and may be made redundant. The curriculum taught at the CTC may well differ from that taught at the former school, as may the age-range of the pupils. Moreover, in *Bostock's* case there was evidence that teachers at a CTC would probably work longer hours than they did at the former school, and thus earn more.[18]

The governors' decision to seek to hold a ballot was also challenged by a group of parents of children at Small Heath School on grounds relating essentially to the content of the information which had been issued to parents concerning grant maintained status and the manner in which it had been disseminated. Much of the press publicity concerning Small Heath had focused on these aspects of the dispute, and in the litigation they raised issues of fundamental importance to the manner in which ballots are held. Central to this aspect of the dispute was the ethnic and linguistic diversity of the parents of children at Small Heath.

Under section 61, the governing body are required, having passed the second resolution in favour of holding a ballot, to 'secure that all necessary arrangements for the ballot are made by such body as may be prescribed'.[19] To this end, they must 'secure that the prescribed body take such steps as are reasonably practicable' to secure that all parents eligible to vote receive specified information concerning the nature and procedures for acquisition of grant maintained status as well as specified information relating to the school concerned.[20] The body which has been 'prescribed' for those purposes by the Secretary of State is the Electoral Reform Society.

The section is silent as to the precise form this information should take, and in particular, whether it should be conveyed in any language other than English. The Secretary of State has, however, issued statutory guidance to governors under section 61(6),[21] which governors are required to 'take into account'. This requires an element of conscious consideration, but it does not mean that it must be slavishly followed. This guidance indicated that the Electoral Reform Society would issue eligible parents with, among other information, a fact sheet concerning grant maintained status. It indicated that it would be for the governors to decide whether to supply any of this information in languages other than English, and that the Electoral Reform Society would for this purpose hold stocks of their fact sheets in Bengali, Chinese, Greek, Gujarati, Hindi, Punjabi, Turkish and Urdu. The headteacher of Small Heath School, acting on behalf of the governors as a whole, requested the Electoral Reform Society to send out the information in English, Urdu and Bengali, but the Society found this impracticable as their packing and despatching machinery did not have the required mechanical facility to do this. As a compromise measure, the fact sheets were sent out only in English, but translated copies were made available on parental request. The availability of translations was made known to parents through the intermediary of the children (by 'pupil post', as it was called). The parents submitted that the governors had failed in their obligation under section 61(3) to secure that the Electoral Reform Society should 'take such steps as are reasonably practicable' to bring the required information to the parents' attention. Lord Justice Woolf concluded that the general presumption was that, where an English statute requires information to be provided, it need be provided only in English. On the facts of this case, given the multiplicity of languages spoken by the parents, it could not reasonably have been expected that the information should be provided in each language spoken. While it would have been desirable for the material to have been provided in the three languages requested by the headteacher, failure to do so did not constitute a breach of section 61(3). By taking the practical steps of ensuring the availability of translations where requested, and making this facility known to parents through 'pupil post', the governors had satisfied the statutory requirements.

The parents went on, however, to challenge certain actions of some of the governors, and in particular of the headteacher, by 'entering the ring in an improper manner and campaigning in favour of the change in status',[22] thereby bringing about a state of confusion in the minds of some of the parents. The governors' response was that the very reason they had 'entered the ring' was to counter misconceptions as to the school's future which had arisen as a result of a large amount of inaccurate information having been issued by several other parties to the dispute. To this end, certain of the governors distributed leaflets to parents through 'pupil post', setting out their viewpoint in favour of the change to grant maintained status, and giving notice of public meetings to discuss the issues. Lord Justice Woolf concluded that there was no legal requirement preventing the governors from taking such steps to counteract inaccuracies and confusions which were then circulating:

> Faced as Mr. Knight (the headteacher) and the governors were with a situation where Christian parents were being told the school would become a Muslim school, where Muslim parents were being told the school would become a Christian school, parents were being told that they would have to pay school fees and pupils would lose the right to free meals and would not be able to use leisure facilities, and all teachers would leave the school and the school would become a Conservative Government school, the course which was adopted by the governors was perfectly understandable and not objectionable.[23]

A final basis for challenge in this context related specifically to the conduct of the headteacher and the two teacher governors in distributing the leaflet through the intermediary of the pupils and explaining the contents of the document to the pupils for them in turn to convey to their parents. This, it was submitted, was in breach of section 45 of the Education (No. 2) Act 1986, a statutory curricular requirement that in maintained schools political issues be presented in a balanced manner. This is believed to be the first legal challenge based on this important curricular requirement, though it is regrettable that it was relegated to the level of a subsidiary challenge in this way. Section 45 imposes a duty on the LEA, the governing body and the headteacher to

> take such steps as are reasonably practicable to secure that where political issues are brought to the attention of pupils while they are . . . at the school . . . they are offered a balanced presentation of opposing views.

The children, it was contended, had been brought into the political conflict: in particular, the views expressed in the document communicated through 'pupil post' had been exclusively in favour of grant maintained status and had thus clearly failed to offer a 'balanced presentation of opposing views', and the headteacher had additionally expressed his views orally to the children. This could be regarded as an unusual context for section 45 to be invoked, the section being primarily intended to operate as an element of constraint on the substantive content of the school curriculum, but the dissemination of material concerning the future status of the school could nonetheless be construed as falling within the ambit of the section. Lord Justice Woolf concluded, however, that, even on the assumption that a proposed change in the school's status was an issue to which section 45 applied, there had on the evidence been no breach: a 'perfectly objective' approach had been adopted in the oral statements to the pupils, and no fault could be found with the written document given the context of the perceived need to take steps to counter the various misconceptions as to grant maintained status circulating at the time among the parents.

As is so often the case, it is almost impossible to disentangle the educational, social and political from the more technically legal considerations in this dispute. The social and political dimension was what attracted most of the press coverage: it is normal for opponents of a particular school opting out to point to the potentially divisive, separatist and elitist impact the change of status would have on the provision of education in the area as a whole. Where that school is one which draws a high proportion of its children from one or more ethnic minority groups, predictions of separatism and divisiveness are still made, though they take on a further social dimension, raising fundamental arguments about multi-cultural education in our society. A majority of the governors and of those parents who voted in the Small Heath ballot expressed the view, doubtless for many different reasons, that their children's educational future and their community would genuinely be better served by the attainment of grant maintained status for their school. The LEA and a group of parents opposed to opting out challenged this by alleging deficiencies in the technical procedures laid down in the Education Reform Act 1988 and in Regulations. As is normal in the judicial review process, what was truly a challenge on social, political and educational grounds was transformed into a challenge on grounds of technical legality. Procedural defects such as failure to consult properly, pecuniary interest and inadequate dissemination of information are, indeed, often fruitful mechanisms of challenge in the courts, and educational disputes have in recent years frequently been the context of such challenges. But parents and others opposed to opting out will be able to derive little comfort from the restrictive interpretation given in this case in the Court of Appeal to governors' pecuniary interests, an interpretation which appears to attach a higher value to practical convenience than to procedural propriety; nor from the apparent judicial endorsement of what could be viewed as seriously inadequate efforts to distribute the fact sheets in languages other than English, and of the involvement of the pupils themselves in transmitting information through them from a section of the governors to parents, while many would say that the involvement of pupils in any way in this context is highly undesirable even if not illegal. This emphasizes the improbability of any successful legal challenge based on the very general phraseology of section 45 of the Education (No. 2) Act 1986.

City of Bath case – Beechen Cliff School

The second major action to have reached the Courts at the time of writing is the challenge brought by Avon County Council against the Education Secretary concerning the latter's approval of proposals by the governors of Beechen Cliff School in Bath for grant maintained status, and his simultaneous rejection of a composite set of proposals by the LEA for reorganization of secondary education in Bath in response to the pressures of falling rolls: *R. v. Secretary of State for Education and Science, ex parte Avon County Council*.[24] Significantly, this was the first judicial consideration of section 73 of the Education Reform Act 1988, a most important provision dealing with the interaction between proposals by an LEA (or governors of a voluntary school) for reorganization under section 12 (or 13) of the 1980 Act, and proposals under section 62 of the 1988 Act by the governors of one of the schools affected by the LEA's (or governors') proposals to opt out rather than face the consequences of reorganization. Given that the majority of opting out proposals have arisen in this context, this first judicial consideration of section 73 was bound to have great significance for other LEAs and governing bodies in a similar relationship – a relationship of considerable stress and perhaps antagonism. The stakes in such a case are high: the governing body is desperate to defend its school from reorganization, perhaps involving amalgamation or closure; the LEA, taking a wider view of educational provision in its area as a whole, is anxious that its co-ordinated plans for school provision in the area should not be thrown into disarray. This was just the relationship between the governors of Beechen Cliff School in Bath and Avon County Council.

Avon County Council had, over a period of years and after extensive consultations, drawn up a composite package of reorganization proposals for the City of Bath, and these were submitted to the Secretary of State under section 12 of the 1980 Act on 22 February 1989.[25] In essence, these proposals involved reducing the number of secondary schools serving Bath City from six to five by the closure of Beechen Cliff Boys School; creating a new sixth form college on the Beechen Cliff site to make centralized provision for sixth form education in the city; and 'decapitating' the remaining five secondary schools of their sixth forms, thus limiting their age range to 11 to 16 years. The governors of Beechen Cliff School were, however, adamant that their school should retain its identity as a secondary school serving the full 11 to 18 years age group, and passed resolutions[26] under section 60 of the 1988 Act in favour of holding a ballot on opting out. In February 1989 a majority of the parents voted in favour of seeking grant maintained status, and formal proposals to this end were then drawn up by the governors and submitted to the Secretary of State under section 62 on 17 April 1989.

The submission of opting out proposals by the governors thus activated the provisions of section 73: this provides that, where an application for grant maintained status is published before an LEA's section 12 proposals have been decided, the Secretary of State must consider both sets of proposals together on their merits, but must make his determination of the grant maintained status proposal first. If he approves the grant maintained status application, he will automatically reject the section 12 proposal in respect of that school, but he must then go on to consider the effect of that decision on the remaining section 12 proposals.[27] It may be that these remaining proposals will be bound to be rejected in the sense that they cannot stand on their own, the newly approved grant maintained school having been severed from their midst, in which case the LEA will have to undertake a complete reappraisal of its proposals. There may, however, possibly be room for a *modified* approval by the Secretary of State of the LEA's remaining proposals, though this may in practice be unlikely as the severance of an entire school from a scheme of proposals is likely to be too radical a change to permit modified approval of the proposals that remain. The Secretary of State in such a case would be in danger of purporting to approve by modification proposals which had never truly been submitted to him under section 12, and this itself would be susceptible to judicial review by those opposed to the modified scheme.[28]

The Secretary of State on 16 August 1989 issued his determinations of both the LEA's and the governors' proposals, and in doing so displayed a most regrettable lack of respect for the interested parties through a virtually total absence of reasoning. His decision letters stated merely that: 'In reaching his decision, the Minister concluded that the merits of the application by the governors of Beechen Cliff School for grant maintained status outweighed those of the authority's proposal.'[29]

Avon County Council were dismayed by the consequences of this decision for their wider proposals on which they had held extensive consultations and which had emerged only after a gestation period going back to the early 1980s, and brought an application for judicial review of the Minister's determination in the High Court. The Minister's reasons, which had been so conspicuously absent from the initial decision letters, were spelled out in an affidavit put before Mr Justice Hutchinson, and the judge found in favour of the LEA chiefly on the grounds that the Minister had misconstrued section 73 by giving the application for grant maintained status *priority* over the section 12 reorganization proposals, when they should properly have been weighed against one another equally in the balance together; and that the Minister had evinced a failure to give proper consideration to the *wider consequences* for the remaining schools in Bath of his decision in favour of grant maintained status for Beechen Cliff School.

The LEA's victory in the High Court was, however, short-lived: the Secretary of State did not appeal against the decision of the Court, but instead took his own decision back for reconsideration in the light of the High Court's findings. On 30 March 1990 he made *identical determinations*, accepting the proposal for grant maintained status for Beechen Cliff and rejecting the Avon proposals in the round, but on this occasion he scrupulously spelled out his reasoning at considerable length and in terms which were far less readily amenable to judicial challenge. He made it explicitly clear that he had adopted a three-stage procedure, as required by section 73(4)(b), namely consideration of the merits and demerits of the grant maintained status application, followed by those of the section 12 reorganization proposals, followed by a consideration of both sets of proposals together.

The Minister took the view that the grant maintained status proposal was sound in that Beechen Cliff was clearly a viable, well-established and popular school of proven worth with a strong sixth form and with every expectation of retaining its existing strong demand for places. The LEA's proposals, on the other hand, although achieving a reduction in surplus capacity, addressing the problem of small sixth forms, keeping capital costs to a minimum and creating more coeducational places in accordance with parental wishes expressed during the consultation process, would nonetheless bring about what the Minister saw as major disadvantages: they involved the closure of Beechen Cliff, one of the stronger and more popular schools in the city; by removing all 11 to 18 provision, they also involved closure of another well-established sixth form of proven worth; they failed to make the most effective possible reduction in surplus capacity; and, above all, through centralization of all sixth form provision in one sixth form college, they eliminated *competition between institutions* and *parental choice* at sixth form level. Both competition and parental choice are, of course, fundamental to the government's philosophy of education and underlie much of the Education Reform Act 1988.

The Minister went on in his decision letter to put forward what he saw as three feasible alternative approaches for consideration by the LEA, each of which might coexist with Beechen Cliff as a grant maintained school:[30]

1 Closure of one school to provide premises for a sixth form college; closure of the sixth forms of either three or four of the remaining schools, and providing either one or two 11 to 18 years schools co-existing with the college (to provide choice and competition at sixth form level).
2 Closure of two schools, one providing premises for a sixth form college; closure of the sixth forms of either two or three of the remaining schools and providing one or two 11 to 18 years schools co-existing with the college.
3 Closure of two schools and leaving the remainder as 11 to 18 years schools with no centralized sixth form college provision.

The Minister then concluded, balancing the grant maintained school proposal against the LEA's reorganization proposals, that it would be preferable to accept the governors' proposals to opt out given the established strength and viability of Beechen Cliff, and that the LEA's proposals were seriously flawed and ought to be reconsidered in the light of the alternative options he had outlined, each of which he considered to be feasible and to avoid the serious flaws he had outlined. He did not feel that the necessary reconsideration and resubmission of fresh LEA proposals ought to delay implementation of the new reorganization scheme by more than one year; nor that his determination would 'inhibit to an unacceptable extent'[31] the options available to Avon; nor that any fresh problems in terms of providing an equal balance between single sex and coeducational provision available to male and female pupils as required by the Sex Discrimination Act 1975 would be irresoluble by the LEA. For all of these reasons he followed his earlier determination.

Again, Avon County Council sought to challenge the Secretary of State's determination: this application for judicial review was heard by the Court of Appeal even though technically it was not an *appeal* against the earlier judgment of Mr Justice Hutchinson but a first instance challenge to the Minister's fresh determinations.[32]

The three major grounds of challenge were that the Minister had unlawfully treated the grant maintained school application as 'paramount', that he had been mistaken in regarding his three alternative solutions as feasible options, and that he had failed to give proper consideration to the difficulties which would be faced by the LEA as a result of their obligations under the Sex Discrimination Act 1975.

The 'paramountcy' argument was very similar to the unlawful priority argument which had been accepted by Mr Justice Hutchinson in the earlier challenge: the Court of Appeal, however, adopted a radically different view of the LEA's submission, emphasizing that the legislation in this context expressly leaves the determination of the issues to the discretion of the Minister, and that it would not be unlawful for him- to adopt policy preferences, provided always that they were not applied inflexibly without taking account of all relevant considerations according to law. As stressed by Lord Justice Ralph Gibson:

> The Acts of 1980 and 1988 . . . empower the Minister to approve or to reject the proposals. They provide no test to be applied. They do not, for example, require the Minister to approve that set of proposals which will, in probability, most nearly accord with the wishes of the majority of parents and schoolteachers . . . The task given to the Minister, however, by the section is to consider both sets of proposals together. The process is not one of fact-finding in the ordinary sense but of *judgment and evaluation*. It includes judgment of the future course of events by reference to the existing facts, to the accumulated knowledge and experience available to the Minister in his Department, to his policy for securing the objects of the legislation, and to his assessment of the prospects for success of that policy in achieving those objects.[33]

It will readily be appreciated that it is extremely difficult to challenge a decision based, as here, on a Minister's *judgment and evaluation* of competing criteria in relation to which he is entitled to adopt policy preferences and have regard to his own and his department's experience and his own underlying educational philosophy. The three judges in the Court of Appeal unanimously rejected this challenge, emphasizing that it could succeed only if shown that the Minister could not rationally have made his determination. The LEA had failed to establish that no rational Minister could have made such a determination on the basis of an unbending priority or paramountcy, but merely that he had applied policy preferences to which he was properly entitled in the light of his judgment and evaluation of the issues.

The court came to a similar conclusion in respect of the challenge to the feasibility of the three alternative solutions propounded by the Minister in his decision letter. Lord Justice Ralph Gibson again pitched the requirement for any successful legal challenge here very high:

> For it to be shown that the Minister in this regard misdirected himself by supposing there to be feasible options, it would, in my judgment, have

to be demonstrated that, on the material before him, he could not reasonably hold the view that such options existed.[34]

The Court of Appeal held that the Minister had, indeed, spelled out his three alternative proposals in his decision letter and, though the LEA or others might well assert that other proposals were educationally preferable for various reasons, this went no distance towards an assertion of illegality as required for a successful legal challenge which involved the taking of a decision which no rational person in the Minister's position could take. Indeed, one assertion by the LEA – that the Beechen Cliff site was the only site that the Minister could rationally entertain as the site for the sixth form college – was, in the Court of Appeal's view, fatally flawed as the LEA itself had proposed another of the schools in the group – Culverhay – as a possible site for the sixth form college in February 1988.[35]

The third main ground of challenge was based on sections 23 and 25 of the Sex Discrimination Act 1975. The assertion was not that the Secretary of State was acting in a discriminatory fashion or had misdirected himself as to the meaning of the provisions in any way, but that he had failed, in considering the proposals submitted by the governors of Beechen Cliff and Avon County Council, to give proper consideration to the difficulties which would be faced by the LEA in complying with *its* obligations under the Sex Discrimination Act to refrain from sexually discriminatory behaviour. This challenge was based on the earlier decisions in *R*. v. *Secretary of State for Education and Science, ex parte Keating*[36] and *Equal Opportunities Commission* v. *Birmingham City Council*,[37] and recognized the obligation of the LEA to make available an equal number of places for male and female pupils in single sex schools or in selective schools (though no obligation to provide any single sex or any selective schools). The Avon proposals had sought to strike a legally acceptable balance, taking into account parental demand for an increase in the number of available co-educational places, through Beechen Cliff ceasing to exist as an 11 to 18 years school for boys and the establishment of a coeducational sixth form college on its premises. Beechen Cliff being permitted, however, to opt out and continue to exist as a school for boys only would plainly have upset the balance of available single sex places in the area, given that in striking this balance an LEA must take account both of schools provided directly by it and of grant maintained (and possibly private) schools in its area. This is indeed likely to be a serious consequence of any single sex school being permitted to opt out in the face of a balanced scheme of LEA proposals for reorganization: the LEA is indeed likely to have to reconsider its obligations under the Sex Discrimination Act and to ensure that its revised proposals remain balanced in terms of the availability of single sex places. As Lord Justice Ralph Gibson commented:

> I see force in the submissions (of Avon County Council) because, on Beechen Cliff achieving grant maintained status, although it will thereafter be maintained by the Minister and not by Avon as local education authority, the places for boys in that single sex school will continue to be available at public expense. It seems at least arguable to me that it would not be open to Avon, without breach of the Sex Discrimination Act, to decide to cease to provide to an equal extent single sex places for girls so as to deprive any girls of the option of attending a single sex school.[38]

Although conceding that the LEA had raised a relevant problem which *they* would have to face, the Court of Appeal rejected the challenge *in relation to the determination by the Secretary of State*, as he had on the facts plainly had regard to the sex discrimination question and had taken the view that it would not be impossible for the LEA on reconsideration to come up with fresh proposals consonant with its obligations under the Sex Discrimination Act.

The Court of Appeal was thus clearly not prepared to accept Avon's three main challenges on grounds of paramountcy, irrationality or sex discrimination.[39] Indeed, the Court described the litigation as fundamentally misconceived in the sense of seeking to challenge under the guise of an application for judicial review what was in essence a disagreement as to educational policy. As Lord Justice Ralph Gibson commented:

> It is, I think, misconceived in so far as it asks the court to intervene in what is, when analysed, a dispute as to educational policy between Avon and the Minister. Avon, including the officials and members who have worked on the task of re-organizing secondary education in the city of Bath, and the teachers and parents who have also worked in the processes of consultation which have been carried out for that purpose, believe that the proposals put forward are the best available for the children of Bath; and they believe, it seems, that it was wrong and unreasonable on the part of the Minister not to approve them and, instead, to approve grant maintained status for Beechen Cliff School. The Minister, however, was acting under powers given by Parliament in the Act of 1988. If he was acting lawfully within those powers, there is no purpose in seeking to demonstrate that the proposals put forward by Avon are, in the view of those putting them forward, superior for the purposes of advancing the quality of secondary education for the children

of Bath. Parliament did not entrust the making of that judgment to the court but to the Minister who is answerable in respect of his decisions to Parliament.[40]

CONCLUSION

This classic expression of judicial restraint in the Avon case reflects how difficult it may be to challenge a decision of the Secretary of State on grounds of *substance* where a statute has vested the decision-making power in him in the widest discretionary terms. It would take a very extreme form of unreasonableness in the shape of a decision no rational Minister could entertain, or clearly taking irrelevant considerations into account or the omission of some clearly relevant factor, before a challenge on grounds of substance would be likely to succeed, in the absence of evidence of bad faith or a Minister acting for an improper purpose. *Procedural* challenge is usually more productive, but very hard to level at a Minister making a determination under section 73, where the statute lays down virtually no procedural formalities for the Minister to follow. Procedural challenge might be successful if levelled by opponents of opting out – as in the Small Heath case – at school governors who *are* under the Act constrained by a multitude of statutory procedural requirements, in the context of passing the initial resolutions, holding the parental ballot and drawing up their formal proposals for submission, but the Avon case shows how difficult it is to challenge a determination by the Secretary of State sheltered as he is by extremely generous discretionary power.

POSTSCRIPT

As already mentioned, further litigation has now arisen elsewhere over opting out, notably in Newham and the government has now proposed to accelerate the pace of opting out through a number of important amendments to the law outlined in its July 1992 White Paper, *Choice and Diversity*, and these have been incorporated in legislation introduced in the autumn of 1992. These developments can only be briefly analysed here.

The Newham dispute centred on the proposal by a group of parents of pupils at Stratford county secondary school to opt out, against the wishes of other parents, of the majority of the school's governors, and of the LEA which had proposed the school's closure as part of a package of re-organization proposals affecting a number of schools in the area. One important motivating factor behind some of those supporting opting out in this case *may* have been the prospect of the governing body coming substantially under Muslim control and the opportunity to run the school effectively as a Muslim school serving the high Muslim population in the area, though it is stressed that this was not uniformly the view of those seeking to opt out. However, much of the furore which surrounded this school *after* it became grant maintained related to the stressful relationships between the headteacher and some of the Muslim governors. Whatever the motivation of the proponents of opting out here, the parents concerned successfully mandated the reluctant governing body of Stratford County school to hold a parental ballot, which marginally favoured opting out. The Secretary of State subsequently endorsed the proposal, and rejected the LEA's composite package of reorganization plans. The Secretary of State argued that the school would be educationally viable as a grant maintained school in the area, would enhance parental choice, and would serve to 'break the mold' of LEA control.

The LEA's challenges by way of judicial review of the Secretary of State's determination were rejected by the High Court,[41] and the school duly joined the grant maintained sector, amid high hopes by many supporters of opting out that it would be seen as a glowing example of a successful inner city grant maintained school. The reality was, however, a damaging and prolonged dispute between the chairperson and some of the members of the governing body on the one hand, and the headteacher on the other, over the internal organization and running of the school and the delivery of the curriculum, becoming one of the most notable and distressing educational disputes of the time. At the heart of the issue is the question of how far the governing body should be permitted, even in a grant maintained school, to intervene in the day-to-day running of the school, and how far the professional expertise and autonomy of the teachers ought to be respected. These fundamental questions are largely unanswered in the Education Reform Act, and, indeed, in the 1992 White Paper: the opportunity ought to have been taken in the White Paper to clarify these relationships.

The White Paper contains wide-ranging proposals, but arguably the most significant relate to the acceleration of the pace of opting out: this the government sees as central to the promotion of greater diversity of provision and parental choice, but it also will bring about a significantly greater undermining of LEA functions. Nowhere is this more clear, both practically and symbolically, than in the proposal to relieve LEAs of their statutory duty to have education committees. The move towards grant maintained status will be the single most important structural change in the maintained schools' system in the coming decade. To manage and to allocate funding for this substantial opted out sector, the government proposes an important new agency – the Funding Agency for Schools. Superficially this looks as if it will operate at 'arm's length' from the government, but its chairperson, its members and its first chief executive will all be appointed by the Secretary of State, and it will be required to operate subject to directions issued by the Secretary of State. The Funding Agency for Schools will carry out its funding duties in accordance with a new common funding formula proposed in the White Paper, but whose details remain substantially unclear. Very importantly, the Agency will also in time take over from LEAs the statutory responsibility for ensuring the provision of sufficient school places. These and other important proposed changes to the legislation on grant maintained schools are likely during the 1990s to bring Baroness Thatcher's vision of schools opting out on a massive scale close to reality.

NOTES

1 Some of the material in this chapter has been published elsewhere in a different form: I am most grateful to Longman (publishers of the journal, *Education and the Law*) and to Routledge (publishers of my own book, *Government, Schools and the Law* (1992)), for permission to incorporate some of that material in this chapter.
2 Grant Maintained Schools – Consultation Paper (July 1987), especially at paras 1–2.
3 See H.C. Deb. Vol. 208, cols. 222–3 (Written Answers) (21 May 1992).
4 Cm. 2021.
5 Para. 3.2.
6 *R. v. Governors of Small Heath School, ex parte Birmingham City Council*; *R. v. Governors of Small Heath School, ex parte Khan and Others*: *The Independent Law Reports*, 30 June 1989 (Divisional Court); *The Independent Law Reports*, 3 August 1989 (Court of Appeal). Available on LEXIS. See P. Meredith, Opting Out: the Birmingham Small Heath Experience (1991) *Education and the Law*, 19.
7 *The Independent*, 27 October 1988, p. 21.
8 Under Education Reform Act 1988, s. 60(1)(a).
9 s. 60(1)(a).
10 Under s. 62.
11 Under s. 62(11).
12 Under s. 63(3)(a).
13 Between 28 and 42 days: s. 60(1)(a).
14 *Per* Lord Justice Woolf, Divisional Court, LEXIS transcript.
15 S.I. 1987 No. 1359.
16 (1989) 87 L.G.R. 583.
17 (1989) 87 L.G.R. 583 at p. 587.
18 Court of Appeal LEXIS transcript.
19 s. 61(1).
20 s. 61(3) and (4).
21 See DES, *School Governors: How to Become a Grant Maintained School* (1988); Revised Edition (1989).
22 Divisional Court LEXIS transcript.

23 *Ibid.*
24 *The Independent Law Reports*, 25 May 1990, Court of Appeal References are to the Court of Appeal LEXIS transcript. This case has since been reported more fully in (1990) 88 L.G.R. 716 (Divisional Court) and (1990) 88 L.G.R. 737 (Court of Appeal). See also P. Meredith, Opting out: the City of Bath Experience (1991) *Education and the Law*, 65.
25 Along with proposals by the governors of one voluntary school submitted under s. 13 of the 1980 Act.
26 On 13 November 1988 and 11 January 1989: LEXIS transcript.
27 This assumes that the s. 12 proposals ranged more widely than the one school to which grant maintained status has been granted.
28 See *Legg* v. *Inner London Education Authority* [1972] 3 All E.R. 177 at p. 188.
29 LEXIS transcript.
30 Para. 13 of decision letter: see LEXIS transcript.
31 LEXIS transcript.
32 This unusual course of action was adopted in order to expedite proceedings. It was taken with the consent of the parties, despite the fact that it involved the loss of one stage in the appellate process.
33 LEXIS transcript (emphasis added).
34 LEXIS transcript.
35 *Ibid.*
36 (1986) 84 L.G.R. 469.
37 (1989) 1 All E.R. 769.
38 LEXIS transcript.
39 There were several other unsuccessful subsidiary grounds of challenge, including failure to take into account the consequences of delay and uncertainty as to the future organization of schools in the area; miscalculation of projected numbers of pupils in the 16–19 age group; and miscalculation of the level of reduction in surplus capacity the LEA proposals would have achieved.
40 LEXIS transcript. Lord Justice Nicholls expressed himself in similarly trenchant terms as to the limited role of the court.
41 These are discussed in detail in P. Meredith, Opting Out – The Newham Experience (1992) *Education and the Law*, 69.

Name index

Subject index